Learning Neo4j 3.x

Second Edition

Effective data modeling, performance tuning, and data
visualization techniques in Neo4j

Jérôme Baton

Rik Van Bruggen

BIRMINGHAM - MUMBAI

Learning Neo4j 3.x

Second Edition

First published: August 2014

Second Edition: October 2017

Production reference: 1171017

Published by Packt Publishing Ltd.
Livery Place
35 Livery Street
Birmingham
B3 2PB, UK.
ISBN 978-1-78646-614-3

www.packtpub.com

Credits

Authors
Jérôme Baton
Rik Van Bruggen

Copy Editor
Tasneem Fatehi

Reviewers
Taffy Brecknock
Jose Ernesto Echeverria
Adriano Longo

Project Coordinator
Manthan Patel

Commissioning Editor
Amey Varangaonkar

Proofreader
Safis Editing

Acquisition Editor
Vinay Argekar

Indexer
Tejal Daruwale Soni

Content Development Editors
Jagruti Babaria
Tejas Limkar

Graphics
Tania Dutta

Technical Editors
Dinesh Chaudhary
Dharmendra Yadav

Production Coordinator
Deepika Naik

About the Authors

Jérôme Baton started hacking computers at the age of skin problems, gaming first then continued his trip by self-learning Basic on Amstrad CPC, peaking on coding a full screen horizontal starfield, and messing the interlace of the video controller so that sprites appeared twice as high in horizontal beat'em up games. Disks were three inches for 178 Kb then.

Then, for gaming reasons, he switched to Commodore Amiga and its fantastic AMOS Basic. Later caught by seriousness and studies, he wrote Turbo Pascal, C, COBOL, Visual C++, and Java on PCs and mainframes at university, and even Logo in high school. Then, Java happened and he became a consultant, mostly on backend code of websites in many different businesses.

Jérôme authored several articles in French on Neo4j, JBoss Forge, an Arduino workshop for Devoxx4Kids, and reviewed kilos of books on Android. He has a weakness for wordplay, puns, spoonerisms, and Neo4j that relieves him from join(t) pains.

Jérôme also has the joy to teach in French universities, currently at I.U.T de Paris, Université Paris V - René Descartes (Neo4j, Android), and Université de Troyes (Neo4j), where he does his best to enterTRain the students.

> *If you would be a real seeker after truth, it is necessary that at least once in your life you doubt, as far as possible, all things.*
>
> *Rene Descartes*

Read more at: https://www.brainyquote.com/authors/rene_descartes.

When not programming, Jérôme enjoys photography, doing electronics, everything DIY, understanding how things work, trying to be clever or funny on Twitter, and spends a lot of time trying to understand his kids and life in general.

Rik Van Bruggen is the VP of Sales for Neo Technology for Benelux, UK, and the Nordic region. He has been working for startup companies for most of his career, including eCom Interactive Expertise, SilverStream Software, Imprivata, and Courion. While he has an interest in technology, his real passion is business and how to make technology work for a business. He lives in Antwerp, Belgium, with his wife and three lovely kids, and enjoys technology, orienteering, jogging, and Belgian beer.

Acknowledgement

I would like to thank many people for this project that is truly a great personal achievement for me.

First of all, Rik Van Bruggen, who is the original author of this book and literally, the giant on whose shoulders I stand. Secondly, Vinay and Jagruti from Packt Publishing for their patience with a slow writer.

Thank you, William LyOn, Cédric FauVEt, Mark NEedham, BenOit Simard, Michael Hunger, Craig Taverner, and Jim Webber from Neo4j for their help and sharing their knowledge over the last few years on Stack Overflow, on Slack, or in person.

This would not have been possible if I myself had not had inspiring teachers such as Daniel 'DG' Guillaume, Françoise Meunier, Florence Fessy-Mesatfa, and Jérôme Fessy from IUT de Paris, and Dr. Robert T Hughes, Richard N Griffith, and Graham Winstanley from the University of Brighton.

Going further in the past, there are more teachers from whom I learned pedagogy and inspired me to share; I remember you, Mrs. Legrand, Mrs. Viala, and Mr. Bouhadda. Also, not being a native English speaker, I was at first very bad at speaking English. Extra energy from Mrs Goddard and Mrs Maluski really unlocked this second language for me.

Teachers change lives!

Also thanks to the doctors of my national health service without whom I would be a souvenir already. Vive la Sécurité Sociale!

Basically, I would like to thank all the people I learned from, be they teachers or not. Including my students.

Thank you, Romin Irani (@iRomin), my friend--you are an example.

Thank you, Anny Naïm, you are a truly shining person.

Above all, love you, kiddos!

I really should make a graph of all the people I would like to thank.

About the Reviewers

Taffy Brecknock has worked in the IT industry for more than 20 years. During his career, he has worked as a software developer, managed development teams, and has been responsible for application design and more recently systems architecture.

He has held roles with both public and private sector organizations. While working with the Australian Government, Taffy got first-hand exposure to the use of connected data in law enforcement. After using relational database systems as the data repository, he is experienced in the short comings of using this paradigm to model such systems.

After learning about graph databases, specifically Neo4j, he has become extremely interested in the many different applications of this technology. He feels that there are few problems in today's business world that cannot benefit from being modeled in a graph.

Jose Ernesto Echeverria started working with relational databases in the 90s, and has been working with Neo4j since 2014. He prefers graph databases over others, given their capabilities for real-world modeling and their adaptability to change. As a polyglot programmer, he has used languages such as Java, Ruby, and R with Neo4j in order to solve data management problems of multinational corporations. He is a regular attendee of GraphConnect, OSCON, and RailsConf. When not working, he enjoys spending time with family, road trips, Minecraft projects with his children, as well as reading and drinking craft beers.

Adriano Longo is a freelance data analyst based in the Netherlands with a passion for Neo4j's relationship-oriented data model.

He is specialized in querying, processing, and modeling data with Cypher, R, Python, and SQL and has worked on climate prediction models at UEA's Climatic Research Unit before focusing on analytical solutions for the private sector.

Today, Adriano uses Neo4j and Linkurious.js to explore the complex web of relationships that nefarious actors use to obfuscate their abuse of environmental and financial regulations--making dirty secrets less transparent, one graph at a time.

www.PacktPub.com

For support files and downloads related to your book, please visit www.PacktPub.com. Did you know that Packt offers eBook versions of every book published, with PDF and ePub files available? You can upgrade to the eBook version at www.PacktPub.com and as a print book customer, you are entitled to a discount on the eBook copy. Get in touch with us at service@packtpub.com for more details. At www.PacktPub.com, you can also read a collection of free technical articles, sign up for a range of free newsletters and receive exclusive discounts and offers on Packt books and eBooks.

https://www.packtpub.com/mapt

Get the most in-demand software skills with Mapt. Mapt gives you full access to all Packt books and video courses, as well as industry-leading tools to help you plan your personal development and advance your career.

Why subscribe?

- Fully searchable across every book published by Packt
- Copy and paste, print, and bookmark content
- On demand and accessible via a web browser

Customer Feedback

Thanks for purchasing this Packt book. At Packt, quality is at the heart of our editorial process. To help us improve, please leave us an honest review on this book's Amazon page at https://www.amazon.com/dp/1786466147.

If you'd like to join our team of regular reviewers, you can email us at customerreviews@packtpub.com. We award our regular reviewers with free eBooks and videos in exchange for their valuable feedback. Help us be relentless in improving our products!

Table of Contents

Preface

Learning Neo4j 3.x will give you the keys to graph databases and Neo4j in particular. From concepts to applications, you will learn a lot about Neo4j and will wonder why using relational databases again.

What this book covers

Chapter 1, *Graph Theory and Databases*, explains the fundamental theoretical and historical underpinnings of graph database technology. Additionally, this chapter positions graph databases in an ever-changing database landscape. It compares the technology/industry with other data technologies out there.

Chapter 2, *Getting Started with Neo4j*, introduces the specific Neo4j implementation of a graph database and looks at key concepts and characteristics.

Chapter 3, *Modeling Data for Neo4j*, covers the basic modeling techniques for graph databases.

Chapter 4, *Getting Started with Cypher*, provides an overview of the Cypher query language.

Chapter 5, *Awesome Procedures on Cypher - APOC*, introduces the APOC library. You will learn how to use it within Cypher queries, get information on it, and find the procedure you need among the hundreds provided by the community.

Chapter 6, *Extending Cypher*, talks about adding functions and procedures to a Neo4j instance. Write your own APOC.

Chapter 7, *Query Performance Tuning*, shows you how to tune your Cypher queries for better performance.

Chapter 8, *Importing Data into Neo4j*, explains how to import data from different kinds of sources.

Chapter 9, *Going Spatial*, covers the geolocation capabilities of Neo4j, APOC, and Neo4j Spatial.

Chapter 10, *Security*, covers authentication and authorization in Neo4j.

Chapter 11, *Visualizations for Neo4j*, shows you how to display your data.

Chapter 12, *Data Refactoring with Neo4j*, explains how to change the data model to fit new requirements.

Chapter 13, *Clustering*, sets up a causal cluster using the Neo4j Enterprise edition.

Chapter 14, *Use-Case Example – Recommendations*, digs into a specific graph database use case--real-time recommendations--and explains it using a specific example dataset/query patterns.

Chapter 15, *Use-Case Example – Impact Analysis and Simulation*, analyzes the impact of a change in the network on the rest of the network. In this part of the book, we will explain and explore that use case.

Appendix, *Tips and Tricks*, provides tips and more knowledge, don't miss it.

What you need for this book

To run the software and examples, you will need a decent developer station with Java 7 or better, with 4 GB of RAM and 2 GB of free disk space.

Examples are provided for the GNU/Linux systems.

Most chapters apply to Neo4j Community Edition and Neo4j Enterprise Edition, except Chapter 10, *Security*, and Chapter 13, *Clustering*.

In the later chapters, two laptops, several Raspberry Pis, and Docker containers are used.

Who this book is for

This book is for developers who want an alternative way to store and process data within their applications or developers who have to deal with highly connected data. No previous graph database experience is required; however, some basic database knowledge will help you understand the concepts more easily.

Conventions

In this book, you will find a number of text styles that distinguish between different kinds of information. Here are some examples of these styles and an explanation of their meaning. Code words in text, database table names, folder names, filenames, file extensions, pathnames, dummy URLs, user input, and Twitter handles are shown as follows: "We mapped the learningneo4j package to the /learningneo4j URL."

A block of code is set as follows:

```
public class StringHacking {
@UserFunction
 @Description("Returns the last word of a string")
 public String getLastWord( @Name("aStr") String aStr){
 if(aStr==null) return null;
 else  {
 int pos = aStr.lastIndexOf(" ");
 if(pos==-1) return aStr;
 else return aStr.substring(pos+1);
 }
 }
}
```

When we wish to draw your attention to a particular part of a code block, the relevant lines or items are set in bold:

```
MATCH (ln:LastName)--(p:Person)
RETURN ln, learningneo4j.randomCount(p.lastName) AS badcount
```

Any command-line input or output is written as follows:

```
mkdir data/ldap/environment -p
mkdir data/ldap/db -p
```

New terms and **important words** are shown in bold. Words that you see on the screen, for example, in menus or dialog boxes, appear in the text like this: "In order to download new modules, we will go to **Files** | **Settings** | **Project Name** | **Project Interpreter**."

Warnings or important notes appear like this.

Tips and tricks appear like this.

Reader feedback

Feedback from our readers is always welcome. Let us know what you think about this book-what you liked or disliked. Reader feedback is important for us as it helps us develop titles that you will really get the most out of. To send us general feedback, simply email feedback@packtpub.com, and mention the book's title in the subject of your message. If there is a topic that you have expertise in and you are interested in either writing or contributing to a book, see our author guide at www.packtpub.com/authors.

Customer support

Now that you are the proud owner of a Packt book, we have a number of things to help you to get the most from your purchase.

Downloading the example code

You can download the example code files for this book from your account at http://www.packtpub.com. If you purchased this book elsewhere, you can visit http://www.packtpub.com/support and register to have the files emailed directly to you. You can download the code files by following these steps:

1. Log in or register to our website using your email address and password.
2. Hover the mouse pointer on the **SUPPORT** tab at the top.
3. Click on **Code Downloads & Errata**.
4. Enter the name of the book in the **Search** box.
5. Select the book for which you're looking to download the code files.
6. Choose from the drop-down menu where you purchased this book from.
7. Click on **Code Download**.

Once the file is downloaded, please make sure that you unzip or extract the folder using the latest version of:

- WinRAR / 7-Zip for Windows
- Zipeg / iZip / UnRarX for Mac
- 7-Zip / PeaZip for Linux

The code bundle for the book is also hosted on GitHub at
`https://github.com/PacktPublishing/Learning-Neo4j-3x-Second-Editon`. We also
have other code bundles from our rich catalog of books and videos available at
`https://github.com/PacktPublishing/`. Check them out!

Errata

Although we have taken every care to ensure the accuracy of our content, mistakes do
happen. If you find a mistake in one of our books-maybe a mistake in the text or the code-
we would be grateful if you could report this to us. By doing so, you can save other readers
from frustration and help us improve subsequent versions of this book. If you find any
errata, please report them by visiting `http://www.packtpub.com/submit-errata`, selecting
your book, clicking on the **Errata Submission Form** link, and entering the details of your
errata. Once your errata are verified, your submission will be accepted and the errata will
be uploaded to our website or added to any list of existing errata under the Errata section of
that title. To view the previously submitted errata, go to
`https://www.packtpub.com/books/content/support` and enter the name of the book in the
search field. The required information will appear under the **Errata** section.

Piracy

Piracy of copyrighted material on the internet is an ongoing problem across all media. At
Packt, we take the protection of our copyright and licenses very seriously. If you come
across any illegal copies of our works in any form on the internet, please provide us with
the location address or website name immediately so that we can pursue a remedy. Please
contact us at `copyright@packtpub.com` with a link to the suspected pirated material. We
appreciate your help in protecting our authors and our ability to bring you valuable
content.

Questions

If you have a problem with any aspect of this book, you can contact us at
`questions@packtpub.com`, and we will do our best to address the problem.

1
Graph Theory and Databases

People have different ways of learning new topics. We know that background information can contribute greatly to a better understanding of new topics. That is why, in this chapter of our *Learning Neo4j 3.x* book, we will start with a bit of background information, not to recount the tales of history, but to give you the necessary context that can lead to a better understanding of the topics.

In order to do so, we will address the following topics:

- **Graphs**: What they are and where they came from. This section will aim to set the record straight on what, exactly, our subject will contain, and what it won't.
- **Graph theory**: What it is and what it is used for. This section will give you quite a few examples of graph theory applications, and it will also start hinting at applications for graph databases, such as Neo4j later on.
- **Databases**: What the different kinds of databases and what they are used for. This section will help you to know what the right database for your projects.

So, let's dig right in.

Introducing Neo4j 3.x and a history of graphs

Many people have used the word **graph** at some point in their professional or personal lives. However, chances are that they did not use it in the way that we will be using it in this book. Most people--obviously not you, otherwise you probably would not have picked up this book--actually think about something very different when talking about a graph. They think about pie charts and bar charts. They think about graphics, not graphs.

In this book, we will be working with a completely different type of subject--the graphs that you might know from your math classes. I, for one, distinctly remember being taught the basics of discrete mathematics in one of my university classes, and I also remember finding it terribly complex and difficult to work with. Little did I know that my later professional career would use these techniques in a software context, let alone that I would be writing a book on this topic.

So, what are graphs? To explain this, I think it is useful to put a little historic context around the concept. Graphs are actually quite old as a concept. They were invented, or at least first described, in an academic paper by the well-known Swiss mathematician, Leonhard Euler. He was trying to solve an age-old problem that we now know as the *Seven Bridges of Königsberg*. The problem at hand was pretty simple to understand.

Königsberg was a beautiful medieval city in the Prussian Empire situated on the river Pregel. It is located between Poland and Lithuania in today's Russia. If you try to look it up on any modern-day map, you will most likely not find it as it is currently known as **Kaliningrad**. The Pregel not only cut Königsberg into left- and right-bank sides of the city, but it also created an island in the middle of the river, which was known as the **Kneiphof**. The result of this peculiar situation was a city that was cut into four parts (we will refer to them as A, B, C, and D), which were connected by seven bridges (labelled a, b, c, d, e, f, and g in the following diagram). This gives us the following situation:

- The seven bridges are connected to the four different parts of the city
- The essence of the problem that people were trying to solve was to take a tour of the city, visiting every one of its parts and crossing every single one of its bridges, without having to walk a single bridge or street twice

In the following diagram, you can see how Euler illustrated this problem in his original 1736 paper:

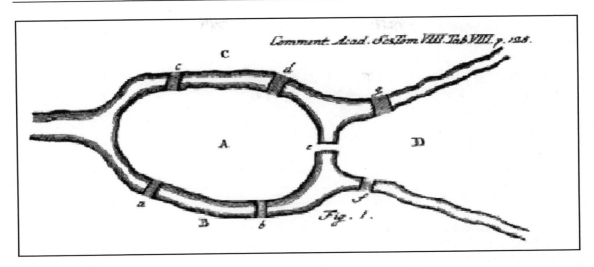

Illustration of the problem as mentioned by Euler in his paper in 1736

Essentially, it was a pathfinding problem, like many others (for example, the **knight's ride** problem, or the **traveling salesman** problem). It does not seem like a very difficult assignment at all now, does it? However, at the time, people really struggled with it and were trying to figure it out for the longest time. It was not until Euler got involved and took a very different, mathematical approach to the problem that it got solved once and for all.

Euler did the following two things that I find really interesting:

- First and foremost, he decided not to take the traditional brute force method to solve the problem (in this case, drawing a number of different route options on the map and trying to figure out--essentially by trial and error--if there was such a route through the city), but to do something different. He took a step back and took a different look at the problem by creating what I call an **abstract version** of the problem at hand, which is essentially a model of the problem domain that he was trying to work with. In his mind, at least, Euler must have realized that the citizens of Königsberg were focusing their attention on the wrong part of the problem--the streets. Euler quickly came to the conclusion that the streets of Königsberg did not really matter to find a solution to the problem. The only things that mattered for his pathfinding operation were the following:
    - The parts of the city
    - The bridges connecting the parts of the city

Now, all of a sudden, we seem to have a very different problem at hand, which can be accurately represented in what is often regarded as **the world's first graph**:

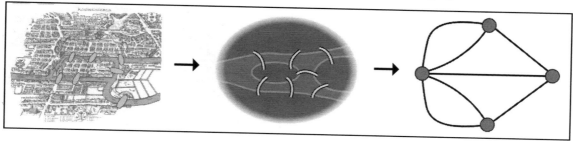

Simplifying Königsberg

- Secondly, Euler solved the puzzle at hand by applying a mathematical algorithm on the model that he created. Euler's logic was simple--if I want to take a walk in the town of Königsberg, then I will have to do as follows:
  - I will have to start somewhere in any one of the four parts of the city
  - I will have to leave that part of the city; in other words, I will have to cross one of the bridges to go to another part of the city
  - I will then have to cross another five bridges, leaving and entering different parts of the city
  - Finally, I will end the walk through Königsberg in another part of the city

Therefore, Euler argues, the case must be that the first and last parts of the city have an odd number of bridges that connect them to other parts of the city (because you leave from the first part and you arrive at the last part of the city), but the other two parts of the city must have an even number of bridges connecting them to the first and last parts of the city, because you will arrive and leave from these parts of the city.

This **number of bridges connecting the parts of the city** has a very special meaning in the model that Euler created, the graph representation of the model. We call this the degree of the nodes in the graph. In order for there to be a path through Königsberg that only crossed every bridge once, Euler proved that all he had to do was to apply a very simple algorithm that would establish the degree (in other words, count the number of bridges) of every part of the city. This is shown in the following diagram:

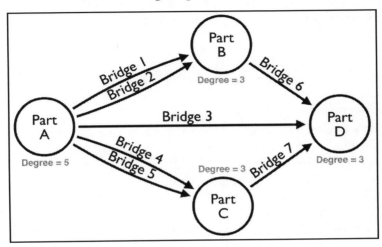

Simplified town

This is how Euler solved the famous *Seven Bridges of Königsberg* problem. By proving that there was no part of the city that had an even number of bridges, he also proved that the required walk in the city could not be done. Adding one more bridge would immediately make it possible, but with the state of the city and its bridges at the time, there was no way one could take such **Eulerian Walk** of the city.

By doing so, Euler created the world's first graph. The concepts and techniques of his research, however, are universally applicable; in order to do such a walk on any graph, the graph must have zero or two vertices with odd degrees and all intermediate vertices must have even degree.

To summarize, a graph is nothing more than an abstract, mathematical representation of two or more entities, which are somehow connected or related to each other. Graphs model pairwise relations between objects. They are, therefore, always made up of the following components:

- **The nodes of the graph, usually representing the objects mentioned previously**: In math, we usually refer to these structures as vertices; but for this book and in the context of graph databases such as Neo4j, we will always refer to vertices as nodes.
- **The links between the nodes of the graph**: In math, we refer to these structures as edges, but again, for the purpose of this book, we will refer to these links as **relationships**.
- **The structure of how nodes and relationships are connected to each other makes a graph**: Many important qualities, such as the number of edges connected to a node (what we referred to as degrees), can be assessed. Many other such indicators also exist.

Now that we have discussed graphs and understand a bit more about their nature and history, it's time to look at the discipline that was created on top of these concepts, often referred to as the graph theory.

Definition and usage of the graph theory

When Euler invented the first graph, he was trying to solve a very specific problem of the citizens of Königsberg, with a very specific representation/model and a very specific algorithm. It turns out that there are quite a few problems that can be addressed as follows:

- Described using the graph metaphor of objects and pairwise relations between them
- Solved by applying a mathematical algorithm to this structure

The mechanism is the same, and the scientific discipline that studies these modeling and solution patterns, using graphs is often referred to as the graph theory and is considered to be a part of discrete mathematics.

There are lots of different types of graphs that have been analyzed in this discipline, as you can see from the following diagram:

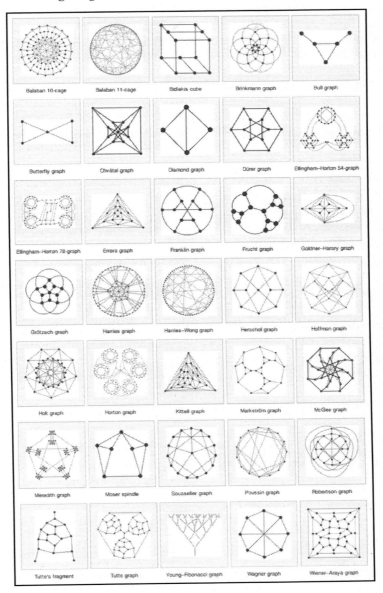

Graph types

Graph theory, the study of graph models and algorithms, has turned out to be a fascinating field of study, which has been used in many different disciplines to solve some of the most interesting questions facing mankind. Interestingly enough, it has seldom really been applied with rigor in the different fields of science that can benefit from it; maybe scientists today don't have the multidisciplinary approach required (providing expertise from graph theory and their specific field of study) to do so.

So, let's talk about some of these fields of study a bit, without giving you an exhaustive list of all applicable fields. Still, I do believe that some of these examples will be of interest for our future discussions in this book and will work up an appetite for what types of applications we will use a graph-based database, such as, Neo4j for.

Social studies

For the longest time, people have understood that the way humans interact with one another is actually very easy to describe in a network. People interact with people every day. People influence one another every day. People exchange ideas every day. As they do, these interactions cause ripple effects through the social environment that they inhabit. Modelling these interactions as a graph has been of primary importance to better understand global demographics, political movements, and--last, but not least--the commercial adoption of certain products by certain groups. With the advent of online social networks, this graph-based approach to social understanding has taken a whole new direction. Companies such as Google, Facebook, Twitter, LinkedIn, and many others have undertaken very specific efforts to include graph-based systems in the way they target their customers and users, and in doing so, they have changed many of our daily lives quite fundamentally. See the following diagram, featuring a visualization of my LinkedIn network:

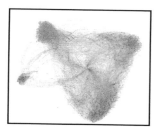

Rik's professional network representation

Biological studies

We often say in marketing taglines: **Graphs Are Everywhere**. When we do so, we are actually describing reality in a very real and fascinating way. Also, in this field, researchers have known for quite some time that biological components (proteins, molecules, genes, and so on) and their interactions can accurately be modelled and described by means of a graph structure, and doing so yields many practical advantages. In metabolic pathways (see the following diagram for the human metabolic system), for example, graphs can help us understand how the different parts of the human body interact with each other. In metaproteomics (the study of all protein samples taken from the natural environment), researchers analyze how different kinds of proteins interact with one another and are used in order to better steer chemical and biological production processes.

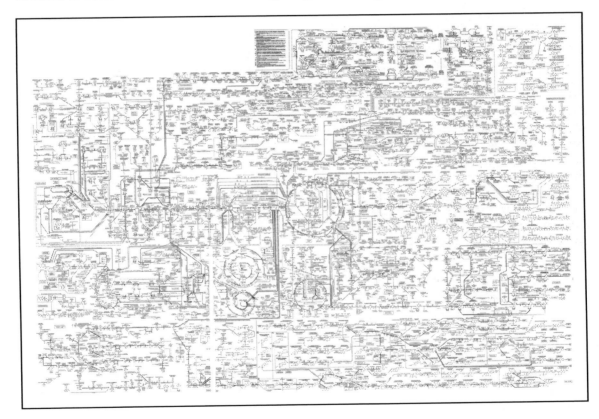

A diagram representing the human metabolic system

Computer science

Some of the earliest computers were built with graphs in mind. Graph Compute Engines solved scheduling problems for railroads as early as the late 19th century, and the usage of graphs in computer science has only accelerated since then. In today's applications, use cases vary from chip design, network management, recommendation systems, and UML modeling to algorithm generation and dependency analysis. The following is an example of a UML diagram:

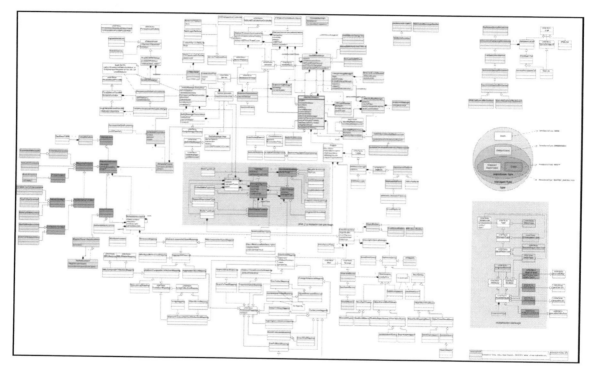

An example of an UML diagram

The latter is probably one of the more interesting use cases. Using pathfinding algorithms, software and hardware engineers have been analyzing the effects of changes in the design of their artifacts on the rest of the system. If a change is made to one part of the code, for example, a particular object is renamed; the dependency analysis algorithms can easily walk the graph of the system to find out what other classes will be affected by that change.

Flow problems

Another really interesting field of graph theory applications is flow problems, also known as **maximum flow problems**. In essence, this field is part of a larger field of optimization problems, which is trying to establish the best possible path across a flow network. Flow networks types of graphs in which the nodes/vertices of the graphs are connected by relationships/edges that specify the capacity of that particular relationship. Examples can be found in fields such as the telecom networks, gas networks, airline networks, package delivery networks, and many others, where graph-based models are then used in combination with complex algorithms. The following diagram is an example of such a network, as you can find it on `http://enipedia.tudelft.nl/`:

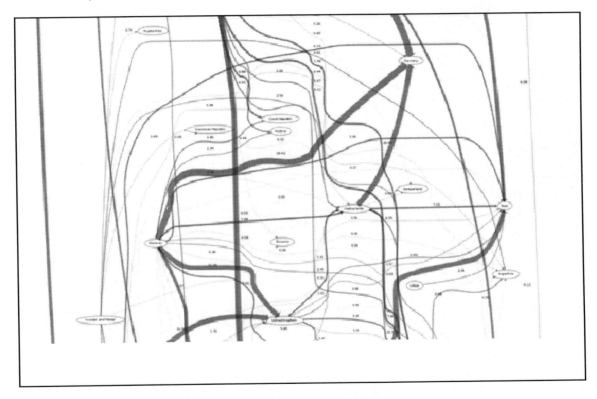

An example of a flow network

These algorithms are then used to identify the calculated optimal path, find bottlenecks, plan maintenance activities, conduct long-term capacity planning, and many other operations.

Route problems

The original problem that Euler set out to solve in 18th century Königsberg was in fact a route planning/pathfinding problem. Today, many graph applications leverage the extraordinary capability of graphs and graph algorithms to calculate--as opposed to finding with trial and error--the optimal route between two nodes on a network. In the following diagram, you will find a simple route planning example as a graph:

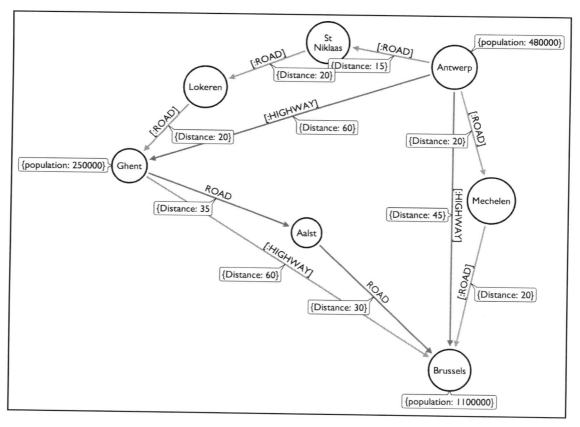

A simple route planning example between cities to choose roads versus highways

A very simple example will be from the domain of logistics. When trying to plan for the best way to move a package from one city to another, one will need the following:

- A list of all routes available between the cities
- The most optimal of the available routes, which depends on various parameters in the network, such as capacity, distance, cost, CO_2 exhaust, speed, and so on

This type of operation is a very nice use case for graph algorithms. There are a couple of very well-known algorithms that we can briefly highlight:

- **The Dijkstra algorithm**: This is one of the best-known algorithms to calculate the shortest weighted path between two points in a graph, using the properties of the edges as weights or costs of that link.
- **The A* (A-star) algorithm**: This is a variation of Dijkstra's original ideas, but it uses heuristics to more efficiently predict the shortest path explorations. As A* explores potential graph paths, it holds a sorted priority queue of alternate path segments along the way, as it calculates the **past path** cost and the **future path** cost of the different options that are possible during the route exploration.

Depending on the required result, the specific dataset, and the speed requirements, different algorithms will yield different returns.

Web search

No book chapter treating graphs and graph theory--even at the highest level--will be complete without mentioning one of the most powerful and widely-used graph algorithms on the planet, **PageRank**. PageRank is the original graph algorithm, invented by Google founder Larry Page in 1996 at Stanford University, to provide better web search results. For those of us old enough to remember the early days of web searching (using tools such as Lycos, AltaVista, and so on), it provided a true revolution in the way the web was made accessible to end users.

The following diagram represents the PageRank graph:

PageRank

The older tools did keyword matching on web pages, but Google revolutionized this by no longer focusing on keywords alone, but by doing link analysis on the hyperlinks between different web pages. PageRank, and many of the other algorithms that Google uses today, assumes that more important web pages, which should appear higher in your search results, will have more incoming links from other pages, and therefore, it is able to score these pages by analyzing the graph of links to the web page. History has shown us the importance of PageRank. Not only has Google, Inc. taken the advantage over Yahoo as the most popular search engine and built quite an empire on top of this graph algorithm, but its principles have also been applied to other fields, such as, cancer research and chemical reactions.

Now, we want to contextualize the concepts around graph databases and understand the historical and operational differences between older, different kinds of database management systems and our modern-day Neo4j installations.

To do this, we will cover the following:

- Some background information on databases in general
- A walk-through of the different approaches taken to manage and store data, from old-school navigational databases to NoSQL graph databases
- A short discussion explaining the graph database category, its strengths, and its weaknesses

This should set us up for some more practical discussions later in this book.

Background

It's not very clear when the first real database management system was formally conceived and implemented. Ever since Babbage invented the first complete Turing computing system (the Analytical Engine, which Babbage never really managed to get built), we have known that computers will always need to have some kind of memory. This will be responsible for dealing with the data on which operations and calculations will be executed. However, when did this memory evolve into a proper database? What do we mean by a database, anyway?

Let's tackle the latter question first. A database can be described as any kind of organized collection of data. Not all databases require a management system--think of the many spreadsheets and other file-based storage approaches that don't really have any kind of real material oversight imposed on it, let alone true management systems. A database management system (or DBMS for short), then, can technically be referred to as a set of computer programs that manage (in the broadest sense of the word) the database. It is a system that sits between the user-facing hardware and software components and the data. It can be described as any system that is responsible for and able to manage the structure of the data, is able to store and retrieve that data, and provides access to this data in a correct, trustable, performant, secure fashion.

Databases as we know them, however, did not exist from the get-go of computing. At first, most computers used **memory**, and this memory used a special-purpose, custom-made storage format that often relied on very manual, labor-intensive, and hardware-based storage operations. Many systems relied on things like punch cards for its instructions and datasets. It's not that long ago that computer systems evolved from these seemingly ancient, special-purpose technologies.

Having read many different articles on this subject, I believe the need for general-purpose database management systems, similar to the ones we know today, started to increase due to the following:

- The number of computerized systems increased significantly.
- A number of breakthroughs in terms of computer memory were realized. Direct Access memory--memory that would not have to rely on lots of winding of tapes or punched cards--became available in the middle of the 1960s.

Both of these elements were necessary preconditions for any kind of multipurpose database management system to make sense. The first real database management systems seem to have cropped up in the 1960s, and I believe it would be useful to quickly run through the different phases in the development of database management systems.

We can establish the following three major phases over the half century that database management systems have been under development:

- Navigational databases
- Relational databases
- NoSQL databases

Let's look at these three system types so that we can then more accurately position graph databases such as Neo4j--the real subject of this book.

Navigational databases

The original database management systems were developed by legendary computer scientists such as Charles Bachman, who gave a lot of thought to the way software should be built in a world of extremely scarce computing resources. Bachman invented a very natural (and as we will see later, graphical) way to model data: as a network of interrelated things. The starting point of such a database design was generally a **Bachman diagram** (refer to the following diagram), which immediately feels like it expresses the model of the data structure in a very graph-like fashion:

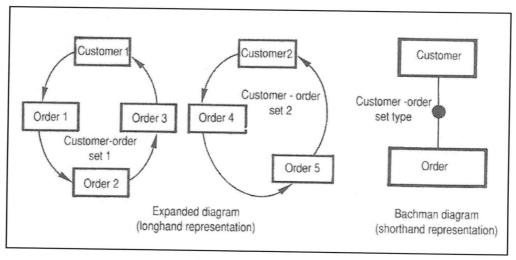

Bachman diagram

These diagrams were the starting points for database management systems that used either networks or hierarchies as the basic structure for their data. Both the network databases and hierarchical database systems were built on the premise that data elements would be linked together by pointers:

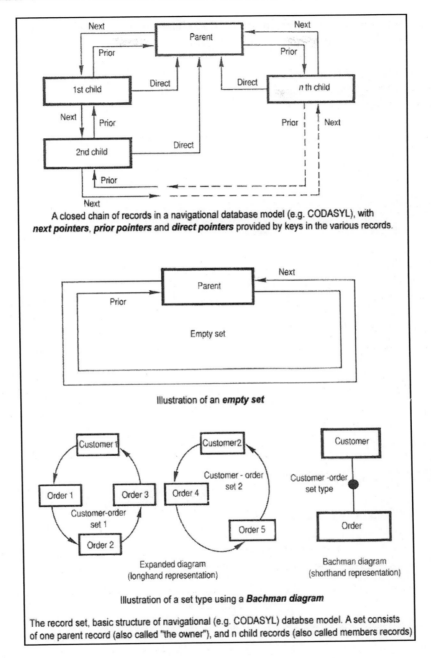

A closed chain of records in a navigational database model (e.g. CODASYL), with **next pointers**, **prior pointers** and **direct pointers** provided by keys in the various records.

Illustration of an **empty set**

Illustration of a set type using a **Bachman diagram**

The record set, basic structure of navigational (e.g. CODASYL) databse model. A set consists of one parent record (also called "the owner"), and n child records (also called members records)

An example of a navigational database model with pointers linking records

As you can probably imagine from the preceding discussion, these models were very interesting and resulted in a number of efforts that shaped the database industry. One of these efforts was the **Conference on Data Systems Languages**, better known under its acronym, **CODASYL**. This played an ever so important role in the information technology industry of the sixties and seventies. It shaped one of the world's dominant computer programming systems (COBOL), but also provided the basis for a whole slew of navigational databases such as IDMS, Cullinet, and IMS. The latter, the IBM-backed IMS database, is often classified as a hierarchical database, which offers a subset of the network model of CODASYL.

Navigational databases eventually gave way to a new generation of databases, the Relational Database Management Systems. Many reasons have been attributed to this shift, some technical and some commercial, but the main two reasons that seem to enjoy agreement across the industry are as follows:

- The complexity of the models that they used. CODASYL is widely regarded as something that can only be worked or understood by absolute experts--as we partly experienced in 1999, when the Y2K problem required many CODASYL experts to work overtime to migrate their systems into the new millennium.
- The lack of a declarative query mechanism for navigational database management systems. Most of these systems inherently provide a very imperative approach to finding data: the user would have to tell the database what to do instead of just being able to ask a question and having the database provide the answer.

This allows for a great transition from navigational to relational databases.

Relational databases

Relational Database Management Systems are probably the ones that we are most familiar with in 21st century computer science. Some of the history behind the creation of these databases is quite interesting. It started with an unknown researcher at IBM's San Jose, CA, research facility--a gentleman called Edgar Codd. Mr. Codd was working at IBM on hard disk research projects, but was increasingly drawn into the navigational database management systems world that would be using these hard disks. Mr. Codd became increasingly frustrated with these systems, mostly with their lack of an intuitive query interface.

Essentially, you could store data in a network/hierarchy, but how would you ever get it back out?

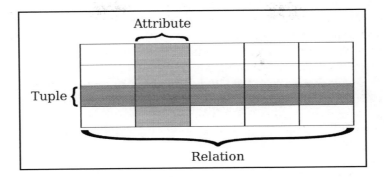

Relational database terminology

Codd wrote several papers on a different approach to database management systems that would not rely as much on linked lists of data (networks or hierarchies) but more on sets of data. He proved--using a mathematical representation called **tuple calculus**--that sets would be able to adhere to the same requirements that navigational database management systems were implementing. The only requirement was that there would be a proper query language that would ensure some of the consistency requirements on the database. This, then, became the inspiration for declarative query languages such as **Structured Query Language (SQL)**. IBM's *System R* was one of the first implementations of such a system, but Software Development Laboratories, a small company founded by ex-IBM people and one illustrious Mr. Larry Ellison, actually beat IBM to the market. Their product, Oracle, never got released until a couple of years later by Relational Software, Inc., and then eventually became the flagship software product of Oracle Corporation, which we all know today.

With relational databases came a process that all of us who have studied computer science know as **normalization**. This is the process that database modellers go through to minimize database redundancy and introduce disk storage savings, by introducing dependency. It involves splitting off data elements that appear more than once in a relational database table into their own table structures. Instead of storing the city where a person lives as a property of the person record, I would split the city into a separate table structure and store person entities in one table and city entities in another table. By doing so, we will often be creating the need to join these tables back together at query time. Depending on the cardinality of the relationship between these different tables (1:many, many:1, and many:many), this would require the introduction of a new type of table to execute these join operations: the join table, which links together two tables that would normally have a many:many cardinality.

I think it is safe to say that Relational Database Management Systems have served our industry extremely well in the past 30 years and will probably continue to do so for a very long time to come. However, they also came with a couple of issues, which are interesting to point out as they will (again) set the stage for another generation of database management systems:

- Relational Database Systems suffer at scale. As the sets or tables of the relational systems grow longer, the query response times of the relational database systems generally get worse, much worse. For most use cases, this was and is not necessarily a problem, but as we all know, *size does matter*, and this deficiency certainly does harm the relational model. A counter example to this could be Google's Spanner, a scalable, multi-version, globally-distributed, and synchronously-replicated database.

- Relational Databases are quite **anti-relational**; they are less relational than graph databases. As the domains of our applications--and therefore, the relational models that represent those domains--become more complex, relational systems really start to become very difficult to work with. More specifically, join operations, where users would ask queries of the database that would pull data from a number of different sets/tables, are extremely complicated and resource-intensive for the database management system. There is a true limit to the number of join operations that such a system can effectively perform, before the **join bombs** go off and the system becomes very unresponsive. See an example of explosive model.

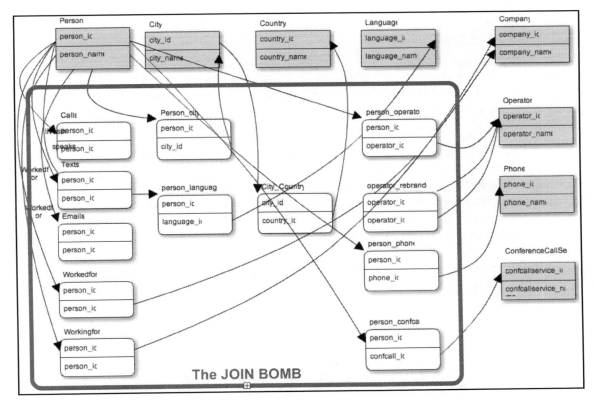

Relational database schema with explosive join tables

- Relational databases impose a schema even before we put any data into the database and even if a schema is too rigid. Many of us work in domains where it is very difficult to apply a single database schema to all the elements of the domain that we are working with. Increasingly, we are seeing the need for a flexible type of schema that would cater to a more iterative, more agile way of developing software.

As you will see in the following sections, the next generation of database management systems is definitely not settling for what we have today, and is attempting to push innovation forward by providing solutions to some of these extremely complex problems.

NoSQL databases

The new millennium and the explosion of web content marked a new era for database management systems as well. A whole generation of new databases emerged, all categorized under the somewhat confrontational name of **NoSQL** databases. While it is not clear where the name came from, it is pretty clear that it was born out of frustration with relational systems at that point in time. While most of us nowadays treat NoSQL as an acronym for Not Only SQL, the naming still remains a somewhat controversial topic among data buffs.

The basic philosophy of most NoSQL adepts, I believe, is that of the **task-oriented** database management system. It's like the old saying goes: *If all you have is a hammer, everything looks like a nail*. Well, now we have different kinds of hammers, screwdrivers, chisels, shovels, and many more tools up our sleeve to tackle our data problems. The underlying assumption then, of course, is that you are better off using the right tool for the job if you possibly can and that, for many workloads, the characteristics of the relational database may actually prove to be counterproductive. Other databases, not just SQL databases, are available now, and we can basically categorize them into four different categories:

- Key-value stores
- Column-family stores
- Document stores
- Graph databases

Let's get into the details of each of these stores.

Key-value stores

Key-value stores are probably the simplest type of task-oriented NoSQL databases. The data model of the original task at hand was probably not very complicated: Key-value stores are mostly based on a whitepaper published by Amazon at the biennial ACM Symposium on Operating Systems Principles, called the **Dynamo paper**. The data model discussed in this paper is that of Amazon's shopping cart system, which was required to always be available and to support extreme loads. Therefore, the underlying data model of the Key-value store family of database management systems is indeed very simple: keys and values are aligned in an inherently schema-less data model. Indeed, scalability is typically extremely high, with clustered systems of thousands of commodity hardware machines existing at several high-end implementations such as Amazon and many others. Examples of Key-value stores include the mentioned DynamoDB, Riak, Project Voldemort, Redis, and the newer Aerospike. The following screenshot illustrates the difference in data models:

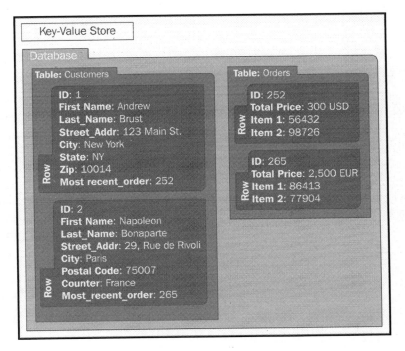

A simple Key-value database

Column-family stores

A **Column-family store** is another example of a very task-oriented type of solution. The data model is a bit more complex than the Key-value store, as it now includes the concept of a very wide, sparsely populated table structure that includes a number of families of columns that specify the keys for this particular table structure. Like the Dynamo system, Column-family stores also originated from a very specific need of a very specific company (in this case, Google), who decided to roll their own solution. Google published their BigTable paper in 2006 at the **Operating Systems Design and Implementation (OSDI)** symposium. The paper not only started a lot of work within Google, but also yielded interesting open source implementations such as Apache Cassandra and HBase. In many cases, these systems are combined with batch-oriented systems that use Map/Reduce as the processing model for advanced querying:

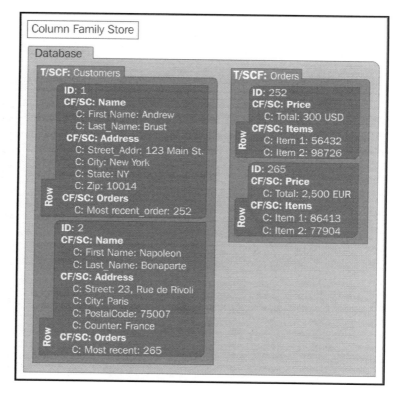

A simple column-family data model

Document stores

Sparked by the explosive growth of web content and applications, probably one of the most well-known and most used types of NoSQL databases are in the document category. The key concept in a document store, as the name suggests, is that of a semi-structured unit of information often referred to as a **document**. This can be an XML, JSON, YAML, OpenOffice, or, MS Office, or whatever other kind of document that you may want to use, which can simply be stored and retrieved in a schema-less fashion. Examples of Document stores include the wildly popular MongoDB, Apache CouchDB, MarkLogic, and Virtuoso:

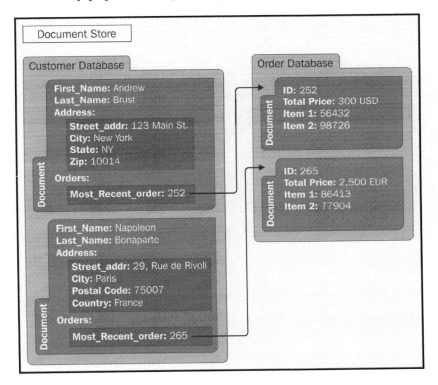

A simple document data model

Graph databases

Last but not least, and of course the subject of most of this book, are the graph-oriented databases. They are often also categorized in the NoSQL category, but as you will see later, they are inherently very different. This is not the case in the least, because the task-orientation that graph databases are aiming to resolve has everything to do with graphs and graph theory. A graph database such as Neo4j aims to provide its users with a better way to manage the complexity of the dense network of the data structure at hand.

Implementations of this model are not limited to Neo4j, of course. Other closed and open source solutions such as AllegroGraph, Dex, FlockDB, InfiniteGraph, OrientDB, and Sones are examples of implementations at various maturity levels.

So, now that we understand the different types of NoSQL databases, it would probably be useful to provide some general classification of this broad category of database management systems, in terms of their key characteristics. In order to do that, I am going to use a mental framework that I owe to Martin Fowler (from his book *NoSQL Distilled*) and Alistair Jones (in one of his many great talks on this subject). The reason for doing so is that both of these gentlemen and share my viewpoint that NoSQL essentially falls into two categories, on two sides of the relational crossroads:

- On one side of the crossroads are the aggregate stores. These are the Key-value, Column-family, and Document-oriented databases, as they all share a number of characteristics:
    - They all have a fundamental data model that is based around a single, rich structure of closely-related data. In the field of software engineering called domain-driven design, professionals often refer to this as an **aggregate**, hence the reference to the fact that these NoSQL databases are all aggregate-oriented database management systems.
    - They are clearly optimized for use cases in which the read patterns align closely with the write patterns. What you read is what you have written. Any other use case, where you would potentially like to combine different types of data that you had previously written in separate key-value pairs / documents / rows, would require some kind of application-level processing, possibly in batch if at some serious scale.

- They all give up one or more characteristics of the relational database model in order to benefit it in other places. Different implementations of the aggregate stores will allow you to relax your consistency/transactional requirements and will give you the benefit of enhanced (and sometimes, massive) scalability. This, obviously, is no small thing if your problem is around scale, of course. Use the following signs:

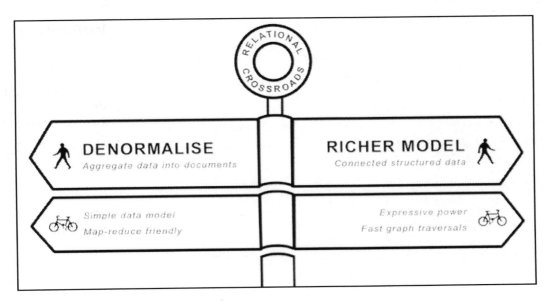

Relational crossroads, courtesy of Alistair Jones

- On the other side of the crossroads are the graph databases, such as Neo4j. One could argue that graph databases actually take relational databases as follows:
    - One step further, by enhancing the data model with a more granular, more expressive method to store data, thereby allowing much more complex questions to be asked of the database, and effectively, as we will see later, demining the join bomb
    - Back to its roots, by reusing some of the original ideas of navigational databases, but of course learning from the lessons of the relational database world by reducing complexity and facilitating easy querying capabilities

With this introduction and classification behind us, we are now ready to take a closer look at graph databases.

The Property Graph model of graph databases

The NoSQL category of graph databases, as we have seen previously, is in a class of its own. In many ways, this is because the underlying data model of graph databases--the Property Graph data model--is of a very specific nature, which we will explain a bit further.

First of all, let's define the Property Graph data model. Essentially, it means that we will be storing our data in the graph database.

A graph structure means that we will be using vertices and edges (or nodes and relationships, as we prefer to call these elements) to store data in a persistent manner. As a consequence, the graph structure enables us to perform the following:

- Represent data in a much more natural way, without some of the distortions of the relational data model
- Apply various types of graph algorithms on these structures

In short, it enables us to treat the graph nature of that data as an essential part of our capabilities. One of the key capabilities that we will find in the remainder of this book is the capability to traverse the graph: to walk on its nodes and relationships and hop from one node to the next by following the explicit pointers that connect the nodes. This capability-- sometimes also referred to as **index free adjacency**, which essentially means that you can find adjacent/neighbouring nodes without having to do an index lookup--is key to the performance characteristics that we will discuss in later paragraphs.

However, it is important to realize that the property graph model is not suited for all graph structures. Specifically, it is optimized for the following:

- **Directed graphs**: The links between nodes (also known as the relationships) have a direction.
- **Multirelational graphs**: There can be multiple relationships between two nodes that are the same. These relationships, as we will see later, will be clearly distinct and of a different type.
- Storing key-value pairs as the properties of the nodes and relationships.

In the different kinds of properties that can belong to the different elements of the graph structure, the most basic ones, of course, are properties assigned to vertices and edges:

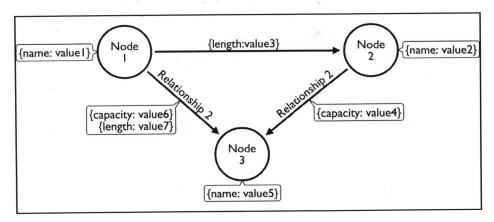

An example of a simple property graph

Let's investigate this model in a bit more detail. When looking closer at this, we find the following interesting aspects of this model:

- There is no fixed schema. The database, in and of itself, does not impose that you have to have a schema; although most software professionals will agree that having some kind of schema as you move closer to production is probably not a bad idea.
- Partly because of the schema-less nature of the database, it seems to be a very nice fit for dealing with semi-structured data. If one node or relationship has fewer or more properties, we do not have to alter the design for this; we can just deal with that difference in structure automatically and work with it in exactly the same way.
- Nodes and node properties seem to be quite easy to understand. In relational terms, one can easily compare nodes with records in a table. It's as if the property graph contains lots and lots of single-row tables, that is, the nodes of the graph. Nodes will have properties just like records/rows in a table will have fields/columns.

- Relationships are a bit different. They always have a start and endpoint, and therefore have a direction. They cannot be dangling, but can be self-referencing (the same node as the start and endpoint). However, the real power lies in the following facts:

  - **Relationships are explicit**: They are not inferred by some kind of constraint or established at query time through a join operation. They are equal citizens in the database; they have the same expressive power as the nodes representing the entities in the database.

  - **Relationships can have properties too**: They can have values associated with them that can specify the length, capacity, or any other characteristic of that relationship. This is terribly important and very different from anything we know from the relational world.

In Neo4j then, this data model has been enriched with a couple of key concepts that extend the core property graph model. Two concepts are important, and related but different: node labels and relationship types.

Node labels

Node labels are a way of semantically categorizing the nodes in your graph. A node can have zero, one, or more labels assigned to it--similar to how you would use labels in something like your Gmail inbox. Labels are essentially a set-oriented concept in a graph structure: they allow you to easily and efficiently create subgraphs in your database, which can be useful for many different purposes, such as querying on only a part of your database content. One of the most important things that you can do with labels is create some kind of typing structure or schema in your database without having to do this yourself (which is what people used to do all the time before the advent of labels in Neo4j 2.0). A node with one label is comparable to a row in a table. There is no comparison with the (so-called) relational world for a node with several labels. Although not required, a node should have at least one label.

Relationship types

Relationship types achieve something similar to what you do with node labels, but with relationships. The purpose of doing so, however, is mostly very different. Relationship types are mandatory properties of relationships (every relationship must have one and only one type--two nodes can be linked by several relations) and will be used during complex, deep traversals across the graph, when only certain kinds of paths from node to node are deemed important by a specific query.

This should give you a good understanding of the basic data model that we will be using during the remainder of this book. Neo4j implements a very well-documented version of the property graph database, and as we will see later, is well-suited for a wide variety of different use cases. Let's explore the reasons for using a graph database like Neo4j a bit more before proceeding.

Why use graph databases, or not

By now, you should have a good understanding of what graph databases are and how they relate to other database management systems and models. Much of the remainder of this book will be drilling into a bit more detail on the specifics of Neo4j as an example implementation of such a database management system. Before that, however, it makes sense to explore why these kinds of databases are of such interest to modern-day software professionals--developers, architects, project and product managers, and IT directors alike.

The fact of the matter is that there are a number of typical data problems, and database system queries are an excellent match for a graph database, but there are a number of other types of data questions that are not specifically designed to be answered by such systems. Let's explore these for a bit and determine the characteristics of your dataset and your query patterns that will determine whether graph databases are going to be a good fit or not.

Why use a graph database?

When you are trying to solve a problem that meets any of the following descriptions, you should probably consider using a graph database such as Neo4j.

Complex queries

Complex queries are the types of questions that you want to ask of your data that are inherently composed of a number of complex join-style operations. These operations, as every database administrator knows, are very expensive operations in relational database systems, because we need to be computing the Cartesian product of the indices of the tables that we are trying to join. That may be okay for one or two joins between two or three tables in a relational database management system, but as you can easily understand, this problem becomes exponentially bigger with every table join that you add. On smaller datasets, it can become an unsolvable problem in a relational system, and this is why complex queries become problematic.

An example of such a complex query would be finding all the restaurants in a certain London neighborhood that serve Indian food, are open on Sundays, and cater for kids. In relational terms, this would mean joining up data from the **restaurant** table, the **food type** table, the **opening hours** table, the **caters** for table, and the **zip-code** table holding the London neighborhoods, and then providing an answer. No doubt there are numerous other examples where you would need to do these types of complex queries; this is just a hypothetical one.

In a graph database, a join operation will never need to be performed: all we need to do is to find a starting node in the database (for example, London), usually with an index lookup, and then just use the index-free adjacency characteristic and hop from one node (London) to the next (Restaurant) over its connecting relationships (`Restaurant-[LOCATED_IN]->London`). Every hop along this path is, in effect, the equivalent of a join operation. Relationships between nodes can therefore also be thought of as an explicitly stored representation of such a join operation.

We often refer to these types of queries as pattern matching queries. We specify a pattern (refer to the following diagram: blue connects to orange, orange connects to green, and blue connects to green), we anchor that pattern to one or more starting points and we start looking for the matching occurrences of that pattern. As you can see, the graph database will be an excellent tool to spin around the anchor node and figure out whether there are matching patterns connected to it. Non-matching patterns will be ignored, and matching patterns that are not connected to the starting node will not even be considered.

This is actually one of the key performance characteristics of a graph database: as soon as you grab a starting node, the database will only explore the vicinity of that starting node and will be completely oblivious to anything that is not connected to the starting node. The key performance characteristic that follows from this is that query performance is very independent of the dataset size, because in most graphs, everything is not connected to everything. By the same token, as we will see later, performance will be much more dependent on the size of the result set, and this will also be one of the key things to keep in mind when putting together your persistence architecture:

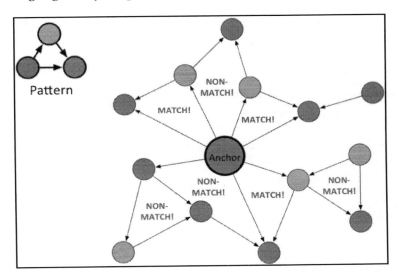

Matching patterns connected to an anchor node

In-the-clickstream queries on live data

We all know that you can implement different database queries--such as the preceding example--in different kinds of database management systems. However, in most alternative systems, these types of queries would yield terrible performance on the live database management systems and potentially endanger the responsiveness of an entire application. The reaction of the relational database management industry, therefore, has been to make sure that these kinds of queries will be done on precalculated, preformatted data that will be specifically structured for this purpose.

This means duplicating data, denormalizing data, and using techniques such as **Extract, Transform, and Load** (ETL), that are often used in business intelligence systems to create query-specific representations (sometimes also referred to as cubes) for the data at hand. Obviously, these are valuable techniques--the business intelligence industry would not be the billion-dollar industry that it is otherwise--but they are best suited for working with data that can be allowed to be more stale, less than up-to-date. Graph databases will allow you to answer a wider variety of these complex queries, between a web request and web response, on data that will not have to be replicated as much and therefore will be updated in near real time.

Pathfinding queries

Another type of query that is extremely well-suited for graph databases is a query where you will be looking to find out how different data elements are related to each other. In other words, finding the paths between different nodes on your graph. The problem with such queries in other database management systems is that you will actually have to understand the structure of the potential paths extremely well. You will have to be able to tell the database how to **jump** from table to table, so to speak. In a graph database, you can still do that, but typically you won't. You just tell the database to apply a graph algorithm to a starting point and an endpoint and be done with it. It's up to the database to figure out if and how these data elements are connected to each other and return the result as a path expression for you to use in your system. The fact that you are able to delegate this to the database is extremely useful, and often leads to unexpected and valuable insights.

Obviously, the query categories mentioned are just that: categories. You would have to apply it to any of the fields of research that we discussed earlier in this chapter to really reap the benefits. We will come back to this in later chapters.

When not to use a graph database and what to use instead

As we discussed earlier in this chapter, the whole concept of the category of Not Only SQL databases is all about task-orientation. Use the right tool for the job. So that must also mean that there are certain use cases that graph databases are not as perfectly suited for. Being a fan of graph databases at heart, this obviously is not easy for me to admit, but it would be foolish and dishonest to claim that graph databases are the best choice for every use case. It would not be credible. So, let's briefly touch on a couple of categories of operations that you would probably want to separate from the graph database category that Neo4j belongs to.

The following operations are where I would personally not recommend using a graph database like Neo4j, or at least not in isolation.

Large set-oriented queries

If you think back to what we discussed earlier and think about how graph databases achieve the performance that they do in complex queries, it will immediately follow that there are a number of cases where graph databases will still work, but not be as efficient. If you are trying to put together large lists of things effectively sets, that do not require a lot of joining or require a lot of aggregation (summing, counting, averaging, and so on) on these sets, then the performance of the graph database compared to other database management systems will be not as favorable. It is clear that a graph database will be able to perform these operations, but the performance advantage will be smaller, or perhaps even negative. Set-oriented databases such as relational database management systems will most likely give just as, or even more, performance.

Graph global operations

As we discussed earlier, graph theory has done a lot of fascinating work on the analysis and understanding of graphs in their entirety. Finding clusters of nodes, discovering unknown patterns of relationships between nodes, and defining centrality and/or in-betweenness of specific graph components are extremely interesting and wonderful concepts, but they are very different concepts from the ones that graph databases excel at. These concepts are looking at the graph in its entirety and we refer to them as graph global operations. While graph databases are extremely powerful at answering graph local questions, there is an entire category of graph tools (often referred to as graph processing engines or graph compute engines) that look at the graph global problems.

Many of these tools serve an extremely specific purpose and even use specific hardware and software (usually using lots of memory and CPU horsepower) to achieve their tasks, and they are typically part of a very different side of the IT architecture. Graph processing is typically done in batches, in the background, over the course of several hours/days/weeks and would not typically be well placed between a web request and web response. It's a very different kind of ball game.

Simple aggregate-oriented queries

We mentioned that graphs and graph database management systems are great for complex queries--things that would make your relational system choke. As a consequence, simple queries, where write patterns and read patterns align to the aggregates that we are trying to store, are typically served quite inefficiently in a graph and would be more efficiently handled by an aggregate-oriented Key-value or Document store. If complexity is low, the advantage of using a graph database system will be lower too.

Hopefully, this gives you a better view of the things that graph databases are good at and not so good at.

Test questions

Question 1: Graph theory is a very recent field in modern mathematics, invented in the late 20th century by Leonard Euler:

> 1. True.
> 2. False.

Question 2: Name one field that graphs are NOT used for in today's science/application fields:

> 1. Route problems.
> 2. Social studies.
> 3. Accounting systems.
> 4. Biological studies.

Question 3: Graphs are a very niche phenomenon that can only be applied to a very limited set of applications/research fields:

> 1. True.
> 2. False.

Question 4: Which other category of databases bears the most resemblance to graph databases?

> 1. Navigational databases.
> 2. Relational Databases.

   3. Column-family stores.
   4. None; graph databases are unique.

Question 5: The data model of graph databases is often described as the proprietary graph data model, containing nodes, relationships, and proprietary elements:

   1. True.
   2. False.

Question 6: Simple, aggregate-oriented queries yielding a list of things are a great application for a graph database.

   1. True.
   2. False.

Summary

In the first chapter of this book, we wanted to give you a first look at some of the concepts that underpin the subject of this book, the graph database Neo4j. We introduced the history of graphs, explained some of the principles that are being explored in the fascinating mathematical field of graph theory, and provided some examples of other academic and functional domains that have been benefiting from this rich, century-long history. The conclusion of this is plain and simple: graphs are everywhere. Much of our world is in reality, dependent on and related to many other things--it is densely connected, as we call it in graph terms. This, of course, has implications on how we work with the reality in our computer systems, how we store the data that describes reality in a database management system, and how we interact with the system in different kinds of applications.

In this chapter, we wanted to give you a bit of context before diving into the wonderful world of graph databases headfirst. It's a good idea, from an architect's point of view, to understand how graph database management systems like Neo4j came about, what problems they are trying to solve, what they are good at, and what they are perhaps less suited for.

With this in mind, we are now ready to get our hands dirty and start with actually playing around with Neo4j, the world's leading graph database.

In the next chapter, we will start applying this context to the specific part of computer science that deals with graph structures in the field of database management systems.

2
Getting Started with Neo4j

In this chapter, we will be taking a much closer look at the real subject of this book, that is, learning Neo4j--the world's leading graph database. In this chapter, we will be going through and familiarizing ourselves with the database management system so that we can start using it in the following chapters with real-world models and use cases.

We will discuss the following topics in this chapter:

- Key concepts and characteristics of Neo4j
- Neo4j's sweet spot use cases
- Neo4j's licensing model
- Installing Neo4j
- Using Neo4j in the cloud
- Using Neo4j Sandbox
- Using Neo4j in a Docker container

Let's start with the first topic straightaway.

Key concepts and characteristics of Neo4j

Before we dive into the details of Neo4j, let's take a look at some of the key characteristics of Neo4j as a graph database management system, specifically. Hopefully, this will immediately point out and help you get to grips with some of the key strengths as well.

Built for graphs from the ground up

Like many open source projects and open source NoSQL database management systems, Neo4j came into existence for very specific reasons. *Scratching the itch*, as this is sometimes called. Grassroots developers who want to solve a problem and are struggling to do so with traditional technology stacks decide to take a radical, new-found approach. That's what the Neo4j founders did early in the 21st century--they built something to solve a problem for a particular media company in order to better manage media assets.

In the early days, Neo4j was not a full-on graph database management system; it was more like a **graph library** that people could use in their code to deal with connected data structures in an easier way. It was sitting on top of traditional, MySQL, and other relational database management systems, and was much more focused on creating a graph abstraction layer for developers than anything else. Clearly, this was not enough. After a while, the open source project took the radical decision to move away from the MySQL infrastructure and build a graph store from the ground up. The key thing here is *from the ground up*. The entire infrastructure, including low-level components such as the binary file layout of the graph database store files, is optimized to deal with graph data. This is important in many ways, as it will be the basis for many of the speed and other improvements that Neo4j will display versus other database management systems.

We don't need to understand the details of this file structure for the basis of this book, but suffice it to say that it is a native, graph-oriented storage format that is tuned for this particular workload. This makes a big difference.

Transactional ACID-compliant database

The **Atomicity, Consistency, Isolation, Durability** (ACID) of transactions ensure that your data will not be corrupt. Neo4j prides itself in being an ACID-compliant database. To explain this further, it's probably useful to go back to what ACID really means, apart from that your data stays surprise-less. Basically, the acronym is one of the oldest summaries of the four goals that many database management systems strive for, and they are shown in the following figure:

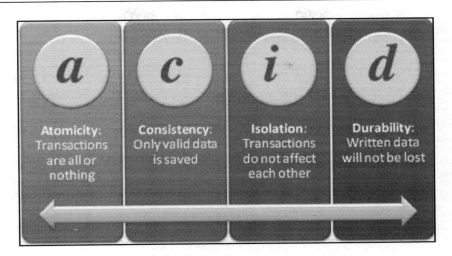

What an ACID base is

- **Atomicity**: This means that changes in the database must follow an *all or nothing* rule. Transactions are said to be **atomic** if when one part of the transaction fails, the consequence is that the entire transaction is rolled back.
- **Consistency**: This means that only consistent or **valid** data will be allowed to be entered into the database. In relational terminology, this often means that the *schema* of the database has to be applied and maintained at all times. The main consistency requirement in Neo4j is actually that the graph relationships must have a start and an end node. Relationships cannot be dangling. Aside from this, however, the consistency rules in Neo4j will obviously be much looser, as Neo4j implements the concept of an **optional** schema.

A schema being optional in Neo4j is a really interesting matter; the idea being that it is actually incredibly useful to have a schema-free database when you are still at the beginning of your development cycles. As you are refining your knowledge about the domain and its requirements, your data model will just grow with you--free of any requirements to pre-impose a schema on your iterations. However, as you move closer to production, schema--and therefore consistency--can be really useful. At this point, system administrators and business owners alike will want to have more checks and balances around data quality, and the C in ACID will become more important. Neo4j fully supports both approaches, which is tremendously useful in today's agile development methodologies.

- **Isolation**: This requires that multiple transactions that are executed in parallel on the same database instance do not impact each other. The transactions need to take their due course, irrespective of what is happening in the system at the same time. One of the important ways that this is used is in the example where one transaction is writing to the database and another is reading from it. In an **isolated** database, the read transaction cannot know about the write that is occurring next to it until the transaction of the write operation is complete and fully committed. As long as the *write* operation is not committed, the *read* operation will have to work with the old data.

- **Durability**: This basically means that committed transactions cannot just disappear and be lost. Persisted storage and transaction commit logs that are forced to be written to disk--even when the actual data structures have not been updated yet--ensure this quality in most database systems, and also in Neo4j.

The summary of all this is probably that Neo4j has really been designed, from the ground up, to be a truly multipurpose database-style solution. It shares many of the qualities of a traditional relational database management system that we know today; it just uses a radically different data model that is well-suited for densely connected use cases.

Made for online transaction processing

The mentioned characteristics help with systems where you really need to return data from the database management system in an online system environment. This means that the queries that you want to ask the database management system will need to be answered in the TimeSpan between a web request and web response. In other words, in milliseconds, not seconds, let alone minutes.

This characteristic is not required of every database management system. Many systems actually only need to reply to requests that are first fired off and then require an answer many hours later. In the world of relational database systems, we call these analytical systems. We refer to these two types of systems as **Online Transaction Processing** (OLTP) and **Online Analytical Processing** (OLAP). There's a significant difference between the two--from a conceptual as well as technical perspective. So let's compare the two in the following table:

	Online Transaction Processing (Operational System)	Online Analytical Processing (Analytical System, also known as the data warehouse)
Source of data	Operational data; OLTPs are the original source of the data	Consolidation data; OLAP data comes from the various OLTP databases
Purpose of data	To control and run fundamental business tasks	To help with planning, problem solving, and decision support
What the data provides	Reveals a snapshot of ongoing business processes	Multidimensional views of various kinds of business activities
Inserts and updates	Short and fast inserts and updates initiated by end users	Periodic long-running batch jobs refresh the data
Queries	Relatively standardized and simple queries returning relatively few records	Often complex queries involving aggregations
Processing speed	Typically very fast	Depends on the amount of data involved; batch data refreshes and complex queries may take many hours
Space requirements	Can be relatively small if historical data is archived	Larger due to the existence of aggregation structures and history data; requires more indexes than OLTP
Database design	Highly normalized with many tables	Typically denormalized with fewer tables; use of star and/or snowflake schemas
Backup and recovery	Backs up religiously; operational data is critical to run the business, data loss is likely to entail significant monetary loss and legal liability	Instead of regular backups, some environments may consider simply reloading the OLTP data as a recovery method

At the time of writing this, Neo4j is clearly in the OLTP side of the database ecosystem. This does not mean that you cannot do any analytical tasks with Neo4j. In fact, some analytical tasks in the relational world are run for more efficiently on a graph database (see the *Sweet spot use cases of Neo4j* section that follows later in this chapter), but it is not optimized for it. Typical Neo4j implementation recommendations would also suggest that you put aside a separate Neo4j instance for these analytical workloads so that it does not impact your production OLTP queries. In the future, Neo Technology plans to make further enhancements to Neo4j that make it even more suited for OLAP tasks.

Designed for scalability

In order to deal with the OLTP workload, Neo4j obviously needs to be able to support critical scalability, high availability, and fault-tolerance requirements. Creating clusters of database server instances that work together to achieve the goals stated before typically solves this problem. Neo4j's Enterprise Edition, therefore, features a clustering solution that has been proven to support even the most challenging workloads. Clustering will be detailed in Chapter 13, *Clustering*.

A declarative query language - Cypher

One of the defining features of the Neo4j graph database product today is its wonderful query language called **Cypher**. Cypher is a declarative, pattern-matching query language that makes graph database management systems understandable and workable for any database user--even the less technical ones.

The key characteristic of Cypher, in my opinion, is that it is a **declarative** language, opposed to other imperative query languages that have existed for quite some time. Why is this so important? Here are your answers:

- Declarative languages allow you to state what you're looking for, declare the pattern that you would like to see retrieved, and then let the database worry about how to go about retrieving that data.
    - In an imperative (query) language, you would have to *tell* the database specifically what to do to get to the data and retrieve it.
- Declarative languages separate the concern of stating the problem from solving it. This allows greater readability of the queries that you write, which is important, as people tend to read their database queries more often than they write them. This piece of your software will therefore become more readable and shareable with others, and long term maintenance of that easy-to-read query becomes so much easier.

- Declarative languages will allow the database to use the information about the nature and structure of the data that it holds to answer your question more efficiently. Essentially, it allows query optimizations that you would never have known of or thought about in an imperative approach. Therefore, declarative languages can be faster--at least over time, as the optimization algorithms mature.
- Declarative languages are great for ad hoc querying of your database, without you having to write complex software routines to do so.

Part of the reason why I feel that Cypher is such an important part of Neo4j is that we know that declarative languages, especially in the database management systems world, are critical to mass adoption. Most application developers do not want to worry about the nitty-gritty of how to best interact with their data. They want to focus on the business logic and that the data *should just be there* when I want it, as I want it. This is exactly how relational database systems evolved in the seventies . (Refer to `Chapter 1`, *Graph Theory and Databases*.) It is highly likely that we will be seeing a similar evolution in the graph database management system space. Cypher, therefore, is in a unique position and makes it so much easier to work with the database. It is already an incredible tool today, and it will only become better with time and the OpenCypher initiative. Cypher will be covered in `Chapter 4`, *Getting Started with Cypher*

Sweet spot use cases of Neo4j

Like with many software engineering tools, Neo4j, too, has its sweet spot use cases--specific types of uses where the tool really shines and adds a lot of value to your process. Many tools can do many things, and so can Neo4j, but only a few things can be done really well by a certain tool. We have already addressed some of this in the previous chapter. However, to summarize specifically for the Neo4j database management system, I believe that there are two particular types of cases, featuring two specific types of database queries, where the tool really excels.

Complex join-intensive queries

We discussed in the previous chapter how relational database management systems suffer from significant drawbacks, as they have to deal with more and more complex data models. Asking these kinds of questions of a relational database requires the database engine to calculate the Cartesian product of the full indices on the tables involved in the query. This computation can take a very long time on larger datasets or if more than two tables are involved.

Graph database management systems do not suffer from these problems. The join operations are effectively precalculated and explicitly persisted in the database based on the relationships that connect nodes together. Therefore, joining data becomes as simple as hopping from one node to another--effectively, as simple as following a pointer. These complex questions that are so difficult to ask in a relational world are extremely simple, efficient, and fast in a graph structure.

Pathfinding queries

Many users of Neo4j use the graph structure of their data to find out whether there are useful paths between different nodes on the network. *Useful* in this phrase is probably the operative word; they are looking for specific paths on the network to perform the following:

- To see whether the path actually exists. Are there any connections between two data elements, and if so, what does this connectivity look like?
- To look for the optimal path. Which path between two things has the lowest cost?
- To look for the variability of the path if a certain component of the path changes. What happens to the path if the properties of a node or relationship change?

Both of these sweet spot use cases share a couple of important characteristics:

- They are **graph local** and they have one or more fixed starting point(s), or **anchors**, in the graph from where the graph database engine can start traversing out
- They are performed on near real-time data (unlike replicated data called cubes in Business Intelligence)

Let's now switch to another key element of Neo4j's success as a graph database management system: the fact that it is an open source solution.

Committed to open source

One of the key things that we have seen happening in Enterprise information technology is the true and massive adoption of open source technologies for many of its business-critical applications. This has been an evolution that has lasted a decade at least, starting with peripheral systems such as web servers (in the days when web servers were still considered to be serving static web pages), but gradually evolving to mission critical operating systems, content management applications, CRM systems, and databases such as Neo4j.

There are many interesting aspects to open source software, but some of the most often quoted are listed as follows:

- **Lower chance of vendor lock-in**: As the code is readily available, the user of the software can also read the code themselves and potentially understand how to work with it (and extend it, fix it, audit it, and so on) independently of the vendor.
- **Better security**: As the code is undergoing public scrutiny and because there is no way for a developer to implement *security through obscurity* (for example, using a proprietary algorithm that no one knows and would have to reverse engineer), open source software systems should be intrinsically more secure.
- **Easier support and troubleshooting**: As both the vendor and customer have access to the source code, it should be easier to exchange detailed, debug-level information about the running system and pinpoint problems.
- **More innovation through extensibility**: By exposing source code, many people left and right will start playing with the software--even without the original author knowing that this is going on. This typically causes these **community contributors** to solve problems that they encounter with the product in their specific use cases, and it leads to faster innovation and extensibility of the solution.
- **Supporting (fundamental and applied) research**: Open source solutions--even the ones equipped with enterprise commercial features such as Neo4j--usually allow researchers to use the software for free. Most researchers also publish their work as open source code. So, it's a two-way street.
- **Cheaper**: Open source software tends to use **fair** licensing models. You only need to pay if you derive value from the software and are not able to contribute your code. This not only allows for cheaper evaluation of the software in the start of the process but also allows enterprises to start with limited investments and grow gradually as the use expands.

I believe that all this is true for Neo4j. Let's look at the different parameter axes that determine the license model. Three parameters, which are explained in the following sections, are important.

The features

Neo4j offers different feature sets for different editions of the graph database management system:

- **Community Edition**: This is the basic, fully functional, high-performance graph database.
- **Enterprise Edition**: This adds a number of typical Enterprise features to the Community Edition: clustering (for high availability and load balancing), advanced monitoring, advanced caching, online backups, and more. Neo Technology has a number of additional features lined up on the Enterprise Edition road map.

Most users of Neo4j start off with the Community Edition, but then deploy into production on the Enterprise Edition.

 Since Enterprise Version 3.2, it is possible to deploy Neo4j as a cluster between different data centers, possibly on different continents, and still ensure that the transactions are ACID.

The support

Different support channels exist for Neo4j's different editions:

- The Community Edition offers **community support**. This means that you are welcome to ask questions and seek support on the public forums (Google Group, Stack Overflow, Twitter, and other channels). However, note the following points:
  - The responses will always need to be publicized (cannot be private)
  - The responses will not be guaranteed or timed
  - Neo Technology does sponsor a significant team of top-notch engineers to help the community users, but at the end of the day, this formula does have its limitations

- The Enterprise Edition offers a professional grade support team that is available 24/7, follows the sun, and has different prioritization levels with guaranteed response times. At the time of writing this, Neo Technology also offers direct access to its engineers that write the product so that customers can literally get firsthand information and help from the people that built Neo4j themselves.

The support program for Neo4j is typically something that is most needed at the beginning of the process (as this is when the development teams the have most questions about the new technology that they are using), but it is often only sought at the end of a development cycle.

The license conditions

For the slightly more complicated bit, Neo Technology has chosen very specific licensing terms for Neo4j, which may seem a tad complicated but which actually really support the following goals:

- Promoting open source software
- Promoting community development of Neo4j
- Assuring long-term viability of the Neo4j project by providing for a revenue stream

This is achieved in the following ways:

- The Community Edition uses the **GNU Public License Version 3 (GPLv3)** as its licensing terms. This means that you may copy, distribute, and modify the software as long as you track changes/dates of in-source files and keep modifications under GPL. You can distribute your application using a GPL library commercially, but you must also provide the source code. It is therefore a very viral license and requires you to open source your code--but only if your code directly interfaces with the Neo4j code through the Java API. If you are using the REST API, then there are little or no contamination effects, and you can just use Neo4j at will.
- The Enterprise Edition uses a so-called dual license model. This means that users of the Neo4j Enterprise Edition can choose one of two options:
    - They adhere to the **Affero GNU Public License Version 3 (AGPLv3)**, which is sometimes also referred to as the **GPL for the web.**

The AGPL license differs from the other GNU licenses in that it was built for network software. Similar conditions apply to the GPL; however, it is even more viral in the sense that it requires you to open source your code not only when you link your code on the same machine (through Neo4j's Java API), but also if you interface with Neo4j over the network (through Neo4j's REST API). So, this means that if you use Neo4j's Enterprise Edition for free, you have to open source your code.

- Get a **Neo Technology Commercial License (NTCL)**. This license is a typical commercial subscription license agreement, which gives you the right to use Neo4j Enterprise Edition for a certain period of time on a certain number of machines/instances.

Neo Technology offers a number of different annual commercial subscription options, depending on the number of instances that you will deploy, the type of company you are (education, start-up, mid-sized corporation, or large corporation), the legal contract requirements of the agreement, and the support contract. For more information on the specifics of these bundles, which change regularly, you can contact `licensing@neotechnology.com`.

With that, we have wrapped up this section and will now proceed to getting our hands dirty with Neo4j on the different platforms available.

Installing Neo4j

In this section, we will take you through the first couple of steps that you need to take to get started with Neo4j. These steps are quite a bit different on different platforms; therefore, we will be going through the different options one by one and looking at the common steps. For most, this will be a simple step, but it's an important one that we cannot afford to skip.

Installing Neo4j on Windows

Like on any platform, installing Neo4j starts with downloading the latest version from the Neo4j website, `http://www.neo4j.org/download`, where the most recent versions can be found (see the following picture):

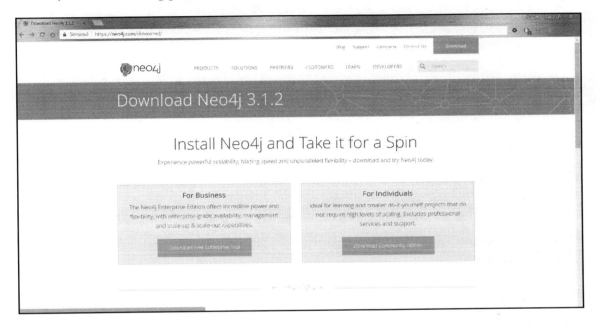

Download Neo4j for Windows

 Currently, interfacing with Neo4j is best done with a webkit-based browser, such as Chrome (which is the browser that we will be using for this section), on all platforms.

Neo4j Community Edition offers an excellent starting point for your exploration of the Neo4j ecosystem, and on Windows, the download process initiated provides you with an executable Windows installer that gives you the smoothest installation experience, which, when run, looks as follows:

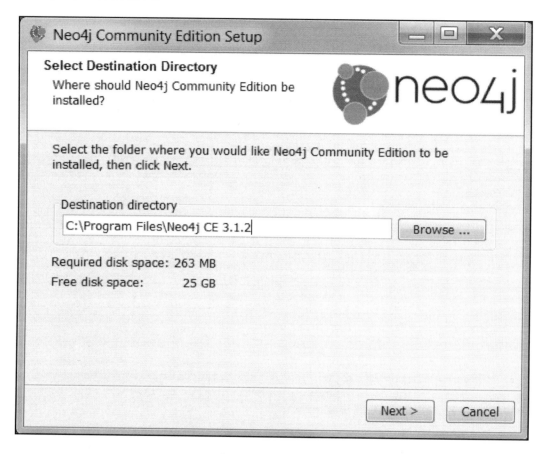

The downloaded Neo4j installer

Once Neo4j is downloaded, the Windows installer provides you with all the necessary options to install Neo4j smoothly and efficiently:

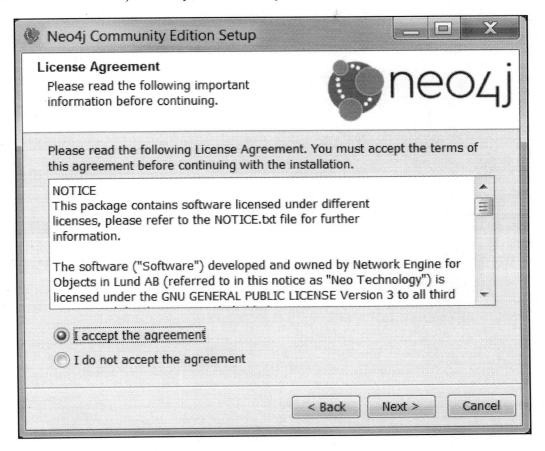

Accept the Neo4j license

After you accept the license agreement, the setup wizard will allow you to immediately run the software:

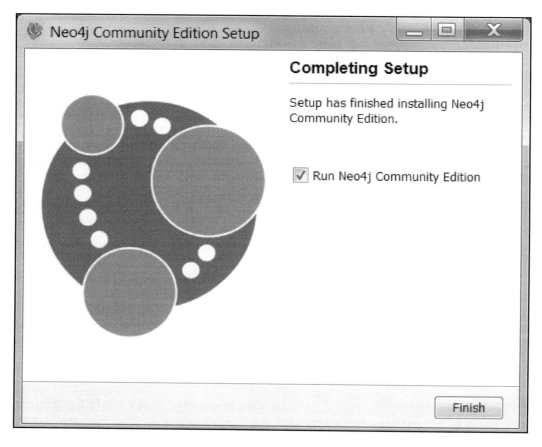

Completed installation of Neo4j

The following screenshot shows that Neo4j is initiated and running when you finish the setup instructions:

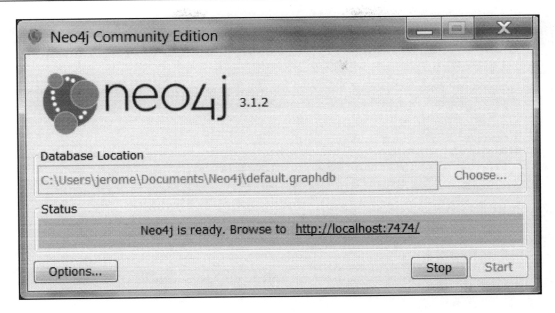

Starting Neo4j

Once Neo4j is running, you can immediately access the server with the Neo4j browser:

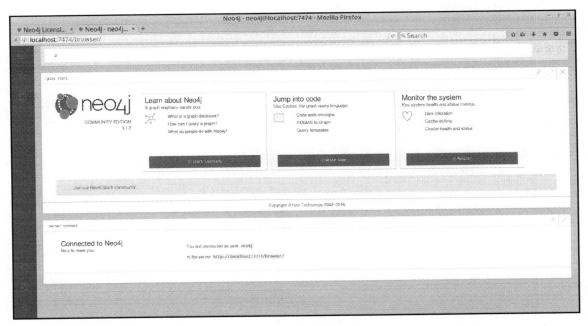

Accessing the Neo4j browser

Accessing the Neo4j server binaries or any of the accompanying tools can be done from the filesystem, which would typically be in the `C:\Program Files\Neo4j Community` directory.

With that, we now have a running server on our Microsoft Windows machine and we are ready to start working with it. We will do so right after we explore some of the other remaining platforms.

Installing Neo4j on Mac or Linux

Downloading Neo4j for the Mac or Linux platforms is very similar. The Neo4j website will automatically detect your platform and start downloading the appropriate version:

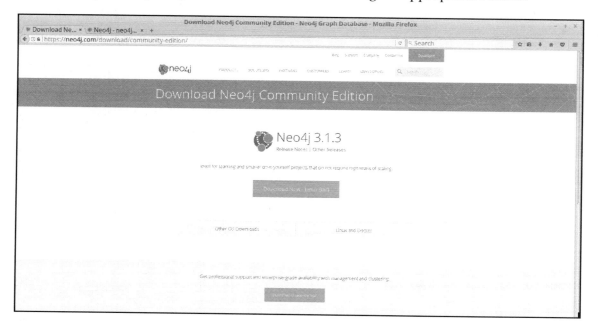

Download Neo4j for OS X/Linux

The only major difference in the download process, however, is in the fact that the Java runtime is not bundled with the downloaded files. On Windows, as we saw previously, there is no need to install anything but the Neo4j installer. On macOS X and Linux, however, you need to make sure that Java 7 is installed and configured to be used as the default Java Virtual Machine. In this book, we will assume that you know how to do this; if not, you may want to search for *Neo4j Java 7 OS X* using a browser to find the required articles to solve this.

I will be using Linux as my home operating system, but the process should be almost identical on OS X.

First, you start by downloading the file that contains Neo4j, as shown in the following screenshot:

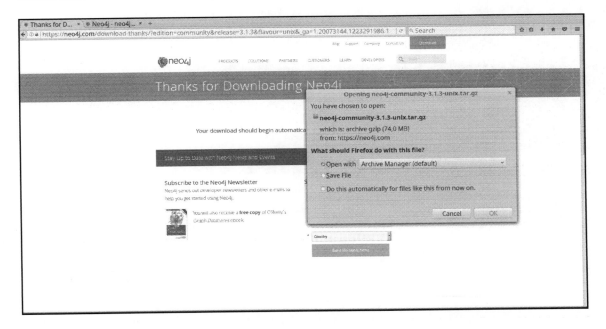

Neo4j is downloaded as a tar ball

Next, you just need to decompress the download in a location of your preference. You can do that with a graphical tool (just double-click on the compressed file) or using the command-line utility that ships with your OS X or Linux distribution. In any case, you will get a file structure similar to the one shown in the following screenshot:

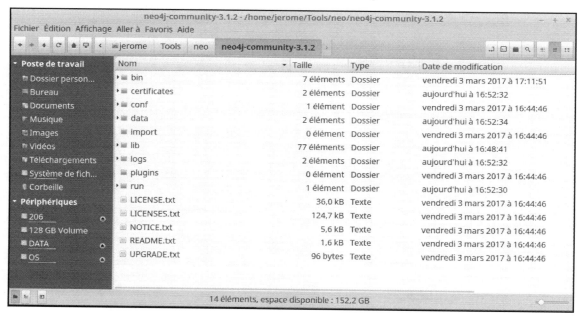

The uncompressed file structure of Neo4j

Next, you should open a Terminal in the directory highlighted in the preceding screenshot. By running a simple command (`bin/neo4j start`), you will start Neo4j at the default location:

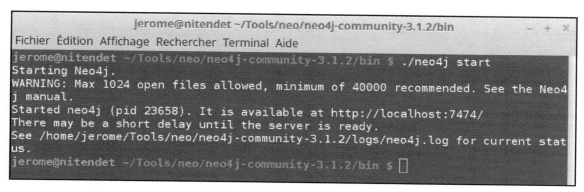

Starting Neo4j from the command line

Accessing Neo4j's browser is completely analogous to the Windows installation illustrated previously; all you need to do is point your browser to `http://localhost:7474` and you should be good to go, having the Neo4j browser in your browser.

The default installation of Neo4j also comes with some tutorials and a simple dataset that you can play around with. Hopefully, this is enough to get you going; it certainly is enough for this chapter of the book.

Using Neo4j in a cloud environment

In this section, we are going to address a third and alternative way of getting started with the Neo4j graph database management system--using a cloud solution. As it turns out, you can try out the power of the database solution without even having to go through the previously mentioned steps of installing the product on an operating system of your own. You can just use a **graph as a service** solution; there are multiple providers out there. At the time of writing this, you can use solutions from the following:

- GrapheneDB
- Heroku
- GraphStory
- GraphGrid
- Azure
- A **roll your own** solution on CleverCloud, OVH, Google Cloud Platform, OpenShift, **Amazon Web Services (AWS)**, and so on, is possible as well

Consider a hosting provider allowing you to use Docker, so you may roll your own image. More details on Docker installation later in this chapter.

Therefore, we are going to explain and illustrate some of the principles of a cloud-based deployment model and how you can use it to get started. To do so, we will be using the **GrapheneDB** platform--probably one of the most simple, elegant, and powerful solutions out there.

Getting started with the cloud platform consists of a few simple steps:

1. Register with GrapheneDB. This is easy enough, as they offer a free tier (depends on the hosting region) to test out the solution and get started:

Starting with GrapheneDB

2. Create a database instance. This is the equivalent of starting up a Neo4j server, but not on your own server hardware:

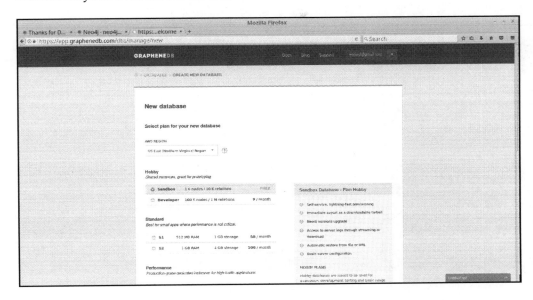

Create a new database 1/2

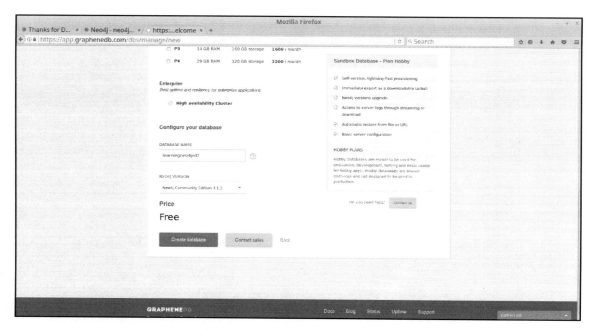

Create a new database 2/2

3. Once the database has been created, we are advised to create a user:

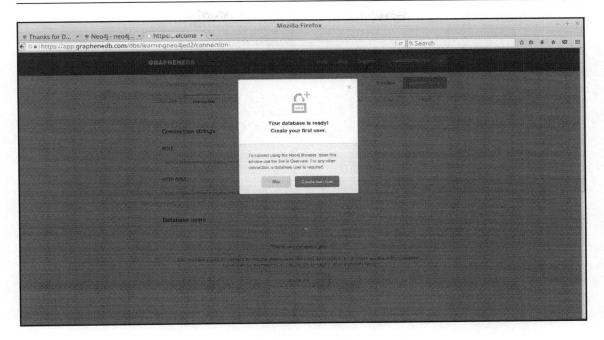

Create a new Neo4j user 1/2

4. For the limited use of our Sandbox, our new user will not expire:

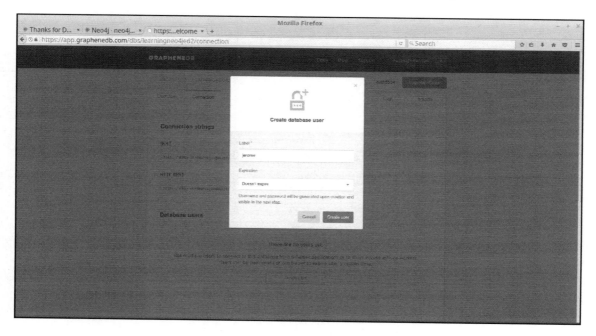

Create a new Neo4j user 2/2

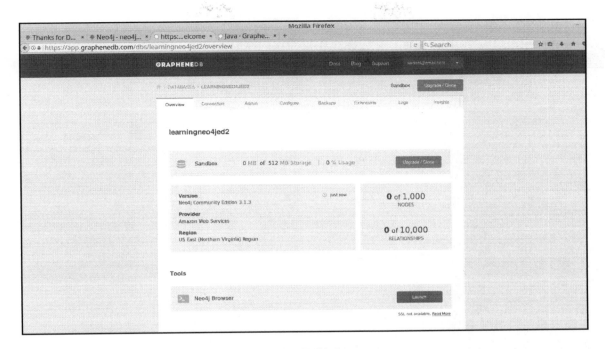

Start using a Neo4j database

5. After validating, go in the **Overview** tab. Click on the **Launch** button in the **Tools** section.

6. In this browser interface, we can do everything we would normally be able to do, except for the fact that this interface is protected by an implicit username/password combination. Running a few queries immediately feels familiar; the experience is nearly identical to that of running a local database server:

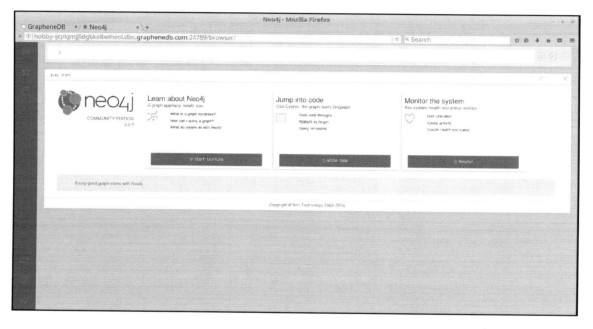

Accessing the Neo4j browser

7. One of the few differences that you will notice is the way you access the REST interface, for example, if you are using specific language bindings. These configurations are very specific and need to be taken into account.

8. Finally, if you want to administer your cloud-based Neo4j system, you can access the following web page to, say, perform exports and imports of your database. The latter is of course interesting and important, as it allows you to create a database on your local machine and then transfer the zipped `graph.db` directory to the Neo4j instance at `http://www.graphenedb.com/` (under the **Admin** tab, look for the **Export database** button).

I hope this gives you a good overview of how you can get started with Neo4j with a provider such as GrapheneDB. It definitely flattens the learning curve even further and makes it easier for people to start using Neo4j in real production environments.

Sandbox

The incredible team at Neo4j managed to offer an even easier opportunity to try Neo4j--the Sandbox. Right off Neo4j's own website, with a few clicks, you will be able to create your own server for free on a public cloud. Of course, there is a major limitation, which is that it will last seven days before it disappears. However, all the work you have done will not be in vain, as it is possible to download the content of your Sandbox. Sounds awesome, right?

Even more awesome is the ability to have a database with some data, even personalized data like your Twitter network (people and tweets).

At this date, other available datasets are as follows:

- The connections around the Trump administration
- Bills and votes from the US Congress
- Movies, in order to generate recommendations

Of course, you may also get a blank Sandbox. You can follow these instructions:

1. We will now create a Twitter-flavored Sandbox. This needs a Twitter account, which you hopefully already have.
2. On the home page of Neo4j.org, click on the **TRY NEO4J SANDBOX** button:

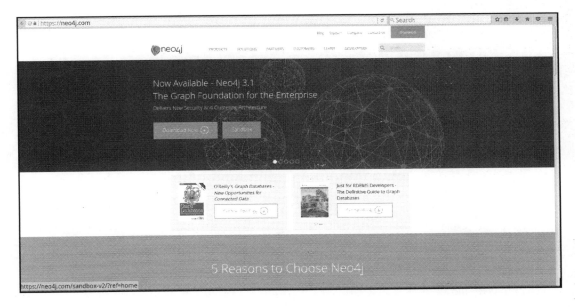

Neo4j home page

3. No download is required; however, a stable internet connection is advised:

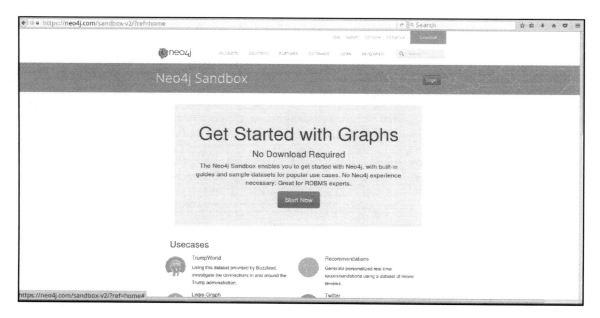

Neo4j Sandbox creation start

4. After we click on **Start Now**, as we are not logged in, this popup appears, inviting us to authenticate through a service of our choice:

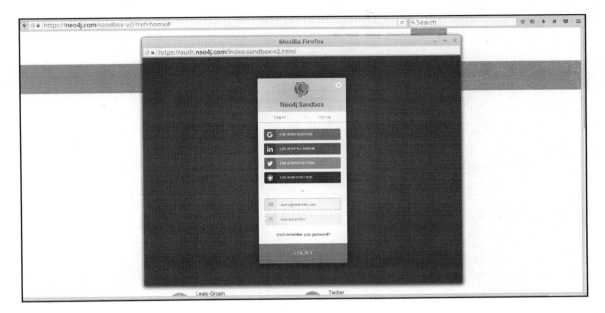

Authentication popup

5. We will choose to **LOG IN** with Twitter. This leads to another popup asking to allow Neo4j permission to consult our Twitter account. You will land on a page like this one:

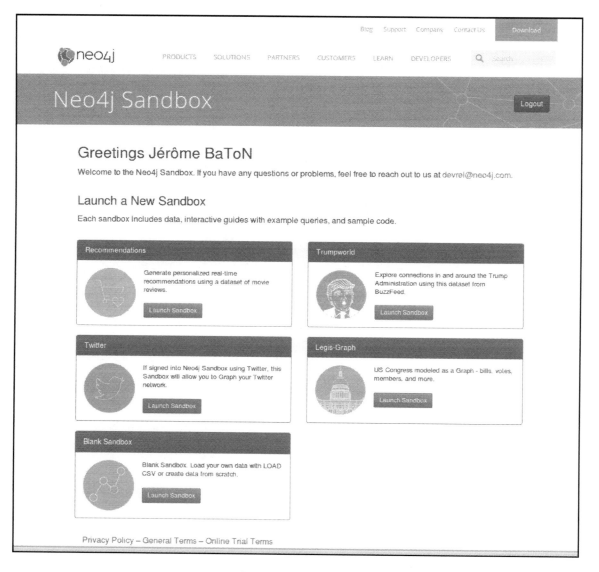

Sandbox home page, authenticated

6. Click on **Launch Sandbox** in the Twitter frame:

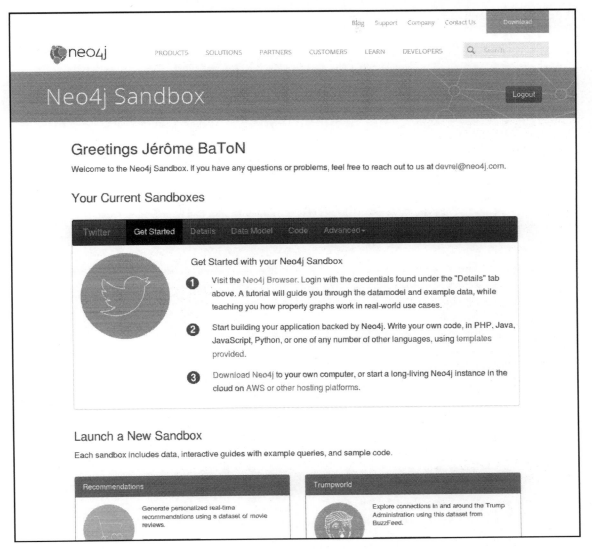

Sandbox home page, authenticated - Get Started

7. After the creation of your first Sandbox, go to the **Details** tab, and middle-click on the **Direct Neo4j HTTP** link to open the Neo4j browser in a new tab:

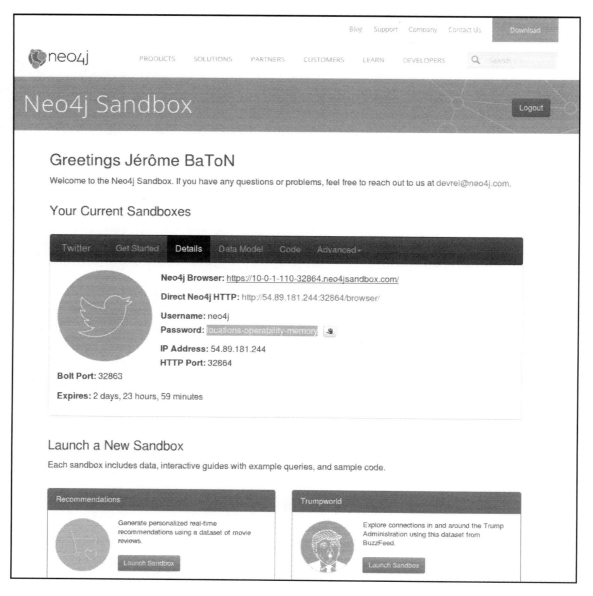

Connection details

8. A card is displayed; click on the right arrow on the right-hand of this card twice, so that you can see the **Your mentions** title:

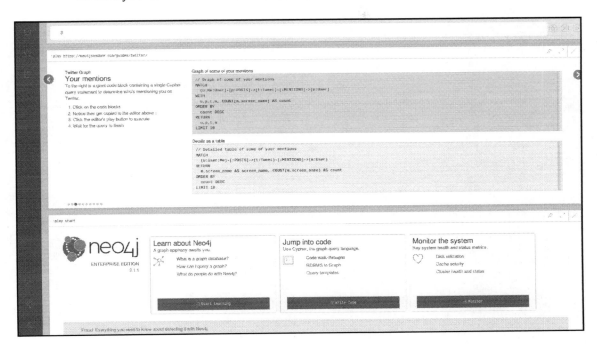

Your Twitter mentions

9. Then, click on the first block of code. This is Cypher code; we will get back to it later, but take a second to appreciate how readable it is. The effect of your click is to copy the code just preceding, in the **prompt** zone.

10. Next, click on the arrow on the right of the prompt zone in order to execute this code. Congratulations, you have executed your first Cypher query!

11. Now, some hacking (not really). Did you notice the **LIMIT 10** at the end of the query? Just like in SQL, its use is to return a limited number of rows. Wait, rows! This is not rows, this is a graph. However, this graph can be displayed as a table if you click on the **Text** tab on the left-hand of the card. You will notice it has ten lines.

12. Click on the same query again in blue frame, and before executing it, change the limit to 300. For me, it looks as follows:

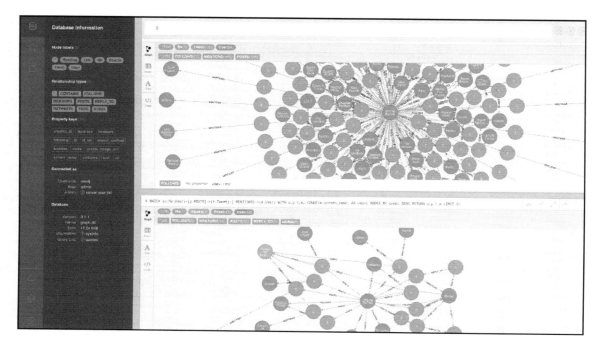

My Twitter mentions, expanded

13. As you can see, increasing the limit decreased the readability. Even if you move the nodes (drag them), it is not very human-friendly.

 Note that because the browser is running inside your web browser, you cannot ask it to display thousands of nodes. You will get warnings indicating that not all nodes are displayed. What you see in the browser will likely always be a partial view of your data. Keep this in mind.

Using Neo4j in a Docker container

Now, what if you want to install Neo4j locally, without really installing it on a server, and not have to face the Cinderella effect of the time limit of the Sandbox? Docker comes to the rescue!

Docker is a technology of virtualization that allows you to run images of a system without the weight of a virtual machine. I encourage you to look at this technology, as it allows you to do **continuous deployment (CD)** of applications.

For Docker-related books, look at this URL on the Packt website: `https://www.packtpub.com/all?search=docker`.

Our goal will be to run a Neo4j Docker image so that we will be able to access the running image as if it was a separate server. For this part, we will use the community edition on Linux Mint, which is based on Ubuntu. Therefore, our examples are given for a GNU/Linux host

Installing Docker

Nothing comes without a little effort, so you need to install docker-ce, if you have not done so already.

Let's not mistaken the different Docker packages. There is a system tray for Gnome named **docker**; the Docker we need used to be packaged as `docker.io`. It is now packaged under the name **docker-ce** (**community edition**).

First, we need to check whether the three prerequisite packages are installed. To check, perform the following:

```
sudo apt-get -y install apt-transport-https ca-certificates curl
```

Then, add the `docker.com` keys to our local keyset:

```
curl -fsSL https://download.docker.com/linux/ubuntu/gpg | sudo apt-key add -
```

Add the Docker repository to our system (Ubuntu users, I assume you use a 64-bit CPU):

```
sudo add-apt-repository "deb [arch=amd64]
https://download.docker.com/linux/ubuntu $(lsb_release -cs) stable"
```

If you use Linux Mint, the `lsb_release -cs` command will not return Docker-supported Ubuntu version names (such as xenial or trusty), but Mint version names such as serena or sarah. Therefore, Linux Mint users should find their equivalent Ubuntu version through `https://fr.wikipedia.org/wiki/Linux_Mint#.C3.89ditions_standards` and `https://wiki.ubuntu.com/Releases` and replace `$(lsb_release -cs)` in the previous command with the result they found (like xenial instead of serena).

Preparing the filesystem

As we want to keep track of the logs and be able to reuse our data, we will need to give the Docker image some access to our filesystem. In our home folder, let's create a Neo4j folder and two subfolders named `logs` and `data`.

This script will do it for you on a GNU/Linux platform:

```
cd ~
mkdir neo4j
cd neo4j
mkdir logs
mkdir data
```

Running Neo4j in a Docker container

Now, run this long command in a Terminal to run Docker with a Neo4j image. Explanations are coming just after:

```
docker run --rm --publish=7474:7474 --publish=7687:7687 --volume=$HOME/neo4j/data:/data \
--volume=$HOME/neo4j/logs:/logs neo4j:3.1.2
```

This triggered some downloading because your **local** Docker repository does not have the Neo4j image available in its 3.1.2 version yet. Meanwhile, a useful magical incantation is to sing "run, baby, run"

Its form is: `docker` **command parameters** `imageName:version`.

Ports used by Neo4j are 7474, 7473, and 7687, for the protocols http, https, and bolt, respectively .

In the parameters part, you can see--volume twice. Its use is to link the folder on your local filesystem to the container filesystem.

Then, providing the port numbers given as parameters were not in use, your Terminal should display something like this:

```
>                                            >

                        jerome@nitendet ~/neo4j                      _ + x
Fichier Édition Affichage Rechercher Terminal Aide
>       --volume=$HOME/neo4j/data:/data \
>       --volume=$HOME/neo4j/logs:/logs \
>       neo4j:3.1.2
Unable to find image 'neo4j:3.1.2' locally
3.1.2: Pulling from library/neo4j
627beaf3eaaf: Pull complete
1de20f2d8b83: Pull complete
74e619d34827: Pull complete
2b3f029f8f8c: Pull complete
5c1be074b03c: Pull complete
c39fa1958707: Pull complete
da1a02f2fbbd: Pull complete
1aa7fae5d370: Pull complete
Digest: sha256:ce7c869a731dfae38732f6a4453938c11e2231da6c5128e521958df240c3bfee
Status: Downloaded newer image for neo4j:3.1.2
Starting Neo4j.
2017-04-27 08:51:23.660+0000 INFO  No SSL certificate found, generating a self-s
igned certificate..
2017-04-27 08:51:25.529+0000 INFO  Starting...
2017-04-27 08:51:26.184+0000 INFO  Bolt enabled on 0.0.0.0:7687.
2017-04-27 08:51:29.339+0000 INFO  Started.
2017-04-27 08:51:30.621+0000 INFO  Remote interface available at http://localhos
t:7474/
```

Docker container started

This informs you that Neo4j is expecting you to connect on port 7474 as usual. So fire your browser and browse to the very same URL we saw earlier, http://localhost:7474, and go graphing! (Your data will be persisted on disk.)

In order to stop Docker running your image, you need to pass not the name (of the image) but the identifier of the running container (based on the image).

So first, in another Terminal, type as follows:

```
docker ps
```

This will list all the containers running, in our case, only one. So we look at the first column, `container_id`, and use it as a parameter:

```
docker stop container_id
```

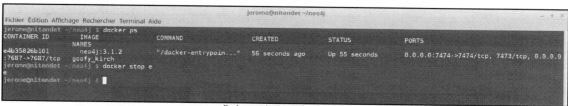

Docker container stopped as it should be stopped

 In fact, the parameter given can only be a part of the ID as long as it strictly identifies a container. In our case, with only one container, the first character is enough.

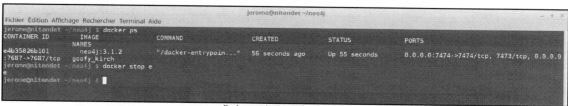

Docker container stopped with laziness

Test questions

Question 1: Neo4j is an ACID database:

1. True
2. False

Question 2: The Enterprise Edition of Neo4j is available in which of the following license formats:

1. A closed-source, proprietary license, to be purchased from Neo Technology
2. An open source license, the Apache 2 License
3. An open source license, the Affero GNU Public license
4. A dual license-either the open source Affero GNU Public license or the open source Neo Technology Commercial License, to be purchased from Neo Technology

Question 3: Neo4j is only available on Linux / Unix / OS X-based systems:

1. True
2. FalseThis allows greater readability of the queries that you write, which is important,

Question 4: Using Docker means I'll lose all my data at every use of the container:

1. True
2. False
3. Depends on the parameters given

Summary

In this chapter, we discussed the background material for Neo4j, specifically, as the world's leading graph database and the topic of the rest of this book. This included an overview of Neo4j's specific implementation of the graph database concepts, its sweet spot use cases, its licensing model, and its installation and deployment considerations in several ways. Honestly, we even went further than getting started, and this should give us the required background to get going with the hands-on part of this book. This is what we will start to address now. The next chapter will help you model your data in the way that is fit for Neo4j.

3
Modeling Data for Neo4j

In this chapter, we will get started with some graph database modeling in Neo4j.
As this type of modeling can be quite different from what we are typically used to with our relational database backgrounds, we will start by explaining the fundamental constructs first and then move on to explore some recommended approaches.

We will cover the following topics in this chapter:

- The four fundamental data constructs
- A graph model--a simple, high-fidelity model of reality
- Modeling pitfalls and best practices

The four fundamental data constructs

As you may already know, the graph theory gives us many different graphs to work with. Graphs come in many different shapes and sizes, and therefore, Neo4j needed to choose a very specific type of data structure that is flexible enough to support the versatility required by real-world datasets. This is why the underlying data model of Neo4j, the labeled property graph, is one of the most generic and versatile of all graph models.

This graph data model gives us four different fundamental building blocks to structure and store our data. Let's go through them:

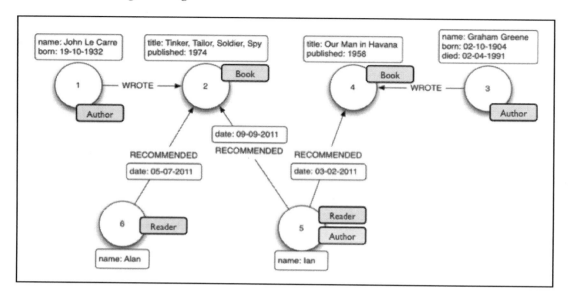

The labeled property graph model

- **Nodes**: These are typically used to store entity information. In the preceding example, these are individual books, readers, and authors that are present in the library data model.
- **Relationships**: These are used to connect nodes to one another explicitly and therefore provide a means of structuring your entities. They are the equivalent of an explicitly stored and precalculated join-like operation in a relational database management system. As we have seen in the previous chapters, joins are no longer a query-time operation--they are as simple as the traversal of a relationship connecting two nodes. Relationships always have a type, a start and an end node, and a direction. They can be self-referencing/looping but can never be dangling (missing a start or end node).
- **Properties**: Both nodes and relationships are **containers** for properties, which are effectively name/value pairs. In the case of the nodes, this is very intuitive. Just like a record in the relational database world has one or more fields or attributes, so can the node have one or more properties. Less intuitive is the fact that relationships can have properties too (like additional columns in a join table). Properties are used to further qualify the strength or quality of a relationship and can be used during queries/traversals to evaluate the patterns that we are looking for.

- **Labels**: This was a fundamental data model construct that was added to Neo4j with version 2.0 at the end of 2013. Labels are a means to quickly and efficiently create subgraphs (categorize nodes). By assigning labels to nodes, Neo4j makes the data model of most users a lot simpler. There is no longer a need to work with a type property on the nodes or a need to connect nodes to definition nodes that provide meta-information about the graph. Neo4j now does this out of the box-- and this is a huge asset, now and for the future. At the time of writing this book, labels are primarily used for the indexing and some limited schema constraints. However, in future, it is likely that the structural understanding that labels provide about the data stored in the graph will be used for other purposes such as additional schema, security, graph sharding/distribution, and perhaps others. In a relational database, a node with one label would be equivalent to a row (node) within a table.
Neo4j allows you to set several labels per node, which has no semantic equivalence in the relational paradigm.
Relations have only one label.

With these four data constructs, we can now start working with Neo4j.

How to start modeling for graph databases

In this section, we will spend some time going through what a graph database model is. Specifically, we would like to clarify a common misunderstanding that originates from our habitual relational database system knowledge.

What we know – ER diagrams and relational schemas

In a relational system, we have been taught to start our modeling with an Entity-Relationship diagram. Using these techniques, we can start from a problem/domain description (what we call a user story in today's agile development methodologies) and extract the meaningful entities and relationships. We will come back to this later, but essentially, we usually find that from such a domain description, we can perform the following:

- Extract the entities by looking at the nouns of the description
- Extract the properties by looking at the adjectives of the description
- Extract the relationship by looking at the operating verbs in the description

These are, of course, generic guidelines that will need to be tried and tested on every domain individually to make sure that it is an appropriate fit. However, for now, let's look at the following diagram:

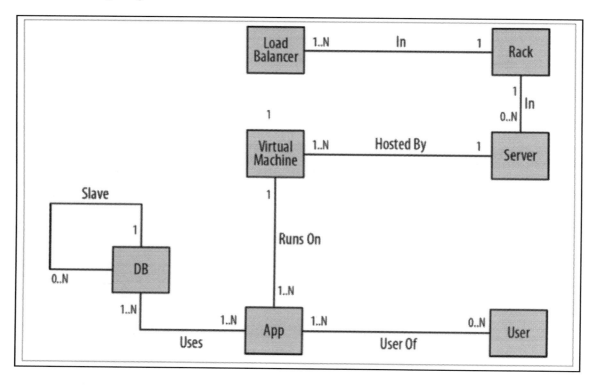

An Entity-Relationship diagram

As you can see from the preceding figure, ER diagrams have the advantage of at least attempting to capture the business domain in a real-world model. However, they suffer from quite a few disadvantages too.

Despite being visually similar to graph visualizations, ER diagrams immediately demonstrate the shortcomings of the relational model to capture a rich domain. Although they allow relationships to be named (something that graph databases fully embrace, but relational stores do not), ER diagrams allow only single, undirected, named but otherwise unqualified relationships between entities.

In this respect, the relational model is a poor fit for real-world domains where relationships between entities are numerous, semantically rich, and diverse. The labeled property graph, as we have seen previously, allows a much richer description of the domain, specifically with regard to the relationships between the entities, which will be multiple, directed, and qualified through properties.

The problem of relational ER modeling becomes even worse when we take the ER diagram to an actual system and are faced with serious limitations. Let's take a look at how one of the relational model's fundamental problems becomes apparent when we take the diagram to a test in a real-world implementation.

Introducing complexity through join tables

Let's take the model, which was described previously, to the database administrator for an actual implementation. What happens then is that, in this implementation, the relational model inherently causes complexity. What you can see in the following diagram is that, for every relationship where we can have n-n combinations, we actually need to introduce something that links the two tables together.

This is what we call a **join table**, and this will be used by every query that requests a combination of the n-n entities:

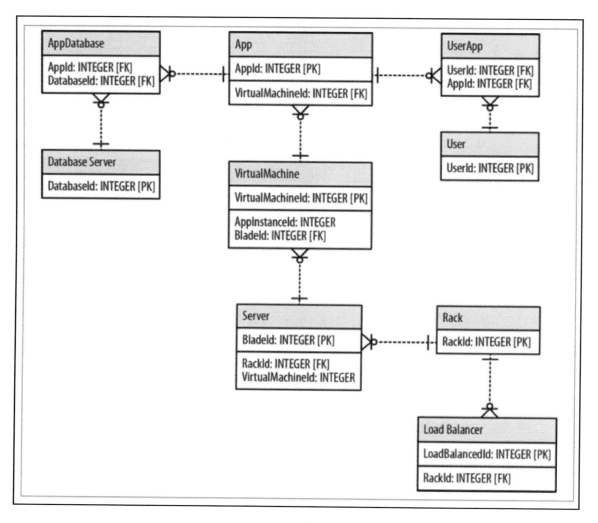

The database schema

In the previous example, we introduced the **AppDatabase** table to link applications to database servers and the **UserApp** table to link **Users** to **Applications**. These join tables are only necessary for dealing with the shortcomings of the relational model, and they complicate our lives as database administrators and application developers. They introduce unwanted complexity.

A graph model – a simple, high-fidelity model of reality

Let's take a quick look at how we can avoid the complexity mentioned previously in the graph world. In the following figure, you will find the graph model and relational model side by side:

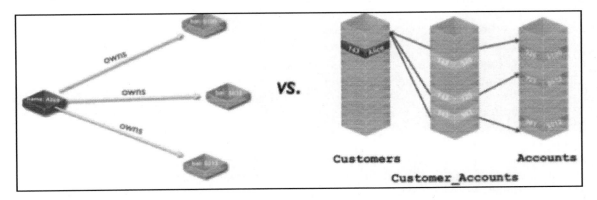

The relational model versus the graph model

On the right-hand side of the image, you will see the three tables in the relational model:

- A **customers** table with a number of customer records
- An **Accounts** table with a number of accounts of these customers
- A typical join table that links customers to accounts

What is important here is the implication of this construction--every single time we want to find the accounts of a customer, we need to perform the following:

1. Look up the customer by their key in the customer table.
2. Join the customer using this key to their accounts.
3. Look up the customer's accounts in the accounts table using the account keys that we found in the previous step.

Compare this with the left-hand side of the figure and you will see that the model is much simpler. We find the following elements:

- A node for the customer
- Three nodes for the accounts
- Three relationships linking the accounts to the customer

Finding the accounts of the customer is as simple as performing the following:

- Finding the customer through an index lookup on the key that we specify in advance
- Traversing out from this customer node using the **owns** relationship to the accounts that we need

In the preceding example, we are performing only a single join operation over two tables. This operation will become exponentially more expensive in a relational database management system as the number of join operations increases and becomes logarithmically more expensive as the datasets involved in the join operation become larger and larger. Calculating the Cartesian product of two sets (which is what relational databases need to do in order to perform the join) becomes more and more computationally complex as the tables grow larger.

We hope to have given you some initial pointers with regard to graph modeling compared to relational modeling, and we will now proceed to discuss some pitfalls and best practices.

Graph modeling – best practices and pitfalls

In this chapter, we will give you an overview of the generic recommendations and best practices for graph database modeling, and we will also provide you with some insight into common pitfalls for you to avoid.
It goes without saying that all of these recommendations are generic recommendations and that there may be exceptions to these rules in your specific domains--just as previously, in the case of your relational database design models.

Graph modeling best practices

In the upcoming sections, we will be discussing a number of practices that have been successfully applied in a number of Neo4j projects.

Designing for query-ability

As with any database management system, but perhaps even more so for a graph database management system such as Neo4j, your queries will drive your model. What we mean with this is that, exactly like it was with any type of database that you may have used in the past or would still be using today, you will need to make specific design decisions based on specific trade-offs. Therefore, it follows that there is no one perfect way to model in a graph database such as Neo4j. It will all depend on the questions that you want to ask of the data and this will drive your design and model.

Therefore, my number one rule, and undoubtedly the most important best practice for graph database modeling, is to start with your user stories. What does the user of the system that you are designing want to know from the data? An example of such a story could be something like this:

> *"As an employee, I want to know who in the company I work for has similar skills to me so that we can exchange knowledge"*

This excerpt tells a little bit about the entities that I need to include in the model and the connections that should exist between these entities. Different domain descriptions would probably add similar or different entities and similar or different connections and will then gradually complete your model.

Aligning relationships with use cases

One of the ways that you can model for query-ability and let your queries drive your model is by using the different relationship types that you can have between nodes for different use cases. Many great graph database models use multiple relationships between two of the same nodes for different use case scenarios.

One of the reasons why this a recommended best practice is actually applicable and of real use in practical development efforts is that the specialization tax, which is the price that you--as a developer--pay (mostly in terms of added model complexity) to introduce a specific relationship between two nodes for a specific use case, is in fact so low. There are no additional tables or schemas to be created, and to be even more specific, there are no additional joins to be computed. All that happens is that the graph traversals will use different paths to establish their course across the network stored in the database.

A key concept to be kept in mind when aligning relationships with use cases is the naming strategy for your relationship types. The general recommendation is to use as few generic names such as **HAS_A** or **IS_PART_OF** as possible, but to be more specific in these naming efforts.

Looking for n-ary relationships

Sometimes, you will find that the first reading of your user stories will not yield optimal results. There can be many reasons for this, but this is often because there are some hidden model elements in these stories that we did not spot at first.

One of the cases where we often see this is when dealing with the so-called n-ary relationships. These types of relationships are often hidden in the model when we want to associate more than two things; in some cases, the natural and convenient way to represent certain concepts is to use relations to link a concept to more than just one concept. These relations are called n-ary relations because they can serve more than two (in fact, n) things or concepts. It is a very common modeling pattern.

When we discover these types of relationships in a graph model, this typically means that there's an additional node to discover that we have split out a new entity, as illustrated here:

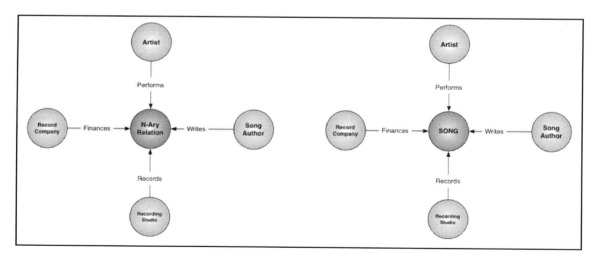

Transforming n-ary relationships into nodes

This is exactly what we have done in the preceding example.

Granulate nodes

The typical graph modeling pattern that we will discuss in this section will be called the **granulate pattern**. This means that in graph database modeling, we will tend to have much more fine-grained data models with a higher level of granularity than we would be used to having in a relational model.

In a relational model, we use a process called **database normalization** to come up with the granularity of our model. Wikipedia defines this process as follows:

> *"...the process of organizing the fields and tables of a relational database to minimize redundancy and dependency. Normalization usually involves dividing large tables into smaller (and less redundant) tables and defining relationships between them. The objective is to isolate data so that additions, deletions, and modifications of a field can be made in just one table and then propagated through the rest of the database using the defined relationships."*

The reality of this process is that we will create smaller and smaller table structures until we reach the third normal form. This is a convention that the IT industry seems to have agreed on: a database is considered to have been normalized as soon as it achieves the third normal form. Visit `http://en.wikipedia.org/wiki/Database_normalization#Normal_forms` for more details.

As we discussed before, this model can be quite expensive as it effectively introduces the need for join tables and join operations at query time. Database administrators tend to denormalize the data for this very reason, which introduces data-duplication--another very tricky problem to manage.

In graph database modeling, however, normalization is much cheaper for the simple reason that these infamous join operations are much easier to perform. This is why we see a clear tendency in graph models to create thin nodes and relationships, that is, nodes and relationships with few properties on them. These nodes and relationships are very granular and have been granulated.

Related to this pattern is a typical question that we ask ourselves in every modeling session--should I keep this as a property or should the property become its own node? For example, should we model the alcohol percentage of a beer as a property on a beer brand? The following diagram shows the model with the alcohol percentage as a property:

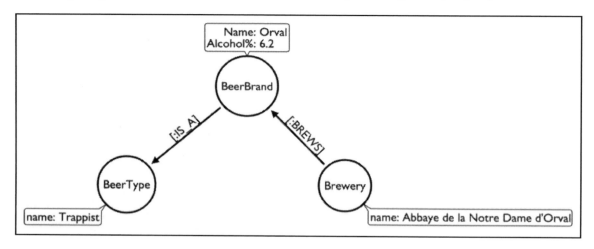

A data model with fatter nodes

The alternative would be to split the alcohol percentage off as a different kind of node. The following diagram illustrates this:

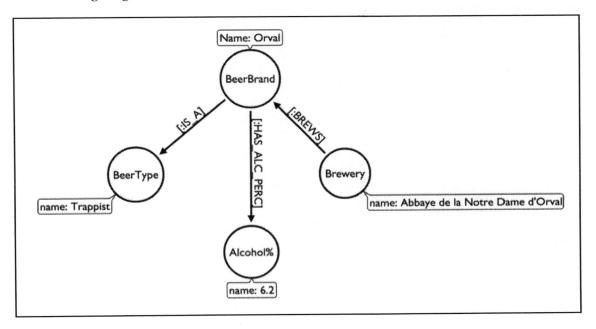

A data model with a granulated node structure

Which one of these models is right? I would say both and neither. The real fundamental thing here is that we should be looking at our queries to determine which version is appropriate. In general, I would present the following arguments:

- If we don't need to evaluate the alcohol percentage during the course of a graph traversal, we are probably better off keeping it as a property of the end node of the traversal. After all, we keep our model a bit simpler when doing this, and everyone appreciates simplicity.
- If we need to evaluate the alcohol percentage of a particular (set of) beer brands during the course of our graph traversal, then splitting it off into its own node category is probably a good idea. Traversing through a node is often easier and faster than evaluating properties for each and every path.

As we will see in the next paragraph, many people actually take this approach a step further by working with **in-graph** indexes.

Using in-graph indexes when appropriate

Taking the granulate pattern even further and knowing that most indexing technologies actually use graphs/trees under the hood anyway, we can apply this pattern to create natural indexes for our data models inside the graph. This can be very useful for specific types of query patterns: range queries, time series, proximity searches, and so on.

Looking at our previous beer model, the alcohol percentages could be a prime candidate for these in-graph indexes. The idea here is that we connect all of the alcohol percentages to one another and create a linked list of alcohol percentages that we could follow upward or downward, for example, to find beer brands with similar alcohol percentages within a certain range. The model is displayed in the following diagram:

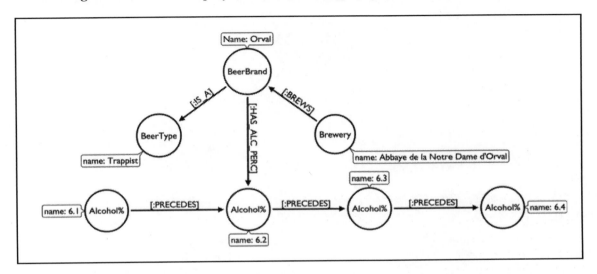

An in-graph index on alcohol percentages

These types of index structures are very often used to deal with time data in a graph structure. In this case, we create more of a time tree instead of a timeline and connect our graph data to this tree instead of putting timestamps as properties on every node or relationship. The following diagram contains an example of such a tree structure:

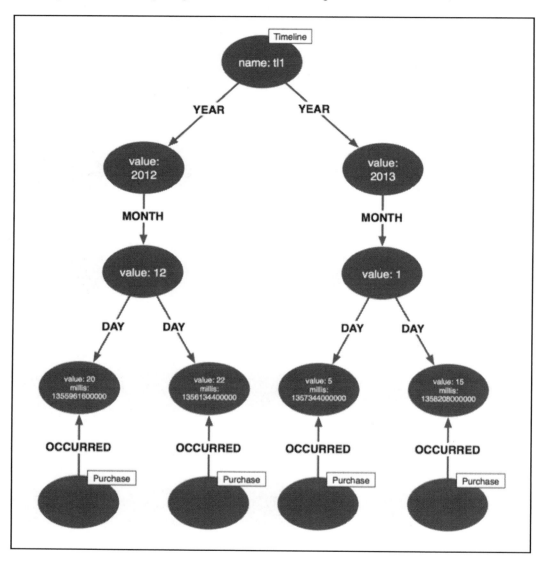

An in-graph time-tree index

All the patterns in the preceding diagram are common modeling patterns that have been used successfully in projects. Use them wisely, and always remember that it's all about the query patterns. Knowing what questions you want to ask of the data will massively impact its design model, and chances are that you will need and want to iterate over that model multiple times to get it to a stable state. Fortunately, graph database management systems such as Neo4j deal with this kind of variation quite elegantly and allow you to do exactly this when appropriate.

Graph database modeling pitfalls

As with any type of database modeling, a graph database will also have some pitfalls that we would should try to. This section will by no means attempt to give you an exhaustive list, but should give you a feel for the types of practices that can lead to poor modeling decisions.

Using rich properties

As it is actually a best practice to have a very granular model in in-graph database systems, the opposite of this can often be an anti-pattern. Using properties on a node that are ostensibly too rich (as shown in the following figure), can be much better solved by leveraging the model, splitting off the properties into separate nodes, and connecting them using a relationship:

name: "Canada"

languages_spoken:
"['English', 'French']"

Using rich properties

Look at the following diagram for a potential solution to this anti-pattern:

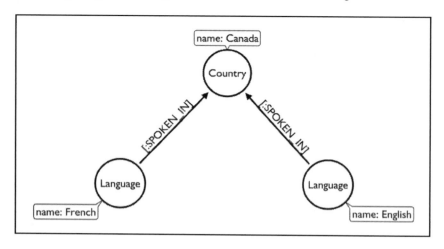

Granulating rich properties

Node representing multiple concepts

Another anti-pattern that we have seen being introduced a number of times is that different concerns or concepts are not separated appropriately in a model. In the model represented in the following figure, we are mingling together the country concept, language concept, and currency concept in one node structure:

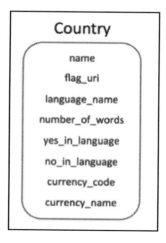

A rich country

This should be a red flag as it will inevitably present us with problems or limitations at query time. It will be far wiser to split off the concepts into separate country, language, and currency node structures, each with their own characteristics and properties. This is what we are trying to convey in the following corrected figure:

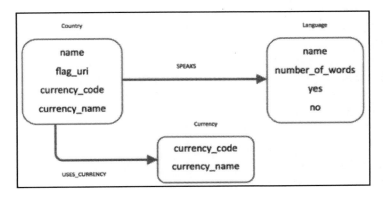

A richer model

Unconnected graphs

An obvious example of graph modeling anti-patterns are unconnected graphs. Graphs are all about the connections between entities, and the power of graph databases is all in the traversals of these connections from node to node.

A pattern like the one displayed in the following image should really not be used in a graph database:

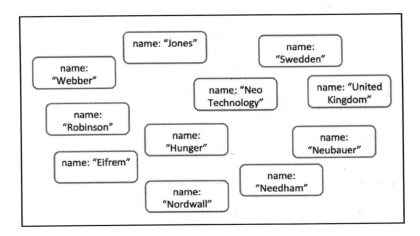

The unconnected graph

Relationships provide structure and query power in a graph, so not using relationships leaves a wealth of opportunities underutilized.

The dense node pattern

We have already discussed how graph queries work in a graph database system. The basic principle was that of a graph local query: starting at a (set of) well-defined starting point(s) and then crawling out from there. The traversal speed is typically very fast and only dependent on the number of parts of the graph that the query will touch or traverse through. Typically, traversal speeds are also very constant with growing dataset sizes, simply because in a normal graph model, everything is not connected to everything. The query will only evaluate the parts of the graph that are connected to the starting points, and therefore, the traversal speeds will be flat.

A very interesting problem that occurs in datasets is where some parts of the graph are all connected to the same node. This node, also referred to as a dense node or supernode, becomes a real problem for graph traversals because the graph database management system will have to evaluate all of the connected relationships to that node in order to determine what the next step will be in the graph traversal. Supernodes can be a real issue in graph database models and should be avoided when setting up your Neo4j instances.

Different strategies exist to deal with this density problem, and Neo Technology is making some important changes to Neo4j to make this problem easier to deal with. However, the fact of the matter is that, on most occasions, we will want to avoid hitting this technical risk by adapting our model. The following diagram highlights one potential strategy that you can use from the music artist/fan graph domain:

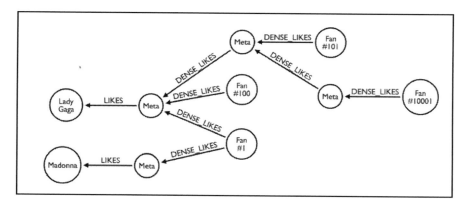

Fan-out strategy for dense nodes

As you can see from the preceding diagram, the strategy essentially consists of *fanning out* the dense relationships to **Lady Gaga** and **Madonna**. Instead of having direct connections from millions of fans to these two popular artists, we create a fan-like structure that connects fans to metanodes, interconnects the metanodes, and then finally connects the top of the metanode hierarchy to the actual artist. The recommendation then becomes that every metanode should have approximately 100 DENSE_LIKES relationships to connect fans to artists and that you can very quickly traverse these relationships to figure out whether there is a variable-length path to connect fans to artists.

Other strategies exist for this, and as we mentioned before, the problem is likely to be significantly reduced in future versions of Neo4j, but just from a modeling perspective, it is very useful to be aware and conscious of this pattern and deal with it proactively.

Test questions

Q1. The four fundamental data constructs of Neo4j are:

1. Table, record, field, and constraint
2. Node, relationship, property, and schema
3. Node, relationship, property, and label
4. Document, relationship, property, and collection

Q2. Normalization is expensive in a graph database model.

1. True
2. False

Q3. If you have a few entities in your dataset that have lots of relationships to other entities, then you can't use a graph database because of the dense node problem.

1. True--you will have to use a relational system.
2. True--but there is no alternative, so you will have to live with it.
3. False--you can still use a graph database but it will be painfully slow for all queries.
4. False--you can very effectively use a graph database, but you should take precautions, such as applying a fan-out pattern to your data.

Summary

In this chapter, we discussed a number of topics that will help you get started when modeling your domain for a graph database management system. We talked about the fundamental building blocks of the model, compared and contrasted this with the way we do things in a relational database management system, and then discussed some often recurring patterns, both good and bad, for the modeling work.

You should also know that modeling is best done as a team in front of a white board, and you should bring non-technical persons as well.

With the model behind us, we can now start tackling more technical matters such as Neo4j's fantastic query language: Cypher.

4
Getting Started with Cypher

Cypher is the **query language** (QL) of Neo4j. Database systems need query languages in order for humans and software applications to interact with them in an efficient way. There are a number of graph query languages out there already (Gremlin, GraphQL and SparQL, to name a few), and some of these have certainly inspired the creation of Cypher, but Cypher is quite different than anything else you may have come across before. No book on Neo4j would be complete without at least spending some time on it--in spite of the fact that there are entire books, presentations, and courses available for you to review. Of course, we will do more than just get started.

In this chapter, we will cover the following topics:

- Writing the Cypher syntax
- Key attributes of Cypher
- Being crude with the data
- Key operative words in Cypher
- Syntax norms
- More that you need to know
- The Cypher refcard
- The openCypher project

Writing the Cypher syntax

I like short examples to set the mind in a good direction, so I'll start with this. If I want to write *Romeo loves Juliet* in Cypher, the Cypher syntax will be as follows:

```
(romeo:Person{name: "Romeo"})-[:LOVES]->(juliet:Person{name:"Juliet"})
```

See, this is almost ASCII-Art. Do you see the **pattern**?

(NODE1)-[:RELATION]->(NODE2)

Now, should you want to create those nodes and relations in your database, type the following in the prompt in the upper part of the Neo4j browser (available at `localhost:7474` if you have started your server):

```
CREATE (romeo:Person{name: "Romeo"})-
[:LOVES]->(juliet:Person{name:"Juliet"})
```

Then, you are greeted with a message telling you about counts of created nodes and relations.

There you are; you have just created data! Did you just say *wow*? Yes, that was easy. Indeed, every person I show Cypher to is impressed. Some students even swear!

As you have just inserted data into a fresh database, use this query if you want to see it:

```
MATCH (n)
RETURN n;
```

It will return all the nodes (and their relations). Let's get back to some history and theory.

Key attributes of Cypher

In making Cypher, Neo Technology and Andres Taylor (`@andres_taylor`) set out to create **a new query language, specifically to deal with graph data structures** like the ones that we store in Neo4j. There were a couple of reasons for this; more specifically, there are four attributes that are not available together in any other query language out there.

Let's quickly examine these attributes, as they are quite important in understanding the way Cypher works in Neo4j:

- **Declarative**: Cypher is a declarative query language, which is very different from the imperative alternatives out there. You *declare* the pattern that you are looking for. You effectively tell Cypher what you want, not how to get it. This is crucial, as imperative approaches always suppose that you--as you interact with the database--have the following qualities:
    - Are a programmer who knows how to tell the database what to do--probably with some procedural logic that will need to be formalized in a program.
    - Are someone that intimately knows the structure, size, and semantics of the dataset being queried in order for the imperative path to the result set to be optimally formed.
    - Both assumptions seem to be quite far-fetched, and for this reason, many database systems have settled on declarative approaches to querying their data. **Structured Query Language (SQL)** is of course the most well-known example.

- **Expressive**: Many people have highlighted that the Cypher syntax is a little bit like ASCII art, and it probably is. With its rounded and square brackets and the arrows connecting the parts of the pattern, it is very easy to understand how the query language expresses what you are looking for. The reason behind **optimizing the syntax to read** is simple and clear: **most code gets read far more often than it gets written**. Expressiveness, therefore, is a very interesting attribute for teams working together on a system that relies on the Neo4j graph database management system.

- **Pattern matching**: Cypher is a pattern matching query language. This is probably one of the more *visual* aspects of the language, as it allows people to sketch and draw complex relationships between different entities in the dataset quite easily. Humans are actually very good at working with patterns; it tends to be very easy for our brains to work with them. Many people therefore experience Cypher as a very easy query language to get started with.

- **Idempotent**: When Neo Technology started working on Cypher, the lead architect of the query language, Andres Taylor, set out to do so using Scala, a functional programming language, on the Java Virtual Machine. One of the key traits of functional programming environments is that they are supposed to be idempotent. In layman's terms, this means that when you operate a function (or in our case, execute a query) in your algorithm, changes in the data should only happen on the first execution of the function. Multiple executions of the same function over the same data should have no effect. This has some great advantages not only in functional programs, but also in the Neo4j database, as state change will be expressed idempotently.

Knowing this, we can now explore some of the key operative words in Cypher and familiarize you with some of these concepts in the real world.

A last key attribute of Cypher is FUN! Cypher is fun to use. Forget the join pains of SQL; see your model in your queries, and vice versa. Thanks, Mr. Taylor!

Being crude with the data

This paragraph is not about swearing at a crew member of a well-known spaceship (while using a language with the name of a crew member of another spaceship). The acronym CRUD stands for Create, Read, Update, and Delete, which are the phases all data eventually goes through. This is the basis of what a database language must offer. This will give you the keys to use your own data. Let's go through the phases and discuss them BY ORDER.

Create data

Obviously, to create data, the keyword is CREATE, as we saw it earlier in our Shakespearean example:

```
CREATE (romeo:Person{name: "Romeo"})-
[:LOVES]->(juliet:Person{name:"Juliet"})
```

Going from left to right in this example, a first node romeo, is created, with the **label** Person and one string property--name valued Romeo. Then, a relation LOVES is linking the first node to a second node, juliet.

A relation is always directed in Neo4j, so basically, we could create a second LOVES relation from `juliet` to `romeo` to model the story better, as follows:

```
CREATE (romeo:Person{name: "Romeo"})-
[:LOVES]->(juliet:Person{name:"Juliet"})
CREATE (juliet)-[:LOVES]->(romeo)
RETURN romeo, juliet;
```

However, this is not mandatory. Not because love sometimes only goes in one way, but because there is a way to test if a relation exists between two nodes without specifying the direction. We will see this in the next paragraph dedicated to reading data.

Note that the first `romeo` and the first `juliet` in lowercase are identifiers **in the scope of this query**. They are made to refer to their respective nodes later in the query if needed.

So, in a simple one-line query, identifiers are useless, and this next syntax is perfectly valid:

```
CREATE (:Person{name: "Romeo"})-[:LOVES]->(:Person{name:"Juliet"})
```

This next one is valid, too, although it is wrong:

```
CREATE (:Person{name: "Romeo"})-[:LOVES]->(:Person{name:"Juliet"})
CREATE (:Person{name:"Juliet"})-[:LOVES]->(:Person{name: "Romeo"})
```

Why is it wrong ? Although powerful, there is (almost) no magic in the query parser.

Four nodes have been created because the query contains four distinct nodes as the query parser has no clue on how to identify nodes. This is because we have not instructed it on what the identifiers of our nodes are. We will get back to how to do that after the CRUD paragraphs.

To end the C part, this query is richer (although they are the same teens from wealthy families):

```
CREATE (romeo:Teen:Person{firstName: "Romeo", lastName: "Montague", age:
13})-[:LOVES{since:"a long time ago",till:"forever",where:
"Verona"}]->(juliet:Teen:Person{name:"Juliet",lastName:"Capulet",age: 13})
CREATE (romeo)<-[:LOVES]-(juliet)
```

This is richer because there are two labels (Teen and Person) on the nodes identified by romeo and juliet. These nodes now have three properties (firstName, lastName, and age). The first LOVE relation also bears information (since, till, and where). The second relation bears no information. As written earlier, it is not mandatory to create it; I just added it to show that it is possible to have the relation's arrow go from right to left.

 Absolutely nothing forces us to put the same properties on the node besides common sense and consistency, which I am sure are qualities you have. What if we want to count all the Teens in the database by age, and some Teens have no age? It will complicate the query and could lead to headaches or false results. So, for the mental health of the future you, please see a Label like a set of properties (0 or n properties; if zero, then it's like a flag). All nodes with a common label **must** have all the label's properties in common.
This is an advice, this is not enforced by Neo4j unless you force it to.

Did you spot the oopsie? The juliet node has a name property and no firstName property, unlike romeo. I swear it was on purpose, to demonstrate that typos are a poison.

Read data

Assuming that you have tried all the previous queries, you have several homonyms in your base:

```
MATCH (n:Person)
WHERE n.name="Juliet" or n.firstName="Juliet"
RETURN n;
```

The important keywords are MATCH and RETURN. This queries the database for nodes with the Person label; we also see a condition on the name property.

Another, richer example of the READ query is as follows:

```
MATCH (n:Person)-[:LOVES]-()
WHERE toLower(n.name)="juliet"
RETURN n ORDER BY n.age ASC
SKIP 2 LIMIT 5 ;
```

Here, we modified the condition with a conversion to lowercase in the condition; there is a sort occurring on the age (from lowest to highest) and nodes without an age property will be at the end of the list. SKIP and LIMIT are used to paginate the results.

Note that in `MATCH`, the non-detailed node `()` has a consequence that the query will only return the Juliets that have a LOVES relation with any kind of node, which could be `(p:PoisonousDrink)` or `(s:Music:Serenade)`.

Did you see that there is no direction on the relation? This is the syntax referred to in the READ paragraph.

An experiment with orienting the relation in both ways is as follows. Try these two similar queries:

```
MATCH (n:Person)-[:LOVES]->()
```

and

```
MATCH (n:Person)<-[:LOVES]-()
```

You saw the results differ.

If we want to return all the `Juliet` loving or being loved by a `Romeo`, a query could be as follows:

```
MATCH (n:Person{name:"Juliet"})-[:LOVES]-(:Person{name:"Romeo"})
RETURN n ;
```

The previous `WHERE` condition is transferred to the node; you can see that it's a copy of the second `CREATE` query.

Update data

The logic is that to update one or more nodes, you need to `MATCH` them. Then, you set the new values of the properties that you want to update. Let's say that a year has passed. We need to update the ages of the `Person` nodes:

```
MATCH (n:Person{name:"Juliet"})
WHERE n.age = 13
SET n.age=14
RETURN n ;
```

In a yearly batch, we can use the following query to update all the `Person` nodes:

```
MATCH (n:Person)
SET n.age=n.age+1
RETURN n ;
```

You will notice how fast it is on our little dataset. It did not take ages.

Note that it is possible to add labels dynamically, and also to remove them.

Add the `Teen` label to that `Person` nodes with an age greater than 12 and lower than 18:

```
MATCH (n:Person)
WHERE n.age>=12 AND n.age <18
SET n:Teen
RETURN n ;
```

You can remove the `Teen` label from the `Person` nodes with an age greater than 18 as follows:

```
MATCH (n:Teen:Person)
WHERE n.age >18
REMOVE n:Teen
RETURN n ;
```

It is also possible to remove a property (use REMOVE n.age).

If we want to add a property in case it does not exist on a node, we use SET:

```
MATCH (n:Person)
WHERE n.age IS NULL
SET n.age = 0
RETURN n ;
```

Certainly, it's not very useful to have ages set to zero, but this is for demonstration purposes.

If we want to add several properties, we can do so as follows, like this:

```
MATCH (n:Person)
SET n.age = 0, n.smell="teenSpirit"
RETURN n ;
```

Or like that:

```
MATCH (n:Person)
SET n.age = 0
SET n.smell="teenSpirit"
RETURN n ;
```

This is it for updating data; now, let's delete it.

Delete data

The first rule when deleting a node is that it is not connected to other nodes anymore. Just like the other operations, it is a matter of matching before deleting a node.

Should we want to DELETE Mr. Montague, the query would be as follows:

```
MATCH (r:Person{lastName:"Montague"})
DELETE r;
```

However, this will fail with an error because of the LOVES relation.

So we either delete the relation first, or we use DETACH DELETE:

```
MATCH (r:Person{lastName:"Montague"}
DETACH DELETE r;
```

Now, Juliet is alone.

We have now covered a solid base of Cypher. We will see more throughout the next chapters, while the next paragraph will be useful as a reference to this basis.

Key operative words in Cypher

Like every database query language, there are a few operative words that have an important meaning in the composition of every query. It's useful for you to know these, as you will be using them to compose your specific queries on your specific datasets.

Keyword	Function	Example
MATCH	This describes a pattern that the database should match. This is probably the most important piece of the query as it is a structural component that always starts your queries (it's one character shorter than SELECT).	`MATCH (me:Person)-[:KNOWS]->(friend)`

Keyword	Function	Example
WHERE	This filters results that are found in the match for specific criteria.	WHERE me.name = "My Name" AND me.age > 18
RETURN	This returns results. You can either return paths, nodes, relationships, or their properties, or an aggregate of the mentioned parameters. This is another structural component, as all read queries and most write queries will return some data.	RETURN me.name, collect(friend), count(*) as friends
WITH	This passes results from one query part to the next. much like RETURN, but instead of including data in the result set, it will be passed to the following part of the query. It transforms and aggregates results and also separates READ and UPDATE statements.	
ORDER BY SKIP LIMIT	These keywords sort and paginate the results.	ORDER BY friends DESC SKIP 10 LIMIT 10
CREATE	This creates nodes and relationships with their properties.	CREATE (p:Person), (p)-[:KNOWS {since: 2010}]-> (me:Person {name:"My Name"})
CREATE UNIQUE	This fixes graph structures by only creating structures if they do not yet exist.	

Keyword	Function	Example

MERGE	This matches or creates semantics using indexes and locks. You can specify different operations in case of a MATCH (part of the pattern already existed) or on CREATE (pattern did not exist yet).	`MERGE (me:Person {name:"My Name"})`
		`ON MATCH me SET me.accessed =`
		`timestamp()`
		`ON CREATE me SET me.age = 42`

SET, REMOVE	This updates properties and labels on nodes and/or relationships.	`SET me.age = 42 SET me:Employee`
		`REMOVE me.first_name REMOVE`
		`me:Contractor`

DELETE	This deletes nodes and relationships.	`MATCH (me)`
		`OPTIONAL MATCH (me)-[r]-() DELETE`
		`me, r`

With these simple keywords, you should be able to start forming your first Cypher queries. After all, it's a bit like ASCII art, a structure similar to the one you could draw on a whiteboard, as shown in the following diagram:

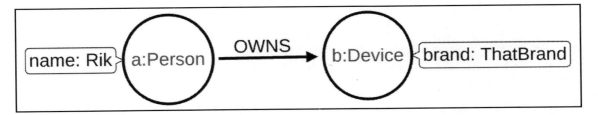

Rick owns a device

This is very easily described in Cypher as follows:

```
(a:Person {name:"Rik")-[:OWNS]->(b:Device {brand:"ThatBrand"})
```

All we need to do to make this a proper Cypher statement is to wrap it in MATCH and RETURN statements:

```
MATCH (a:Person {name:"Rik")-[r:OWNS]->(b:Device {brand:"ThatBrand"})
RETURN a,r,b;
```

We have seen a few simple (and less simple) examples of how you would start using Cypher. More complex examples can, of course, be found elsewhere in this book.

Syntax norms

In order to be consistent with ourselves and other Cypher users, we strongly advise you to follow these syntax norms:

- nodeAliases are in lower camel case (start with lowercase)
- Labels are in upper camel case (start with uppercase)
- RELATIONS are in upper snake case (like IS_A)
- Property names are in lower camel case
- KEYWORDS are in uppercase

Remember, we read code more than we write it.

More that you need to know

I would definitely have started this paragraph with One more thing; but there is more than one. Here are a few points I would have liked to know when I started using Cypher.

When a syntax error arises, as it happens to the best of us, sometimes the error message can be improved:

- Check whether all nodes are closed; it's easy to miss a closing parenthesis just after a closing curly bracket
- The semicolon before the name of a relation is mandatory (so far, I'm lobbying against this)

Check what you return, because the graph view in the browser will show you a view of your results. This is why you get relations when you only return a few nodes. The neighbors (nodes connected) are displayed up to the maximum count of displayable items, which is 300 by default. Keep this in mind. Neighbors give the context, but the truth is in the Rows and Text tabs.

To see and change the default settings for the browser, click on the Settings icon (a gear) at the bottom left of the screen. The following screenshot will be the output:

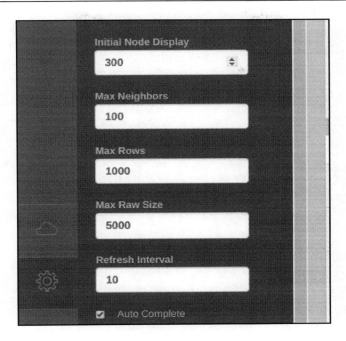

Neo4j browser settings

Last but not least, let's not forget how to set identifiers. Of course, each node has its technical identifier for use by the system.

However, you must not use it. This is not for you; do not make this mistake (technical IDs may be re-affected to new nodes). Back to how to identify a node. First, you have to decide which field (or fields) is the unique identifier (like a primary key in relational databases). This field is to be present for all nodes having a given label. (Remember, you enforce consistency!)
The syntax speaks for itself:

```
CREATE CONSTRAINT ON (p:Person) ASSERT p.identifier IS UNIQUE
```

Its effect is the creation of a constraint that will be enforced on the creation and an update of a Person node. Note that it is enforced only if there is a value for the property identifier.

If you want to remove the constraint, drop it!

```
DROP CONSTRAINT ON (p:Person) ASSERT p.identifier IS UNIQUE
```

There is more in Cypher that we will see throughout the following chapters.

Prepare for numerical conversions, string operations, lists and maps usage, and advanced conditions.

For now, let me give you some WOW effect!

With a little help from my friends

Among the improvements that graph databases bring compared to relational databases is a usage typical for dating sites and recommendation sites (find the friend of a friend or contacts of your contacts).

To demonstrate this, we need a little more data in our graph. Let's consider this as a tree with three levels of Dude (a new Label). There are no identifiers here, thus no constraint, just a name property. We will use this notation dudeA1:Dude for the first (1) node of the first level, our starting point being (leBig:Dude). This dude will have three friends (on level B) called (dudeB1:Dude), (dudeB2:Dude), and (dudeB3:Dude), who will have four friends each on level C.

To create these nodes, a Cypher code to run in the Neo4j browser is as follows:

```
CREATE (leBig:Dude {name: "Lebowski"})
CREATE (dudeA1:Dude {name: "A1"})
CREATE (dudeA2:Dude {name: "A2"})

CREATE (leBig)<-[:FRIEND_OF]-(dudeA1)
CREATE (leBig)<-[:FRIEND_OF]-(dudeA2)

CREATE (dudeB1:Dude {name: "B1"})
CREATE (dudeB2:Dude {name: "B2"})
CREATE (dudeB3:Dude {name: "B3"})
```

And next:

```
CREATE (dudeA1)<-[:FRIEND_OF]-(dudeB1)
CREATE (dudeA1)<-[:FRIEND_OF]-(dudeB2)
CREATE (dudeA1)<-[:FRIEND_OF]-(dudeB3)
CREATE (dudeA2)<-[:FRIEND_OF]-(dudeB1)
CREATE (dudeA2)<-[:FRIEND_OF]-(dudeB2)
CREATE (dudeA2)<-[:FRIEND_OF]-(dudeB3)

CREATE (dudeC1:Dude {name: "C1"})
CREATE (dudeC2:Dude {name: "C2"})
```

```
CREATE  (dudeC3:Dude {name:  "C3"})
CREATE  (dudeC4:Dude {name:  "C4"})

CREATE  (dudeB1)<-[:FRIEND_OF]-(dudeC1)
CREATE  (dudeB1)<-[:FRIEND_OF]-(dudeC2)
CREATE  (dudeB1)<-[:FRIEND_OF]-(dudeC3)
CREATE  (dudeB1)<-[:FRIEND_OF]-(dudeC4)

CREATE  (dudeB2)<-[:FRIEND_OF]-(dudeC1)
CREATE  (dudeB2)<-[:FRIEND_OF]-(dudeC2)
CREATE  (dudeB2)<-[:FRIEND_OF]-(dudeC3)
CREATE  (dudeB2)<-[:FRIEND_OF]-(dudeC4)

CREATE  (dudeB3)<-[:FRIEND_OF]-(dudeC1)
CREATE  (dudeB3)<-[:FRIEND_OF]-(dudeC2)
CREATE  (dudeB3)<-[:FRIEND_OF]-(dudeC3)
CREATE  (dudeB3)<-[:FRIEND_OF]-(dudeC4)
```

You can now see the result of the graph:

```
MATCH (d:Dude) RETURN d
```

Uh oh! Isolated nodes! How bizarre!

Do you notice grey nodes with no names when you double-click on isolated nodes ?
Yes, but why ? You will ask.

Because variables scope, my dear reader!

The names we use as IDs (like dudB4) are variable names, understood by the query parser during ONE call.

We made two calls. My fault; I wanted to demonstrate this to you, so I tricked you. Yes, I am that kind of teacher; I think that it is better to fall in traps during education time than during work time.

Should we want some Neo magic and to use the previously created nodes, we should MATCH them back.

So first, let's remove all the dudes:

```
MATCH (d:Dude) DETACH DELETE d
```

Now, replay the first block of Cypher commands. Use this block instead of the second one:

```
MATCH  (dudeA1:Dude {name: "A1"})
MATCH  (dudeA2:Dude {name: "A2"})
MATCH  (dudeB1:Dude {name: "B1"})
MATCH  (dudeB2:Dude {name: "B2"})
MATCH  (dudeB3:Dude {name: "B3"})
CREATE (dudeA1)<-[:FRIEND_OF]-(dudeB1)
CREATE (dudeA1)<-[:FRIEND_OF]-(dudeB2)
CREATE (dudeA1)<-[:FRIEND_OF]-(dudeB3)
CREATE (dudeA2)<-[:FRIEND_OF]-(dudeB1)
CREATE (dudeA2)<-[:FRIEND_OF]-(dudeB2)
CREATE (dudeA2)<-[:FRIEND_OF]-(dudeB3)

CREATE (dudeC1:Dude {name: "C1"})
CREATE (dudeC2:Dude {name: "C2"})
CREATE (dudeC3:Dude {name: "C3"})
CREATE (dudeC4:Dude {name: "C4"})

CREATE (dudeB1)<-[:FRIEND_OF]-(dudeC1)
CREATE (dudeB1)<-[:FRIEND_OF]-(dudeC2)
CREATE (dudeB1)<-[:FRIEND_OF]-(dudeC3)
CREATE (dudeB1)<-[:FRIEND_OF]-(dudeC4)

CREATE (dudeB2)<-[:FRIEND_OF]-(dudeC1)
CREATE (dudeB2)<-[:FRIEND_OF]-(dudeC2)
CREATE (dudeB2)<-[:FRIEND_OF]-(dudeC3)
CREATE (dudeB2)<-[:FRIEND_OF]-(dudeC4)

CREATE (dudeB3)<-[:FRIEND_OF]-(dudeC1)
CREATE (dudeB3)<-[:FRIEND_OF]-(dudeC2)
CREATE (dudeB3)<-[:FRIEND_OF]-(dudeC3)
CREATE (dudeB3)<-[:FRIEND_OF]-(dudeC4)
```

As you can see, we had to MATCH the nodes we previously created, so as not to have isolated nodes. You can now see the result of the graph:

```
MATCH (d:Dude) RETURN d
```

The graph should look as follows:

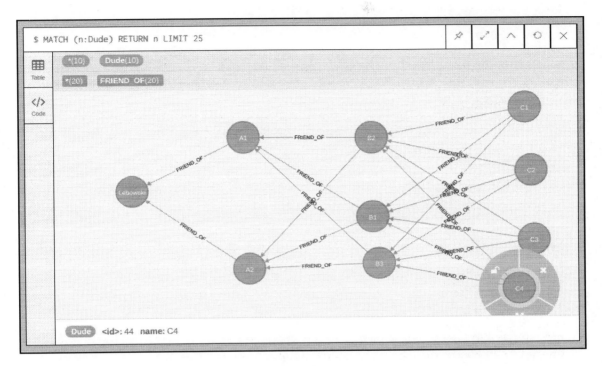

A friendly tree

You do not need to double-click on the nodes to verify if there are grey nodes in between.

Now for some queries.

To list the friends of `Lebowski`:

```
MATCH (le:Dude {name:"Lebowski"})<-[:FRIEND_OF]-(some:Dude)
RETURN some
```

This returns A1 and A2.

To list the friends of the friends of `Lebowski`, here are two forms:

```
MATCH (le:Dude {name:"Lebowski"})<-[:FRIEND_OF]-(someA:Dude)<-[:FRIEND_OF]-
(someB:Dude)
RETURN someB
```

Let's stop a moment and imagine the equivalent SQL with a `DUDES` table and a `DUDE_FRIEND` join table on `DUDES`. It already uses quite a few characters to get the friends of someone, and even more for the **friends of a friend (FoF)**.
So, imagine the SQL for the **friends of friends of friends (FoFoF)** of someone. I would disagree to putting it in this book because it would be a long waste of space and ink. The following is the FoFoF query in Cypher:

```
MATCH (le:Dude {name:"Lebowski"})<-[:FRIEND_OF*3]-(some:Dude)
RETURN DISTINCT some
```

Wow, isn't it? It returns the nodes C1 to C4, just as expected.
Two side notes: First, I have added DISTINCT, in case you look at the Table (or Text) views of the result. Try it with and without, as an exercise. Second, the direction of the relation is here to box the result, or else the nodes A1 and A2 would be returned, too, as they are friends (F) of B1, B2, and B3, which are FoF of Lebowski. An F of an FoF is an FoFoF, which is what is asked in the query.

Should we want to get the FoFoFoF (after having added some friends to C1, for example), the query would need a one character change (just replace the 3 with a 4 in the previous example), and presumably two pages in SQL. I'm not talking about the execution times getting longer and longer with an RDBMS (Am I?).
Wow, again !

The Cypher refcard

Cypher is the declarative query language for Neo4j, the world's leading graph database, and it keeps evolving with time. The language is constantly documented in a reference card that is updated for every new version of Neo4j. You can find the complete Cypher Ref Card online at `https://neo4j.com/docs/cypher-refcard/current/`.

The refcard is also available from the Neo4j browser, the third tab on the left of the screen ("Documents") has a *Cypher Refcard* link.

Although URL schemes changed between versions, like `http://neo4j.com/docs/2.0/cypher-refcard/` for version 2.0 and `http://neo4j.com/docs/cypher-refcard/3.1/` for version 3.1, older versions of the refcard are still available.

> My advice is to download the PDF versions of the refcard for the Neo4j version(s) you use. This keeps me safe from network issues at the office. I also have one on my smartphone because it helps solve syntax errors.

The PDF refcard for version 3.2 is available at `https://neo4j.com/docs/pdf/cypher-refcard-3.2.pdf`

The openCypher project

Since October 2015, the openCypher project has aimed to provide an open grammar, language specification, technical compatibility kit and reference implementation of parser, planner, and runtime for Cypher.

This is how the Neo4j website presents openCypher. Not only is this query language awesome, but this initiative of freeing it means that knowing Cypher does not limit you to only one vendor, be it the best graph database of the market or otherwise. This is intrinsically good for you.
Currently, the other vendors involved in the openCypher project are Oracle, Apache Spark, Tableau, and Structr, but there are, of course, open source projects coming from the community. These projects may not offer the full language and may make use of other databases to persist data, such as PostgreSQL or Redis.

The openCypher website is `http://www.opencypher.org`.

Summary

You did it, you can resist you because you learned the Cypher-fu.

In 'Being CRUD to the data', you understood the syntax, saw the patterns, and learned how to do CRUD things.

Now, you are a data master on your way to the first dan, it is just a matter of more practice.

You are aware that through openCypher, your Cypher-fu will be useful with other servers.

And I hope you enjoyed your training too.

Now, let's move on to the next dojo, err chapter, for more awesomeness with APOC, a collection of procedures.

Go !

5
Awesome Procedures on Cypher - APOC

Apoc was the technician and driver on board of the Nebuchadnezzar in the Matrix movie. He was killed by Cypher.

That was for those among you who know how Neo4j is tinted with Matrix love. However, that does not explain what APOC of in our context. APOC stands for both of the following:

- A Package Of Components
- Awesome Procedures On Cypher

Both are right.

Started in 2009, APOC is a collection of functions and procedures that are available for use in Cypher. They cover the following subjects:

- Collection operations (sorting, min, max, and so on)
- Graph operations (indexes and refactoring)
- Text search
- Conversions
- Ranking
- Geospatial operations
- Data integration
- Reporting
- Getting a meta graph representing your graph

So, contrarily to the Matrix universe, Cypher does not kill APOC, not even the contrary. APOC gives more procedures, more life to Cypher.

Installing APOC

The first step is to download the APOC version corresponding to your Neo4j version (same major and minor number), which can be seen in the Neo4j browser after clicking on the first tab in the upper-left corner of the screen. The next steps vary, depending on how you run Neo4j.

On a hardware server

If you have installed Neo4j on a hardware machine, whether it runs Windows, OS X, or Linux, stop your Neo4j server with the following command:

```
neo4j stop
```

Then copy the downloaded jar in the `plugins` subfolder and restart your server:

```
neo4j start
```

You can now jump to the paragraph *Verifying APOC installation*.

On a Docker container

First, you have to stop your container, as seen previously.

Then, providing you followed the instructions of the `Chapter 2`, *Getting Started with Neo4j*, `cd` into the `neo4j` folder you created and create a `plugins` directory:

```
cd ~/neo4j
mkdir plugins
```

In this new folder, copy the APOC JAR archive that you have downloaded.

Then, we will restart the container with a new file mapping for this `plugins` folder:

```
docker run --publish=7474:7474 --publish=7687:7687 --
volume=$HOME/neo4j/data:/data
--volume=$HOME/neo4j/logs:/logs
--volume=$HOME/neo4j/plugins:/plugins
neo4j:3.1.2
```

Verifying APOC installation

With your server started, you may now go to your Neo4j browser and input the following query:

```
CALL dbms.functions() YIELD name
WHERE name STARTS WITH 'apoc.'
RETURN count(name)
UNION
CALL dbms.procedures() YIELD name
WHERE name STARTS WITH 'apoc.'
RETURN count(name)
```

This is a UNION query that will return two lines, fortunately with non-zero numbers. My result at the time of writing this is 98, then 201. Note that this is not using APOC, but built-in functions.

 A UNION query returns the concatenation of the results of two queries returning the same columns.

This means 98 functions and 201 procedures. I presume that soon, the formidable community and the uncomparable Michael Hunger (@mesirii) will reach 365 functions or procedures and we will have a new APOC calendar to go with the old wisdom that says:

One APOC a day keeps verbosity away.

I just made up this old wisdom, of course.
Nevertheless, using APOC will keep the verbosity away from your queries because, in effect, when you have a main method in code and create methods called in main one so that the main one remains short and readable.

Functions and procedures

As I mentioned before, APOC contains functions and procedures; let's see how they differ. The keyword is **complexity**.

Functions are giving simpler services than procedures.
Functions are designed to return a single value after a computation that only reads the database. Consequently, as you will have inferred, procedures can make changes to the database and return several results.

Procedures have to be CALL-ed. Functions can be referenced directly in a Cypher query (function is in bold).

```
CREATE (p:Person{GUID:apoc.create.UUID()})
```

We will see in a later chapter how to write our own functions and procedures.

My preferred usages

Before we see the key usages of APOC, I would like to show you my preferred ones; you will notice that calling them looks a lot like one half of the UNION query previously seen, as the keyword to use APOC procedures goodness is CALL.

A little help from a friend

Considering there are almost 300 items in APOC, it is user-friendly to provide this function: an entry-point to APOC. Should we want to find all the procedures and functions that contain the word meta in their name or description, we should use this query:

```
CALL apoc.help('meta')
```

The result is as follows:

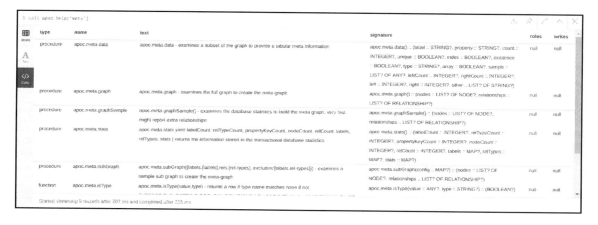

Meta-related APOC search result

The text field will give you a clear text description.

The signature field details the parameters and the values returned. Don't get impressed with it.

This query is very useful; I added it as a favorite (by pressing the Star button at the right of the query input zone) for quicker access.

Graph overview

This query will give you an overview of your database:

```
CALL apoc.meta.graph    // This is for versions of Neo4j up to 3.1
```

Or:

```
CALL db.schema()    // For version 3.2 and above
```

The overview is currently rather poor (unlike the Capulet and Montague families):

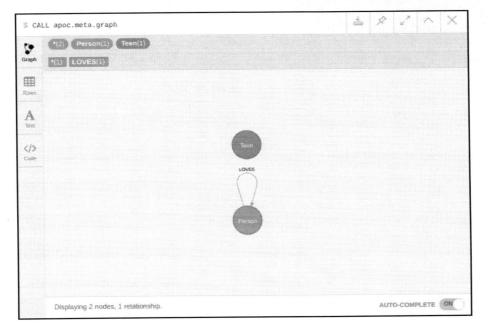

Overview of our database

As you can see, what we defined as labels are now shown as nodes.

I advise you to add this query as a favorite (by pressing the Star button at the right of the query input zone):

This query is very useful; I added it as a favorite for quicker access even if it is already available in the Favorites tab then Sample Scripts / Common Procedures / Show meta-graph:

Favorites

To reuse your favorite queries, just click on them in the Star tab on the left of the screen. If we had added the Movie dataset, the overview would look richer, and maybe a little fishy, as you can see:

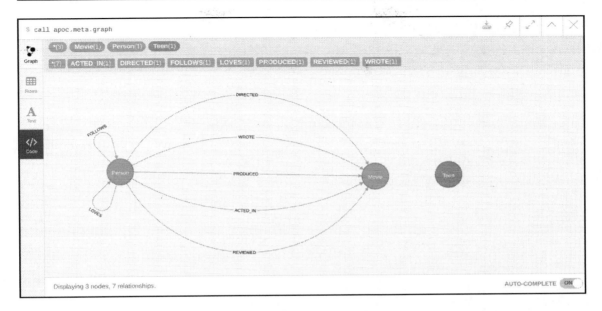

Overview of our database (called Wanda?)

Several key usages

Let's see some key usages; others will be seen in dedicated chapters, such as Chapter 8, *Importing data into Neo4j*.

Setup

First, we need to grant permissions to the APOC functions and procedures, so we need to add the following line to the end of the conf/neo4j.conf file; otherwise, we would get an error message like this one--apoc.algo.pagerank is not available due to having restricted access rights, check configuration:

```
dbms.security.procedures.unrestricted=apoc.*
```

Random graph generators

Well, not so random graph generators, for there is an algorithm to choose and parameters to input. I call it random because it's meaningless:

```
CALL apoc.generate.ba(1000, 2, 'Person', 'FRIEND_OF')
```

This example uses the **Barabasi-Albert (ba)** model to generate a thousand nodes with the label Person that have two FRIEND_OF relations. As Person is a common label, each node will have a name property, which looks as follows, added automatically:

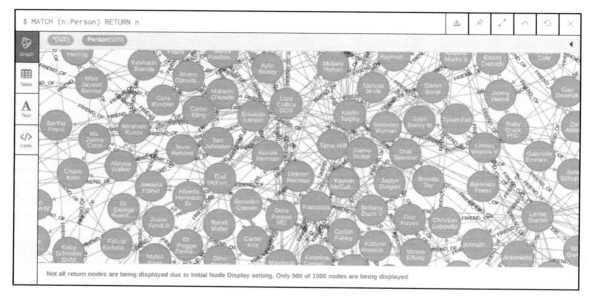

A lot of friends, connected

Be aware that this can create the relation from a node to itself, which is rather funny with example. So to find all the People who are friends of themselves, the query is as follows:

```
MATCH (p:Person)-[FRIEND_OF]-(p)
RETURN p
```

There are, as of today, five algorithms that you can find at https://neo4j-contrib.github. io/neo4j-apoc-procedures/index31.html#_generating_graphs.

PageRank

PageRank is the algorithm that made Google stand out from the competition of search engines by ranking websites. It counts both the number and quality of a relation and deduces an importance for this node.

The rules are:

- The more relations, the more important the node
- The more relations with important nodes, the more important the node

First, let's create a thousand nodes:

```
FOREACH (id IN range(0,1000) | CREATE (n:Node {id:id}))
```

And, at most, a million relations:

```
MATCH (n1:Node),(n2:Node) WITH n1,n2 LIMIT 1000000 WHERE rand() < 0.1
CREATE (n1)-[:TYPE_1]->(n2)
```

Then, let's call the pageRank algorithm:

```
MATCH (node:Node) WITH collect(node) AS nodes
CALL apoc.algo.pageRank(nodes) YIELD node, score
RETURN node, score
ORDER BY score DESC
```

In this quick example, having a list of nodes and scores might not seem very useful; nevertheless, if you apply this to more meaningful data like **Buzzfeed's Trumpworld**, it will become clearer how powerful this is.

Timeboxed execution of Cypher statements

If we want to run a Cypher query that must not take more than a given amount of time, there is a way:

```
CALL apoc.cypher.runTimeboxed(CypherStatement, params, timeoutInMs)
```

Neat, but what is it good for? You may use it to restrain how much CPU time you give to some users of your database, not with standing the roles that are given in your application:

```
CALL apoc.cypher.runTimeboxed('MATCH (n) return n',NULL, 2)
```

Provided you still have numerous nodes in your database, it's unlikely that a complete result can be reached in under two milliseconds. So the result will be an error, as shown in the following image:

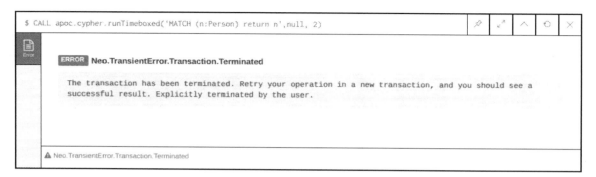

Out of time, man -> terminated

Be aware that the returned result uses the database cache that is shared between users. So, if a user with more time credit already ran the query, the result is available for all users (until the cache is invalidated).

Linking of a collection of nodes

Among the features that apply to a collection of nodes, there is linking. Calling a single procedure will make it possible to create ONE (same) relation between all the nodes of a collection.

This example creates the relation EARTHBRO_OF between the nodes, as follows:

```
MATCH (p:Person)
WITH collect(p) AS persons
CALL apoc.nodes.link(persons, 'EARTHBRO_OF')
RETURN length(persons)
```

If we want to check whether there is only one EARTHBRO_OF, a Cypher query can be as follows:

```
MATCH (p:Person)-[r:EARTHBRO_OF]->(m:Person)
RETURN p, count(r)
```

There's more in APOC

There is more in APOC; we could write a full book dedicated to it. Among the other topics covered by this awesome library are the following:

- **Triggers**: They add a behavior to the database, such as adding a label to nodes that had another label removed.
- **Refactoring**: Modifying the existing datamodel
- **Auto-expiring data**: This gives your nodes a **time to live (TTL)**
- Dates manipulations (conversions from strings, add days, and so on)
- Interactions with other databases (CouchDB, ElasticSearch, MongoDB, and so on)

We encourage you to browse the documentation (available at `https://neo4j-contrib.github.io/neo4j-apoc-procedures/`); you will see how broad it is.

Test questions

Question 1: APOC is an awesome collection of procedures and functions

1. True.
2. False.

Question 2: APOC is a single man project

1. True.
2. False.

Question 3: There is a "dial 911" (US), "dial 112" (EU) command in APOC, is it:

1. CALL apoc.help("me Micheal")
2. CALL apoc.112("me, Benoit")

Question 4: APOC allows to limitate resource usage:

1. True.
2. False.

Question 5: Which APOC innovation allows you to get a bird's eye view on your graph ?

1. CALL db.schema()
2. CALL apoc.meta.graph()
3. both, depending on context

Question 6: What is APOC made of ?

1. Pectin
2. Coffee
3. Bits
4. All of that

Question 7: What is TTL ?

1. Acronym of *through the lens*, a way to measure light for cameras
2. The *time to live* of nodes, for data that would be meaningful after a period

Summary

In this chapter, you have learned what is APOC, how to install and use it, what APOC is made of (not pectin), what are the differences between functions and procedures. We went through some key usages and listed others.

By knowing how to find information about the subjects that arouse your curiosity in APOC, you gained autonomy on this topic. You now know that APOC is good for you and probably already has the functions/procedures you are looking for.

Now, let's move on to the next chapter to learn how to extend the Cypher language.

6
Extending Cypher

Now that we have seen Cypher and the famous APOC project, we will talk about adding functions and procedures to a Neo4j instance, just like writing your own APOC for your projects, except that your extensions are more directly related to your business.

In this chapter, we will cover the following topics:

- Building an extension project (plugin)
- User-defined functions
- User-defined procedures
- Custom aggregators
- Unmanaged extensions
- Streaming JSON responses

Let's empower ourselves with more knowledge.

Building an extension project

The kind people at Neo4j are always keen to ease the workload of their users, so they have created a Maven-based template project on GitHub for us to get a quickstart on our functions and procedures. This way, no time is wasted looking for the dependencies.

Cheers guys!

The project is hosted at https://github.com/neo4j-examples/neo4j-procedure-template. You can either download or clone it, and then open your copy in your favorite Java IDE. In the pom.xml file, update the neo4j.version property with the value corresponding to the version of the Neo4j server that you use. In my case, it is the following:

```
<properties>
  <neo4j.version>3.2.0</neo4j.version>
</properties>
```

Build the project with your IDE. There should be no error at this stage. We will use the same project for all kinds of code we will write.

Creating a function

This is not rocket science, a function is just a method in a Java class. This method must be annotated with @UserFunction and @Description (both in the org.neo4j.procedure package).

To start, let's create a function that returns true if the given parameter is an odd number, and its even counterpart. The source code is as follows:

```java
package learningneo4j;

import org.neo4j.procedure.Description;
import org.neo4j.procedure.Name;
import org.neo4j.procedure.UserFunction;


public class OddEven {
    @UserFunction
    @Description("Returns true if the given number is odd")
    public Boolean isOdd(@Name("number") Long number){
        if(number!=null) return number%2==1;
        else
            return false;
    }

    @UserFunction
    @Description("Returns true if the given number is even")
    public Boolean isEven(@Name("number") Long number){
        if(number!=null) return number%2==0;
        else
            return false;
    }
```

```
}
```

To deploy, my preferred way is to switch to the command line and fire the usual command:

```
mvn clean package
```

This will create a JAR archive in the target subfolder of the project. When installing our functions, the process is the same as when installing APOC.

Copy this `JAR procedure-template-1.0.0-SNAPSHOT.jar` to the `plugins` subfolder of your Neo4j installation. Then, restart Neo4j.

 It is a good idea to script this, because it's probably a process you will repeat during development.

We could check whether they are present by listing the functions as we did earlier. To test the functions, we will create a few nodes as follows:

```
CREATE (t:Test {val:15})
```

Repeat several times, changing the value of val to odd and even values. Then, run the following query:

```
MATCH (t:Test) WHERE learningneo4j.isOdd(t.val)
RETURN t
```

As you can see, it is mandatory to use the package name. Therefore, it's better to use a cool and short name and not what is usual in Java, such as `com.company.project`.

APOC helps you create test data quickly. Try this query

```
UNWIND apoc.coll.randomItems(range(0,1000),15) AS random
WITH random
CREATE (t:Test{val:random})
RETURN t
```

It will create fifteen nodes out of a thousand values.

As an exercise, have a look at the help for `apoc.coll.randomItems`

Another example of function

```
public class StringHacking {
@UserFunction
 @Description("Returns the last word of a string")
```

```
public String getLastWord( @Name("aStr") String aStr){
if(aStr==null) return null;
else  {
int pos = aStr.lastIndexOf(" ");
if(pos==-1) return aStr;
else return aStr.substring(pos+1);
}
}
}
```

Now, let's see how to create a procedure.

Creating a procedure

The principle for procedures is the same; custom code needs to be annotated as well. Our example will be simple: to save the trees.

Procedures may change the content of the graph. Consequently, they are powerful tools. We could imagine a procedure that could perform the following:

- Consume an Internet source (RSS, JSON, and so on) to add content to the graph
- Clean up the graph from old data

It could be a procedure that creates valuable data or relations from the existing data.

From the generated graph of friends that we saw in Chapter 04, *Getting Started with Cypher*, on APOC, we will create nodes for each last name and link the Persons to their corresponding LastName node. Each LastName labeled node will have a lastName property.

We need to ensure the uniqueness of each lastName value, thus let's create a unicity constraint:

```
CREATE CONSTRAINT ON (ln:LastName) ASSERT ln.lastName IS UNIQUE
```

Let's make sure that there is no LastName-labeled node:

```
MATCH (n:LastName)
```

This should return zero results. The procedure that we wish to create will run a pair of Cypher queries within a transaction. Its code is as follows:

```
@Procedure
@Description("Regroup all :Person nodes to newly (re)created :LastName
nodes. Recreates all.")
```

```
public void regroupByLastName() {

    /* We assume
        CREATE CONSTRAINT ON (ln:LastName) ASSERT ln.lastName IS UNIQUE
    has been run but you can add it to this procedure as an exercise.
    */

    Driver driver = GraphDatabase.driver("bolt://localhost",
                            AuthTokens.basic("neo4j", "password"));

    try (Session session = driver.session()) {
        try (Transaction tx = session.beginTransaction()) {
            tx.run("MATCH (ln:LastName) DETACH DELETE (ln)");

            tx.run("MATCH (p:Person) " +
                    "WITH learningneo4j.getLastWord(p.name) as lw, p " +
                    "MERGE (ln:LastName {lastName: lw}) " +
                    "WITH ln,p,lw " +
                    "CREATE (p)-[:IS_NAMED]->(ln)");

            tx.success();
        }
    }
}
```

This procedure runs this first query:

```
MATCH (ln:LastName) DETACH DELETE (ln)
```

This deletes all the nodes with a LastName label.

Then it runs the following code:

```
MATCH (p:Person)
WITH learningneo4j.getLastWord(p.name) as lw, p
MERGE (ln:LastName {lastName: lw})
WITH ln,p,lw
CREATE (p)-[:IS_NAMED]->(ln)
```

To create they are a node labeled LastName, create the relation between it and the processed Person.

This introduces the keyword WITH, which we have not seen yet. WITH is like RETURN; it allows you to separate the query in parts. WITH keyword's role to continue variables scope to the next instruction.

A more comprehensive way to write the preceding query is as follows:

```
MATCH (p:Person)

WITH learningneo4j.getLastWord(p.name) as lw, p
MERGE (ln:LastName {lastName: lw})

WITH ln,p
CREATE (p)-[:IS_NAMED]->(ln)
```

The first MATCH restricts the query to all the :Person nodes. Each one will be used with the following commands. The first WITH passes the p (as per James Brown "pass the peas") variable while declaring an lw variable containing the result of the learningneo4j.getLastWord function for the name property of each Person node. MERGE is like CREATE but it won't fail if the node already exists. Finally, a relation IS_NAMED is created between the considered Person node and the considered LastName node.

You can see the result of this procedure by running the following query:

```
MATCH (a)<-[r:IS_NAMED]-(p:Person)
RETURN a,r,p LIMIT 50
```

Now, if we want the procedure to return the nodes created as a result, the code would be as follows:

```
@Procedure(mode = Mode.WRITE)
public Stream<StringResult> regroupByLastNameVerbose() {
    /* We assume
        CREATE CONSTRAINT ON (ln:LastName) ASSERT ln.lastName IS UNIQUE
    has been run
    */

    Driver driver = GraphDatabase.driver("bolt://localhost",
                    AuthTokens.basic("neo4j", "password"));

    try (Session session = driver.session()) {
        try (Transaction tx = session.beginTransaction()) {
            tx.run("MATCH (ln:LastName) DETACH DELETE (ln)");

            StatementResult result = tx.run("MATCH (p:Person) " +
                    "WITH learningneo4j.getLastWord(p.name) as lw, p " +
                    "MERGE (ln:LastName {lastName: lw}) " +
                    "WITH ln,p,lw " +
                    "CREATE (p)-[:IS_NAMED]->(ln) "
            +       " RETURN ln.lastName");
```

```
                tx.success();
                return result.list(r -> new StringResult(r.get(0).toString())
    ).stream();
            }
        }
    }
```

A user-defined procedure either returns void or a list of records. These records are to be declared as **public static final** classes.

Here, I use `StringResult`, which is part of APOC, in a Java 8 lambda expression in the return statement. The lambda will apply to each `ln.lastName` returned by the Cypher query. The first column is transformed into a `StringResult` instance. All instances are returned as a stream.

Custom aggregators

Some of the most common aggregators in the SQL world are `count`, `sum`, `min`, or `max`. They are used in conjunction with the `GROUP BY` instruction. Here is an example of aggregator usage in Cypher:

```
MATCH (p:Person)-[IS_NAMED]-(ln:LastName)
RETURN ln.lastName, count(p)
```

Since version 3.2, Neo4j allows you to create your own aggregators, which is fairly simple. To illustrate, we will see how to code a random count: a count aggregator that returns a random value. The Java code is as follows:

```
package learningneo4j;

import org.neo4j.procedure.*;

public class RandomCount {
    @UserAggregationFunction("learningneo4j.randomCount")
    @Description( "learningneo4j.randomCount - mostly returns a wrong value
" )
    public RandomAggregator randomAggregator() {
        return new RandomAggregator();
    }

    public static class RandomAggregator {
        private long count;

        @UserAggregationUpdate
        public void repeated(@Name("string") Object obj ){ // parameter
```

```
    given as example
        count +=1;
    }

    @UserAggregationResult
    public Long result(){
        return Long.valueOf( (int)(count * Math.random() + 0.5) );
    }
  }
}
```

The following is an example of use of this procedure, to be used in the Neo4j browser:

```
MATCH (ln:LastName)--(p:Person)
RETURN ln, learningneo4j.randomCount(p.lastName) AS badcount
```

You can see that I have used the value given to `@UserAggregationFunction` in the Cypher code.

As you can see from the Java code, I have created a new class. Its name is not important apart from code hygiene; what is important is that the inner class is declared as public and static, which actually does the work. This topic brings three new annotations:

- `@UserAggregationFunction`
- `@UserAggregationUpdate`
- `@UserAggregationResult`

The `@UserAggregationFunction` is made to register the name under which the aggregator will be used. As you can see, short names are better. Mind that there is currently no way to list the custom aggregators installed on a server.

Unmanaged extensions

Unmanaged extensions (UE) are a way to serve content from the Neo4j server but outside of its usual API endpoints. Strictly put, this is YOUR code, running on the server, in order to serve your data. More precisely, this is JAX-RS 2.0 code.

 JAX-RS is a Java API originating in Java EE 6, whose goal is to help develop web services according to the **Representational State Transfer (REST)** paradigm. The corresponding JSR is #339, and its expert group is constituted of Java gurus such as Adam Bien or Bill Burke.

In order to create a Maven-based project, after the initial creation with your favorite IDE, add those two dependencies to the pom.xml file:

```
<dependency>
  <groupId>org.neo4j</groupId>
  <artifactId>neo4j</artifactId>
  <version>${neo4j.version}</version><!-- This is a Maven property  -->
  <scope>provided</scope>
</dependency>

<dependency>
  <groupId>javax.ws.rs</groupId>
  <artifactId>javax.ws.rs-api</artifactId>
  <version>2.0</version>
  <scope>provided</scope>
</dependency>
```

You may also only add the javax.ws.rs-api dependency to the project used for the custom functions, procedures, and aggregator.

HTTP and JAX-RS refreshers

Of the several HTTP methods that exist (GET, POST, PUT, DELETE, HEAD), we will concentrate on the GET method. A GET call is made by an HTTP client, like a browser, when the user validates an address (URL) in the address bar.

The best practice is to create a class whose name ends with Resource in a package whose full name contains **webservices**. The class must be annotated with @Path and this annotation must be valued. The value of an annotation is what is inside its parentheses when no parameter name is provided, such as in @Path("/thisisthevalue"). This value will then be part of each service that you write to this class.

Each service will also have its own @Path annotation and the @GET annotation as well so that the service is registered in the server as code that answers to GET HTTP calls (with the URL corresponding to the two @Path values). We will get back to this soon.

As we will create code that produces JSON formatted data, we must annotate the method with @Produces(MediaType.APPLICATION_JSON).

The following example code will return the list of the last names in use in the database:

```
package learningneo4j;

import org.neo4j.graphdb.*;
import javax.ws.rs.GET;
import javax.ws.rs.Path;
import javax.ws.rs.Produces;
import javax.ws.rs.core.MediaType;
import java.util.ArrayList;
import java.util.List;

@Path("/persons")
public class PersonResource {

    private final GraphDatabaseService database;

    public PersonResource( @javax.ws.rs.core.Context
        GraphDatabaseService database )  {
        this.database = database;
    }

    @GET
    @Path("/lastnames")
    @Produces(MediaType.TEXT_PLAIN)
    public String getLastNames(){
        try (Transaction tx = database.beginTx() ) { // A transaction
          is mandatory
          ResourceIterator<Node> nodes =
            database.findNodes(Label.label("LastName"));
              List<String> lastNames = new ArrayList<String>();
              Node n = null;
              while (nodes.hasNext()) {
                  n = nodes.next();
                  lastNames.add((String) n.getProperty("lastName"));
              }
              nodes.close();
              tx.success();
              return lastNames.toString();
        }
    }
}
```

Registering

Before you can use your brand new web service, you must register its package and map it to a URL.

Open the configuration file, `conf/neo4j.conf`, and add this line:

dbms.unmanaged_extension_classes=learningneo4j=/learningneo4j

Now we have mapped the `learningneo4j` package to the `/learningneo4j` URL.

Accessing

Consequently, you can access your web service via the following URL:

`http://localhost:7474/learningneo4j/persons/lastnames`

Its form is `protocol://server:port`, followed by the value of the `@Path` annotation of the class, and then the value of the `@Path` annotation of the method.

Streaming JSON responses

Preparing the result of an HTTP call may lead to storing a lot of objects on the server side and thus triggering more garbage collection by the JVM than needed. To keep a lower memory footprint, there is the possibility of streaming the results.

We will get the list of friend's names of someone whose name is given as a parameter.

Create a new class with this code:

```
package learningneo4j;

import org.codehaus.jackson.JsonEncoding;
import org.codehaus.jackson.JsonGenerator;
import org.codehaus.jackson.map.ObjectMapper;

import java.io.IOException;
import java.io.OutputStream;

import javax.ws.rs.GET;
import javax.ws.rs.Path;
import javax.ws.rs.PathParam;
import javax.ws.rs.WebApplicationException;
import javax.ws.rs.core.Context;
```

```java
import javax.ws.rs.core.MediaType;
import javax.ws.rs.core.Response;
import javax.ws.rs.core.StreamingOutput;

import org.neo4j.graphdb.GraphDatabaseService;
import org.neo4j.graphdb.Label;
import org.neo4j.graphdb.Node;
import org.neo4j.graphdb.Relationship;
import org.neo4j.graphdb.RelationshipType;
import org.neo4j.graphdb.ResourceIterator;
import org.neo4j.graphdb.Transaction;

import static org.neo4j.graphdb.Direction.INCOMING;
import static org.neo4j.graphdb.Direction.OUTGOING;

@Path("/friends")
public class FriendsResource {
    private GraphDatabaseService graphDb;
    private final ObjectMapper objectMapper;

    private static final RelationshipType FRIEND_OF =
RelationshipType.withName("FRIEND_OF");
    private static final Label PERSON = Label.label("Person");

    public FriendsResource(@Context GraphDatabaseService graphDb) {
        this.graphDb = graphDb;
        this.objectMapper = new ObjectMapper();
    }

    @GET
    @Path("/{personName}")
    public Response findFriends(@PathParam("personName") final String
      personName) {
        StreamingOutput stream = new StreamingOutput() {
            @Override
            public void write(OutputStream os) throws IOException,
              WebApplicationException {
                JsonGenerator streamingOutput =
                  objectMapper.getJsonFactory().createJsonGenerator(os,
                    JsonEncoding.UTF8);
                streamingOutput.writeStartObject();
                streamingOutput.writeFieldName("friends");
                streamingOutput.writeStartArray();

                try (Transaction tx = graphDb.beginTx();
                  ResourceIterator<Node> persons =
                    graphDb.findNodes(PERSON, "name",
                  personName)) {
```

```
            while (persons.hasNext()) {
              Node person = persons.next();
            for (Relationship relationshipTo :
            person.getRelationships(FRIEND_OF, OUTGOING)) {
            Node friend = relationshipTo.getEndNode();
            streamingOutput.writeString(friend.getProperty
              ("name").toString());
            }
            for (Relationship relationshipFrom :
              person.getRelationships(FRIEND_OF, INCOMING)) {
                Node friendComing =
                    relationshipFrom.getStartNode();
          streamingOutput.writeString(friendComing.getProperty
            ("name").toString());
                }
            }
            tx.success();
        }
        streamingOutput.writeEndArray();
        streamingOutput.writeEndObject();
        streamingOutput.flush();
        streamingOutput.close();
      }
    };
    return
Response.ok().entity(stream).type(MediaType.APPLICATION_JSON).build();
    }
}
```

From the imports, you can see that this uses the `jackson` library; therefore, I added a new dependency to the `pom.xml` file:

```
<dependency>
  <groupId>org.codehaus.jackson</groupId>
  <artifactId>jackson-mapper-asl</artifactId>
  <version>1.9.7</version>
  <scope>provided</scope>
</dependency>
```

`Jackson` is a powerful library for everything related to JSON. The version number may have evolved by the time you read these lines.

Reinstall your plugin project (You did a script, didn't you?) and open your browser. Click on the `Person` label in the column on the left so that the following query is included in the input:

```
MATCH p=()-[r:FRIEND_OF]->() RETURN p LIMIT 25
```

Execute it. Now pick a person and read his/her friend's names. I picked `Damion Hand`.

Open a new tab and browse to your variant of this URL:
`http://localhost:7474/learningneo4j/friends/Damion%20Hand`

The `%20` corresponds a space, as the URL was encoded by the browser. A new annotation is used, `@PathParam`, in conjunction with `@Path`. The value of `@PathParam` is a variable name (here, `personName`). It has to be part of the value of `@Path`. This value is set into the method's parameter variable by the JAXRS framework.

In my case, the value of the `personName` variable is `Damion Hand` as the framework has decoded the encoded value from the encoded URL requested by the browser.

The code is mostly done in the write method. After fetching the `Person` (or several) with the given name, with `graphDb.findNodes`, the `FRIEND_OF` relations to this node are examined (outbound, then inbound) and the name of the end node and start nodes are added to the `streamOutput` object.

The line that returns the result is as follows:

```
return
Response.ok().entity(stream).type(MediaType.APPLICATION_JSON).build();
```

The result is an OK (HTTP code 200) response, based on the stream built into the chosen type. The rest (pun intended!) of the code is mostly JSON boilerplate code.

Summary

We came in to this chapter to learn how to add strings to our bow so that we can now create our own functions and procedures, specific to our projects (and models).

We saw that functions are for small tasks, and procedures are for tasks updating the graph. We saw what custom aggregators are made of. We saw that unmanaged extensions are custom REST entry points to the Neo4j server. We saw new possibilities to put into action in our projects.

We came, we saw, we conquered, or as Caesar would say: Veni, Vidi, Vici

```
(you:Reader)-[:LEARNED]->(s:Sentence {language: "latin", meaning: "I came,
I saw, I overcame"}
```

In the next chapter, we will see if we need to improve the performance of our queries, and if so, how to do it. Get ready !

7
Query Performance Tuning

In this chapter, you will learn how to estimate if our queries are under performing. It may well happen, and if this is the case, what are the rules to apply to improve them? The rule of thumb is to reduce the number of db hits.

A DB hit is a unit of work for the database. So, how do we do this?

We will cover the following topics in the chapter:

- Explain and profile instructions
    - Query plan
    - Operators
- Indexes
- Rule of thumb for improving performance

Explain and profile instructions

Explain and profile are the two Cypher instructions that will help us get facts where we see possible performance issues.

Explain will give you the execution plan of your query without executing it, while profile will execute the query and return results.

The execution plan is not determined by a hitman but out of the text defining the query by a component of Cypher named the planner; there are two planners: cost planner and rule planner. Cost planner is used by default; it appeared in version 2.2. Its action is to smoothly turn a text into a list of *operators* (remember this name).

A query plan

To illustrate, here is an example of a query plan, which reads from top to bottom. You can see the related query in the image; it is based on the Movies dataset that is available if you follow the slides tied to the :play movies command:

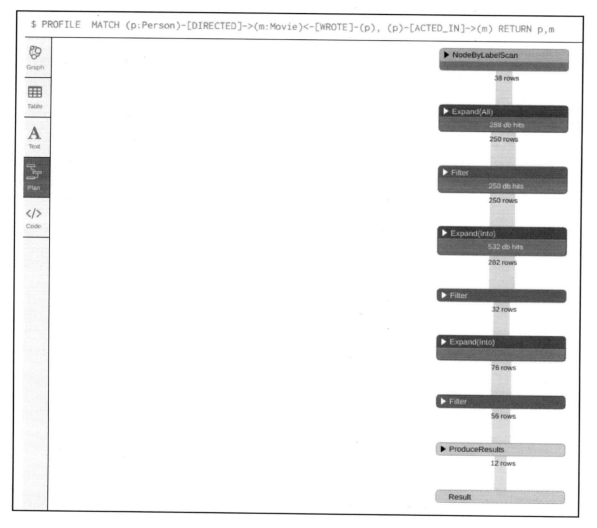

A short execution plan

The first operator is `NodeByLabelScan` because I mentioned the labels. If I drop them, the execution plan becomes the following:

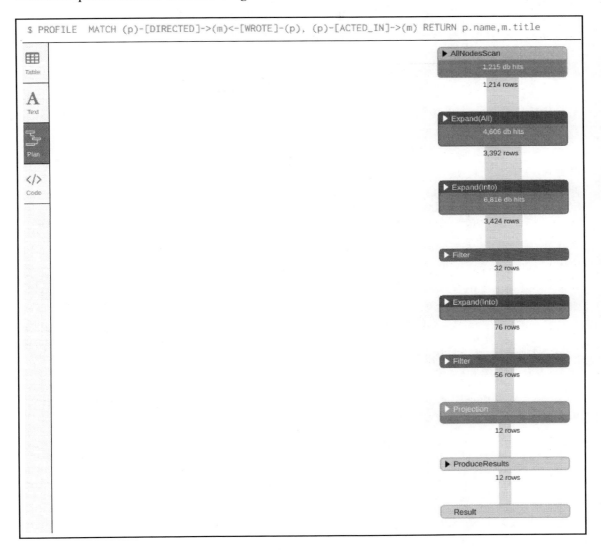

A longer execution plan

As you will notice, it starts with the operator `AllNodesScan`, which means that all the nodes in the database are evaluated to see if they match the query. We notice that the DB hits numbers are higher, and the link between the operator is larger in the first operators.

These are bad sign, so we'd better put the label back!

 When using cypher shell, the execution plan must be read from bottom to top.

Operators

Operators are actions from the server. They are of several kinds and, to make a comparison, they are like CPU instructions. Some take longer to execute than others. As stated by Petra Selmer and Mark Needham, the operators to look for are as follows:

- All nodes scan
- Label scan
- Node index seek
- Node index scan

Obviously, scanning all the nodes is the most expensive operator, and the remaining ones become less and less expensive. Among the different possibilities to execute each analyzed query, the cost planner chooses the cheaper one.

For this goal, it uses statistics updated on each query execution. (The rule planner does not use these statistics.)

As query plans are cached, it would be better to use parameters instead of literals so that the query does not have to be parsed again and again.

To define a parameter `title` with the value `Unforgiven`, the syntax is as follows:

```
#In Neo4j browser
:param title:"Unforgiven"

#In Cypher shell
:param title:"Unforgiven"
```

Then, to use it, as follows:

```
MATCH (n:Movie)
```

```
WHERE n.title=$title
RETURN n
```

or:

```
MATCH (n:Movie)
WHERE n.title={title}
RETURN n
```

Providing you have imported the movie graph, you will get one result.

To get the list of defined parameters, use the following command:

```
:params
```

When using the HTTP API, you will write MATCH (n:Person {name: {myparam}}) and not MATCH (n:Person {name: 'Dennis'}) if there is a lot of traffic using this query.

In the Neo4j browser, you can paste this query:

```
:POST /db/data/cypher
{
"query" : "MATCH (n:Movie {title: {title}}) RETURN n",
"params" : {"title" : "Unforgiven"}
}
```

Indexes

In Neo4j, indexes are used to find the starting points of the queries. You can count on them. Indexes are automatically created on properties that have a constraint. Otherwise, you can create an index with a query like the following:

```
CREATE INDEX ON :LabelName(propertyName)
```

However, refrain from creating an index for every property of each label as they need to be maintained by the server when data is inserted. It is taken care of here, but there is no magic.

The command to get the list of indexes in use in your graph is as follows:

```
CALL db.indexes
```

Force index usage

You may force the use of an index by specifying it in your query, as follows:

```
MATCH (t:Tower {name: ""})
 USING INDEX t:Tower(name)
 RETURN ...
```

Force label usage

You may also force the planner to start by evaluating nodes for a label instead of an index. This is particularly useful if you are querying for nodes having two labels and you know that one of the labels is more restrictive than the other.

In this example, we could have a billion locations in Japan so why look all of them to see if they have the Tower label? It's better to do it the other way.

```
MATCH (t:Location:Tower)
USING SCAN t:Tower
WHERE t.country='JPN'
RETURN t
```

Rules of thumb

Here is a list of rules to help you make your queries the most performant possible.

Explain all the queries

Once written and their results verified, explain all your queries on a decent dataset to look for possible bottlenecks, as explained earlier in this chapter.

Rows

In your query plans, the row counts should decrease rapidly from top to bottom. If not, did you use enough labels? Enough indexes? Are the properties you use indexed?

Do not overconsume

Virtual resources are resources too. Do not waste CPU cycles, memory, and energy by returning more data than you need. Do not get the full nodes if you only want to use a few properties of each.

Cartesian or not?

Unless authorized, you should not do a cartesian product in your queries. You may already know this, but sometimes it happens. For example, here is one, the most obvious:

```
MATCH (n),(m)
RETURN n,m
```

Mind that the number of results is the square of the number of nodes. Recognize cartesian products by the lack of relation expressed between different kinds of nodes.

Simplicity

A good way to avoid accidental cartesian products in order to make the queries more readable is to cut your query into several chunks using the WITH Cypher command. WITH allows you to pass variables from one chunk to another. You can pass nodes, lists, or values.

Summary

We have seen how to check whether our queries are wasting resources and how to correct them, because CPU cycles are time and electric power, and your time is precious! Notwithstanding the fact that it generates heat and the climate is already a mess.

We saw Neo4j's execution plans, how to read them, and spot what may be an issue. We saw what the parameters are and how they might remind you of JDBC's PreparedStatements. We saw how to force the use of indexes or labels (you may have to do a comparison of the performances of both, depending on your graph and queries). Remember this old saying that elders transmit to younger disciples of our profession: Make it work, then, and only then, optimize!

Now, let's switch to something totally different: Chapter 8, *Importing data into Neo4j*.

The import queries can be profiled too!

8
Importing Data into Neo4j

What is a database without data? An empty shell!

There are numerous ways to import data into a Neo4j server. We have already seen the rich GUI approach of typing it in the Neo4j browser using Cypher. Fortunately, as Neo4j is a big data categorized database, there are other ways, such as the following:

- Importing CSV data with `LOAD CSV`
- Importing from a JSON source
- Importing from a JDBC source
- Importing from an XML source

Restoring a backup is also a way but we will leave that for later in the `Appendix`, *Tips and Tricks*.

Knowing how to load data will open for you the doors of all the open data that the internet has to offer. It is my opinion that there are combinations of open datasets that would prove to be the base for useful and enriching projects. My students tend to love the dataset of Parisian cafés selling a coffee for one euro, but there are many more! Let's get started.

LOAD CSV

`LOAD CSV` is a built-in Cypher instruction that can be used with the filename of a CSV file, and Cypher instructions to play for each line of the CSV file.

CSV stands for **comma-separated value**. Normally, each column of the file is separated by a comma, which was not a good idea. It is far more common to see the semicolon character used as a separator, which is a better choice, but my personal choice is to use the Unix pipe character | as a separator.
The first line may be a list of headers.
CSV is text; you do not need a spreadsheet to open CSV files.

Here is a simple example taken from the Neo4j website. It will load data from a URL and, for each line of this source, will run the CREATE command. I have highlighted the points that I'll discuss in this chapter:

```
LOAD CSV WITH HEADERS FROM
'https://neo4j.com/docs/cypher-refcard/3.2/csv/artists-with-headers.csv' AS
line
CREATE (:Artist {name: line.Name, year: toInt(line.Year)})
```

LOAD CSV WITH HEADERS means that the first line of the CSV input will contain a list of headers (column names). This way, it is possible to use the columns by their names.

The (short!) content of this file is as follows:

```
"Id","Name","Year"
"1","ABBA","1992"
"2","Roxette","1986"
"3","Europe","1979"
"4","The Cardigans","1992"
```

Know your datasource: WITH HEADERS is optional (the datasource may not have a first line with headers but start with data), as this is also a perfectly valid datasource content:

```
"1","ABBA","1992"
"2","Roxette","1986"
"3","Europe","1979"
"4","The Cardigans","1992"
```

In that case, the corresponding Cypher syntax would be as follows:

```
LOAD CSV FROM
'https://neo4j.com/docs/cypher-refcard/3.2/csv/artists.csv' AS line
CREATE (:Artist {name: line[1], year: toInt(line[2])})
```

Now, what is the meaning of AS line?

Simply put, this is the reference to use in your Cypher statement to designate the current line of data processed. Whether the datasource has headers or not, you will be able to reuse those (column) names in your Cypher. If not, you will have to use the column indexes, which start at zero. Using indexes is way more error prone than names.

I have an anecdote about importing data from a datasource published as open data by a French authority: some column names were several words long, others had a single quote. The single word Birthday we in I.T. use in preference to *birth date* was *Date de naissance*. Two spaces here. Commented field names were present too, like *Description (not taking account of 07/2015 reform)*.

That clearly led to some swearing, so I learned that it is possible to use inverted quotes around the column names:

```
LOAD CSV WITH HEADERS FROM
'https://neo4j.com/docs/cypher-refcard/3.2/csv/artists-with-headers.csv' AS
line
CREATE (:Artist {name: line.`Name`, year: toInt(line.`Year`)})
```

As this example was to be repeated, I chose a short one.

However, know the following points:

- The Cypher statement applied can have more than one line
- You may apply several LOAD CSV to the same datasource (preferably a local file)

Yes, you may use files located on the server itself. The good folks at Neo4j have prepared an import folder to your server installation. It is a good practice to load local data only from this location. First, because of portability, as the following command works but is not very portable among admins:

```
LOAD CSV WITH HEADERS FROM
'file:////home/jerome/Tools/neo/neo4j-
community-3.2.0/import/level1/artists-with-headers.csv' AS line
CREATE (:Artist {name: line.Name, year: toInt(line.Year)})
```

So, you should go in `$NEO_HOME/conf/neo4j.conf` and uncomment this line:

```
dbms.directories.import=import
```

As such, the given path will be related to import as the root (after server restart).

Say you have the artists file to import in `$NEO_HOME/import/level1/`, then the Cypher syntax would be as follows:

```
LOAD CSV WITH HEADERS FROM
'file:///level1/artists-with-headers.csv' AS line
CREATE (:Artist {name: line.Name, year: toInt(line.Year)})
```

Keep in mind that there are three slashes!

A last word about `toInt(line.Year)`; this is the conversion of the `String` read in the datasource into a `Integer` typed data field.

By default, all data is imported as strings. Among other conversion functions, there are the following:

- `toFloat`
- `toBoolean`

You may have created your own conversion procedures too.

Scaling the import

If your CSV file is large has (many columns, such as preceding 50, I even saw 100+) and long (has many lines), you may face an `OutOfMemoryException` crashing your import. To avoid this, a solution is to make the transaction commit periodically. To benefit from this, just add the following:

```
USING PERIODIC COMMIT n
LOAD CSV ....
```

Here, the value of n is the number of rows processed by the transaction.

Now, let's import some JSON data!

Importing from a JSON source

To import a JSON datasource, we need to use APOC (see `Chapter 5`, *Awesome Procedures on Cypher – APOC*). Therefore, make sure that you have installed it.

We will use a JSON file that contains the list of the countries of the world. You can find it here in a human-readable form, `https://github.com/mledoze/countries/blob/master/countries.json`, and in a computer-processable form at `https://raw.githubusercontent.com/mledoze/countries/master/countries.json`, which I saved in the import folder.

To use the local copy, set the following in your `neo4j.conf` (and restart the server):

```
apoc.import.file.enabled=true
```

However, at this time, it's the full path that must be given as a parameter, so adapt the following examples to your system.

Try this query to get a view of the data:

```
WITH "file:////home/jerome/Tools/neo/neo4j-
community-3.2.0/import/countries.json" AS url
CALL apoc.load.json(url) YIELD value
RETURN value.cca2, value.cca3,value.name.common, value.name.official,
value.capital, value.borders, value.languages;
```

As you can see in the result, there are collections of country codes (as `cca2`) for the borders and for the languages, such as `["BRA","GUF","GUY"]` and `{"nld":"Dutch"}` for the country named ;Suriname. Should there be several languages, such as in Tanzania, the languages value would be `{"eng":"English","swa":"Swahili"}`.

Now, before importing the data, let's explain the first two lines:

```
WITH "file:////home/jerome/Tools/neo/neo4j-
community-3.2.0/import/countries.json" AS url
```

This permits you to define a variable named `url` and use it with the next Cypher command:

```
CALL apoc.load.json(url) YIELD value
```

This calls an `apoc` procedure with the defined variable (`url`) as a parameter and `YIELD` results into a variable named `value`.

If, like me, you are not a native English speaker and have not used yield often, keep in mind that it means to produce in this case.

Now let's do some importing We will create nodes with a `Country` label. First, let's start with some constraints:

```
CREATE CONSTRAINT ON (c:Country) ASSERT c.cca2 IS UNIQUE
CREATE CONSTRAINT ON (c:Country) ASSERT c.cca3 IS UNIQUE
```

Run the query:

```
WITH "file:////home/jerome/Tools/neo/neo4j-
community-3.2.0/import/countries.json" AS url
CALL apoc.load.json(url) YIELD value
CREATE (c:Country)
SET c.cca2=value.cca2, c.cca3=value.cca3, c.name=value.name.common,
c.officialName=value.name.official, c.capitalCity=value.capital ;
```

Now, should we want to create language nodes and link them to the countries and create relations between countries that share borders, it becomes less straightforward. We need a new constraint:

```
CREATE CONSTRAINT ON (l:Language) ASSERT l.code IS UNIQUE
```

To create the countries, we can perform the following:

```
WITH "file:////home/jerome/Tools/neo/neo4j-
community-3.2.0/import/countries.json" AS url
CALL apoc.load.json(url) YIELD value
MERGE (c:Country {cca3: value.cca3})
ON CREATE SET c.cca2=value.cca2, c.cca3=value.cca3,
c.name=value.name.common, c.officialName=value.name.official,
c.capitalCity=value.capital;
```

`MERGE` is a very useful keyword. If the node is not found via the `cca3` field, then the node will be created and the `SET` command defined after `ON CREATE` will be run.

 If you run this command several times, it is not an issue. Should the `MERGE` be a `CREATE`, then running it a second time would lead to an error about a node already existing.

We can import the languages along the countries but we need to wait to have imported all the countries if we want to create the relations inferred from the borders:

```
WITH "file:////home/jerome/Tools/neo/neo4j-
community-3.2.0/import/countries.json" AS url
CALL apoc.load.json(url) YIELD value
MERGE (c:Country {cca3: value.cca3})
ON CREATE SET c.cca2=value.cca2, c.cca3=value.cca3,
```

```
      c.name=value.name.common, c.officialName=value.name.official,
      c.capitalCity=value.capital

WITH c, value, keys(value.languages) AS ki
FOREACH(k IN ki |
      MERGE (l:Language{code: k} ) ON CREATE SET l.name = value.languages[k]
      MERGE (c)-[:HAS_LANGUAGE]->(l)
)
```

This example is a little tougher and is a good opportunity to see more Cypher. It starts with the same creation (or not) of the countries and is followed by the creation of languages.

As the languages list read is not really a list but more of a map, such as {"eng":"English","swa":"Swahili"}, we need to isolate the keys (here: eng and swa) to use them in a given property (code, the identifier for which we created a unicity constraint). This is what happens with keys(value.languages) AS ki, a new variable ki is created, containing the list of the keys (of the map value.languages).

Then, we iterate this list and merge a Language node, setting its name by accessing the map.

Last, merge a relation between the country and the language.

> Note the structure of the FOREACH command: the variable declaration (k IN ki), then the unix pipe to separate, then the commands to execute, and the closing parenthesis.

To list the different languages and in how many countries they are officially used, try this query:

```
MATCH (c:Country)--(l:Language)
RETURN l.code, count(c.cca3) AS count ORDER BY count DESC, l.code ASC
```

Now that all countries are in our graph, it is possible to create relations between them according to the 'borders' list in the JSON source. Remember the value for Suriname? It's ["BRA","GUF","GUY"] and looks like a list of cca3 codes, which is good because we have a cca3 property in our Country nodes. So, as we just saw how to use lists, I encourage you to write the code that creates the different HAS_BORDER_WITH relations.

Should you not succeed in the first try, the query to remove all countries, languages, and their relations is as follows:

```
MATCH (c:Country)--(l:Language)
DETACH DELETE c,l
```

Then rerun the query that loads them. To check your result, execute the following query, which will return results for Suriname:

```
MATCH (c:Country) WHERE c.name STARTS WITH "Suri" RETURN c
```

Double-click on the node to expand it. Move your mouse pointer above the other countries, read their details, and notice that the `cca3` codes are correct. A solution is as follows:

```
WITH "file:////home/jerome/Tools/neo/neo4j-
community-3.2.0/import/countries.json" AS url
CALL apoc.load.json(url) YIELD value
MATCH(c:Country {cca3:value.cca3})
WITH c, value
FOREACH( bc IN value.borders |
    MERGE (c)-[:HAS_BORDER_WITH]->(co:Country {cca3: bc})
)
```

 If you are confident enough in your new skills, you may add more content to your countries graph using the data available at `https://github.com/opendatajson/factbook.json`.
It is very rich and is known as the CIA factbook.

Importing from a JDBC source

Using Apoc, it's also possible to import data from a relational database, providing it has a Java driver. The first thing that you have to do is download the JDBC driver for your database and drop it into the plugins folder of your Neo4j installation. In this example, we will use MySQL. Let's set it up.

Test setup

In case you do not wish to install MySQL, you can use `docker` and run this command to start a MySQL running on port `3306`, without a password for the `root` user:

```
docker run -e MYSQL_ALLOW_EMPTY_PASSWORD=yes -p 3306:3306 mysql
```

Connect with your favorite client (I use Squirrel) to enter some commands to create the data that we will import thereafter:

```
CREATE DATABASE learning
use learning;
CREATE TABLE operating_systems (id long not null, name VARCHAR(50), familly
VARCHAR(50));
```

```
INSERT INTO operating_systems VALUES (1, "DEBIAN", "UNIX");
INSERT INTO operating_systems VALUES (2, "UBUNTU LINUX", "UNIX");
INSERT INTO operating_systems VALUES (3, "LINUX MINT", "UNIX");
INSERT INTO operating_systems VALUES (4, "ANDROID", "UNIX");
INSERT INTO operating_systems VALUES (5, "KALI LINUX", "UNIX");
```

Importing all the systems

To sum up, this method is similar to importing from a JSON data source apart from a few differences. This effort toward consistency is the mark of top-level professionals and is to be saluted.

So, now that we have a MySQL database named `learning` running on the same server, using default ports, we want to import the operating systems into nodes with the `Os` label and a `FROM` relation that goes to a node labeled `OsFamily`. The ID column will not be reused. This means that we have a pair of constraints to create, as follows:

```
CREATE CONSTRAINT ON (o:Os) ASSERT o.name IS UNIQUE
CREATE CONSTRAINT ON (of:OsFamily) ASSERT of.name IS UNIQUE
```

Creating these constraints is not mandatory unless you run the import that follows several times, because that would lead to the creation of several nodes with the same names. My goal is to make you develop good habits.

To access the database, the JDBC driver must be loaded into memory. This is done with the following instruction:

```
CALL apoc.load.driver("com.mysql.jdbc.Driver");
```

The Cypher code to import the operating systems is the following:

```
WITH "jdbc:mysql://localhost:3306/learning?user=root" as url
CALL apoc.load.jdbc(url,"operating_systems") YIELD row AS line
MERGE (o:Os {name: line.name})
MERGE (of:OsFamily {name: line.familly})
MERGE (o)-[:FROM]->(of)
```

As you can notice, it is very similar to importing JSON data. However, you may wonder what `YIELD row as line` means. It is because the `apoc.load.jdbc` procedure returns a result called *row* that is renamed `line` for use in our query.

The query to verify the result is as follows:

```
MATCH (o:Os)-[:FROM]->(of:OsFamily)
RETURN o,of
```

Now, let's import some XML.

Importing from an XML source

If you have to import data from an XML source, APOC has your back again. Valid XML sources have a main advantage to already have been validated against an XSD schema (or a DTD).

Let's import some countries again, but this time by continent. Here is the XML, it is hand-written and voluntarily short, so do not feel offended if you do not find your country in this list:

```
<?xml version="1.0"?>
<earth>
 <continent name="Africa">
    <country name="Morocco" money="Dinar"/>
 </continent>
 <continent name="Europe">
    <country name="France" money="Euro"/>
    <country name="Germany" money="Euro"/>
 </continent>
 <continent name="Asia">
   <country name="China" money="Yuan"/>
   <country name="Japan" money="Yen"/>
 </continent>
</earth>
```

There are countries sharing a continent, and others sharing money. As usual, constraint creation takes place before importing:

```
CREATE CONSTRAINT ON (c:Continent) ASSERT c.name IS UNIQUE
CREATE CONSTRAINT ON (mo:Money) ASSERT mo.name IS UNIQUE
```

The principle used to import XML is to create a multimap, a map of maps (knowing that those maps may contains maps too and so on) in memory and then applying Cypher to that map.

The Cypher query is as follows:

```
WITH 'file:///home/jerome/Tools/neo/neo4j-
```

```
community-3.2.0/import/countries.xml' as url
CALL apoc.load.xml(url) YIELD value as earth
UNWIND earth._children as continent
 MERGE (co:Continent {name: continent.name})
 WITH continent,co
 UNWIND continent._children as cou
 WITH continent, co, cou
 MERGE (existingCountry:Country {name: cou.name})
 MERGE (money:Money {name: cou.money})
 MERGE (existingCountry)-[:INSIDE]->(co)
 MERGE (existingCountry)-[:HAS_CURRENCY]->(money)
```

Of course, you should update the path. Unfortunately, at this date, it does not behave like the JSON import and thus, the full path of the file must be given.

That brings us a new Cypher command: UNWIND, which creates an iterator and will walk it.

You may wonder what is _children. It is an attribute of the map that has been created when the XML was loaded. It contains a list of all the child elements of the current element. So, imagine that each country was defined with a child element instead of attributes, as follows:

```
<country>
 <name>France</name>
 <money>Euro</money>
</country>
```

This is very verbose but also a common way to write XML, which would lead to another level of complexity in the Cypher code. You would have to iterate over the children and use the CASE statement (see Cypher refcard) to do conditional testing to behave accordingly to the values of the _type attribute (here, name them money) and get the value by using _text.

As I value you, dear reader, avoid importing verbose XML for your own sanity.

If you use your own datasource while reading this chapter, remember to check the performance of your queries.

That closes this chapter on importing data.

Summary

In this chapter, we saw how to import data from different kinds of sources into our graph and saw which one is preferable. We know we can do funny and interesting things like importing the 1€ cafés dataset and a dataset of free wifi credentials.

More seriously, we know how to import datasets and how to combine them. It is up to you to find the datasets of your interest. This can really open the doors of perception of the world when you import data and then look at your graph.

Imagine you can combine statistics of crime rates, poverty, alcohol sales, and education levels.

We will now get back to Earth and deal with geolocalized data in the next chapter, Chapter 9, *Going Spatial*.

9
Going Spatial

No, this chapter will not train you to become a cosmonaut. Sorry.

However, as you have seen so far, using a graph database is not rocket science. You cannot say it is well beyond your understanding. Enough with the puns and let's deal with this spatial aspect.
First, we have to agree that Earth's shape is close to a sphere; this world is not a disc wandering through space on the back of a tortoise. So say we all? So let's start our trek toward a new frontier for our skills.

We will cover the following topics in this chapter:

- Revise the geo concepts
- See the geo features of Neo4j and of APOC
- Neo4j spatial

What is spatial?

Spatial refers to giving a location to nodes, like answering the question, *Where in the world is the new Dennis Ritchie?*

Refresher

Every location (or point) on Earth can be localized via its spatial coordinates--latitude and longitude. Both are angular values; they measure an angle from the center of Earth. Latitude zero is shared by all points on the equator. Positive latitude is for all points north of the equator. Negative latitude is for all points located south of the equator.

All points with the same latitude form a virtual horizontal line (circle); whereas all points with the same longitude form a line (circle) called meridian. Longitude zero is currently defined by the meridian going through Greenwich near London in the United Kingdom, where the royal observatory (not a people's magazine) is located. The legend says that the Greenwich meridian replaced the Paris meridian as longitude zero in exchange of England adopting the metric system.

Unfortunately, it has not worked so far. Someone must have crossed his fingers while swearing.

Of course, there are two standards in use when writing spatial coordinates: lat-long and long-lat.

We will use lat-long.

Not faulty towers

We will use three towers in our examples, the Eiffel tower and its two replicas.
The latitude of The Eiffel Tower, Paris, France is 48.858093 and the longitude is 2.294694 and the elevators happen to be out of order sometimes, making the old lady a faulty tower (?qué ?). There is a restaurant there but the kitchen is underground.

The latitude of The Eiffel tower, Las Vegas, Nevada, USA is 36.112474 and the longitude is -115.172737. It has a restaurant too.

The latitude of The Tokyo tower, Tokyo, Japan is 35.659053 and the longitude is 139.745228 and, like the French one, is used to broadcast signals. Is there a restaurant?

What is so spatial then?

The answer is:

Neo4j is spatial, APOC is spatial too, and of course, Neo4j Spatial is more spatial.
Let me explain.

Spatial capabilities are present in these three pieces of software. Their spatialness goes from basic to advanced in that order.

However, as the last two (APOC and Neo4j Spatial) are plugins that you install in the first software (Neo4j), spatial features add up. The package names change in order to call the procedures. We will see this now.

Neo4j's spatial features

Neo4j has a limited built-in spatial support since Neo4j 3.0. There is default support for **point** and **distance**. This support assumes that you will set property keys named latitude and longitude for the nodes you want to use as points.

You can use them to calculate the distance between two nodes, but first let's build the towers, starting with the good habit of creating a constraint:

```
CREATE CONSTRAINT ON (t:Tower) ASSERT t.name IS UNIQUE
CREATE (paris:Tower {name: "Eiffel Tower",country:"FRA",
latitude:48.858093, longitude:2.294694})
CREATE (vegas:Tower {name: "Vegas Eiffel Tower",country:"USA",
latitude:36.112474, longitude:-115.172737})
CREATE (tokyo:Tower {name: "Tokyo Tower",country:"JPN",
latitude:35.659053,longitude:139.745228})
```

Now, let's see the distance between the `Eiffel tower` and the other towers, using this query:

```
MATCH (et:Tower {name:'Eiffel Tower'}), (other:Tower)
RETURN et.name, other.name, round(distance(point(et), point(other))/10)/100
as dist_km
```

The keywords here are `point`, which that creates a point out of a node that has latitude and longitude properties, and `distance`, which that calculates a distance between two points.

As round(value), rounds to the nearest integer value, I used this little trick (/10/100) that you can see rounds a value to have two decimal digits:

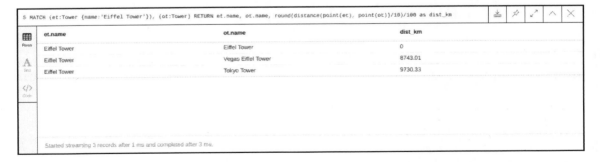

Distances between towers

We are getting those values, which are corroborated by the site `http://distance.` `to` although the match is not exact for the towers do not mark the center of their home town.

As there are only three towers, should we want to know the distance between the Tokyo tower and the Las Vegas tower, we can do very bad things (a movie that takes place in Las Vegas), like a Cartesian product, with the following query:

```
MATCH (t1:Tower),(t2:Tower)
RETURN t1.name, t2.name, round(distance(point(t1), point(t2))/10)/100 as
dist_km
```

This returns three power two, that is nine lines of results. This is safe, as there is no resource overuse here and it's also a good opportunity to see how to write one. In any other case, do not do cartesian products (please):

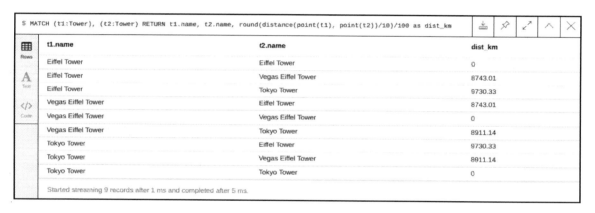

Encouraged cartesian product

Now, let's up our spatial capabilities with APOC.

APOC spatial features

You can get the list of the spatial procedures of APOC by querying as follows:

```
CALL apoc.help("spatial")
```

APOC offers the possibility to do geocoding, which is transforming an address into spatial coordinates and sorting paths by distance. That is all so far.

Although it is just mapping an address to coordinates, not to say two floats, geocoding is not easy--it takes a lot of storage, wandering cars taking pictures, and CPU cycles to identify numbers in pictures--and certainly a lot of coffee that engineers transform in code line.

Therefore, our preferred software cannot do it by itself and relies on a provider that will be transparently called by APOC.

Geocoding

Geocoding is the transformation of an address into geographical coordinates. The two main providers that I know are **OpenStreetMap (OSM)** and Google. Only one can be used at a time. It takes a little configuration and a restart to set or change the provider.

Setting up OSM as provider

Open the usual `neo4j.conf` file and add these two lines:

```
apoc.spatial.geocode.provider=osm
apoc.spatial.geocode.osm.throttle=5000
```

They define the provider and specify a throttle of five seconds to avoid hammering the OSM servers because it is only normal to be kind to an organisation that provides a *free* service. It is education: netiquette.

Setting up Google as provider

To use Google as a provider, you must get a key for a project via the API console. To do this, follow the guidelines on the page at `https://developers.google.com/maps/documentation/geocoding/get-api-key`. When you reach the limit--2,500 hits per day--you have to activate billing and expect to be billed.

The configuration keys to set in `neo4j.conf` are as follows:

```
apoc.spatial.geocode.google.throttle=10
#delay between queries to not overload servers and/or explode your billing,
in ms

apoc.spatial.geocode.google.key=xxxx
#API key for google geocode access, like
AIzaSyCGOqPxaXkODpAKg_teles7tprisqu3icro3yaitpren7dre
```

I must underline that a third provider is supported by APOC, named OpenCage (`https://geocoder.opencagedata.com/`).

Like Google, it is a paying solution with a free tier of 2,500 hits per day. Give them a try; they claim to have the most permissive licence, that is, you may store the results you got in return from them. Do not laugh, Google's terms forbid it.

Now, for example, I want to know the coordinates of where I give lectures:

```
CALL apoc.spatial.geocodeOnce('143 Avenue de Versailles,75016, PARIS
FRANCE') YIELD location
RETURN location.latitude, location.longitude
```

Neo4j spatial

Neo4j Spatial (later NS) is a plugin, like APOC, discussed in Chapter 5, *Awesome Procedures on Cypher - APOC*. The homepage of this plugin is `https://github.com/neo4j-contrib/spatial`.

Just like APOC, you should take care to install a version compatible with the version of your Neo4j server. See the `releases` tab on their GitHub landing page. The release notes and the release filenames are self-explanatory. (Thank the project leader, Craig Taverner.)

Online demo

William Lyon (`https://twitter.com/lyonwj`) from Neo4j has made an online demo available at this address, `http://www.lyonwj.com/scdemo/index.html`.

Use the polygon tool in the toolbar on the left to define a shape, double-click inside it, and you will get markers on the map to indicate restaurant locations. Let's find some restaurants in Phoenix, in an almost successfully drawn butterfly shape:

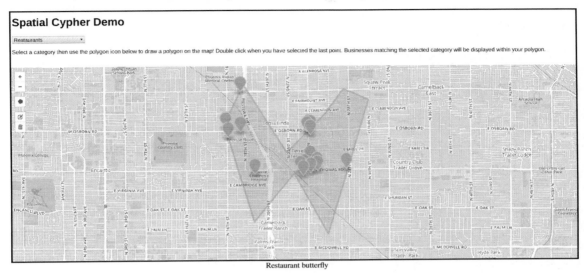

Restaurant butterfly

While we are in the lexical field of food, let's say the demo was an *amuse-bouche* (appetizers) or a starter, and move on to the features of NS.

Features

To list all the features given by the version of Spatial you installed, run this query:

```
call spatial.procedures()
```

The result will be as follows:

```
$ call spatial.procedures()
```

name	signature
spatial.decodeGeometry	spatial.decodeGeometry(layerName :: STRING?, node :: NODE?) :: (geometry :: ANY?)
spatial.removeLayer	spatial.removeLayer(name :: STRING?) :: VOID
spatial.importShapefile	spatial.importShapefile(uri :: STRING?) :: (count :: INTEGER?)
spatial.intersects	spatial.intersects(layerName :: STRING?, geometry :: ANY?) :: (node :: NODE?)
spatial.updateFromWKT	spatial.updateFromWKT(layerName :: STRING?, geometry :: STRING?, geometryNodeId :: INTEGER?) :: (node :: NODE?)
spatial.getFeatureAttributes	spatial.getFeatureAttributes(name :: STRING?) :: (name :: STRING?)
spatial.bbox	spatial.bbox(layerName :: STRING?, min :: ANY?, max :: ANY?) :: (node :: NODE?)
spatial.addLayer	spatial.addLayer(name :: STRING?, type :: STRING?, encoderConfig :: STRING?) :: (node :: NODE?)
spatial.procedures	spatial.procedures() :: (name :: STRING?, signature :: STRING?)
spatial.withinDistance	spatial.withinDistance(layerName :: STRING?, coordinate :: ANY?, distanceInKm :: FLOAT?) :: (node :: NODE?, distance :: FLOAT?)
spatial.layers	spatial.layers() :: (name :: STRING?, signature :: STRING?)
spatial.importOSMToLayer	spatial.importOSMToLayer(layerName :: STRING?, uri :: STRING?) :: (count :: INTEGER?)
spatial.addPointLayer	spatial.addPointLayer(name :: STRING?) :: (node :: NODE?)
spatial.addWKT	spatial.addWKT(layerName :: STRING?, geometry :: STRING?) :: (node :: NODE?)
spatial.addLayerWithEncoder	spatial.addLayerWithEncoder(name :: STRING?, encoder :: STRING?, encoderConfig :: STRING?) :: (node :: NODE?)
spatial.importOSM	spatial.importOSM(uri :: STRING?) :: (count :: INTEGER?)
spatial.addNode	spatial.addNode(layerName :: STRING?, node :: NODE?) :: (node :: NODE?)
spatial.addPointLayerXY	spatial.addPointLayerXY(name :: STRING?, xProperty :: STRING?, yProperty :: STRING?) :: (node :: NODE?)
spatial.asExternalGeometry	spatial.asExternalGeometry(geometry :: ANY?) :: (geometry :: ANY?)
spatial.setFeatureAttributes	spatial.setFeatureAttributes(name :: STRING?, attributeNames :: LIST? OF STRING?) :: (node :: NODE?)
spatial.closest	spatial.closest(layerName :: STRING?, coordinate :: ANY?, distanceInKm :: FLOAT?) :: (node :: NODE?)
spatial.addWKTs	spatial.addWKTs(layerName :: STRING?, geometry :: LIST? OF STRING?) :: (node :: NODE?)
spatial.layerTypes	spatial.layerTypes() :: (name :: STRING?, signature :: STRING?)
spatial.asGeometry	spatial.asGeometry(geometry :: ANY?) :: (geometry :: ANY?)
spatial.importShapefileToLayer	spatial.importShapefileToLayer(layerName :: STRING?, uri :: STRING?) :: (count :: INTEGER?)
spatial.addNodes	spatial.addNodes(layerName :: STRING?, nodes :: LIST? OF NODE?) :: (count :: INTEGER?)
spatial.layer	spatial.layer(name :: STRING?) :: (node :: NODE?)
spatial.addWKTLayer	spatial.addWKTLayer(name :: STRING?, nodePropertyName :: STRING?) :: (node :: NODE?)
spatial.addPointLayerWithConfig	spatial.addPointLayerWithConfig(name :: STRING?, encoderConfig :: STRING?) :: (node :: NODE?)

Spatial procedures

While the obvious point is that there are many procedures, we can see some keywords that require an explanation. While you already know OSM, we have yet to see what are layers, WKT, shapefiles, and bbox?

Layers are to be seen like named subsets--subsets of the set of nodes that you have imported whether by adding them one by one (`spatial.addPoint`), or by list (`spatial.addPoints`), or by importing a file (`spatial.importOSMFile`).

When you add points, they are transparently added to an index tree. This index is then used by the procedures of the library.

See the layers as branches of the tree. They fulfill a role comparable to the Labels we saw earlier as they constrain the amount of nodes to search.

There are also different kinds of layers, which are SimplePoint, WKT, WKB, and OSM.

The easiest way to get started is create a SimplePoint layer with the following:

```
call spatial.addPointLayer("Paris")
```

Now that there is a `Paris` layer, let's add the `Eiffel Tower` to it:

```
MATCH (etp:Tower {name: "Eiffel Tower"})
CALL spatial.addNode("Paris", etp) YIELD node
RETURN node
```

Now let me issue you a warning: when you remove a layer, you remove all the nodes within it from the database! Relations with nodes that are not in a layer are removed. The following code steps are used to demonstrate this:

1. Let's create a layer:

```
call spatial.addPointLayer("MyWorld")
```

2. Now, let's create a `Person` and add it to the layer:

```
CREATE (me:Person {name:"me", longitude: 1.1, latitude: 2.2})
WITH me
CALL spatial.addNode("MyWorld", me) YIELD node
RETURN node
```

You noticed the `longitude` and `latitude` properties, which are mandatory.

3. Let's create a second person:

```
CREATE (you:Person {name:"you", longitude: 1.1, latitude: 2.2})
```

4. Now let's create a relation:

```
MATCH (you:Person {name:"you"}), (me:Person {name:"me"})
CREATE (you)-[:READ]->(me)
```

5. Inspect your data and find two persons and one relation:

```
MATCH (n:Person) RETURN n LIMIT 25
```

6. Remove the layer:

```
CALL spatial.removeLayer("MyWorld")
```

7. Check your data:

```
MATCH (n:Person) RETURN n LIMIT 25
```

Oops, a person has disappeared, like in a magic show (so Las Vegas!)

Importing OpenStreetMap data

OpenStreetMap is an open data community-driven initiative that regroups and shares geographical data of the world (streets, roads, stations, bus stops, and so on).

To get data, we have different options. First, we have the OSM site that allows you to export the data for the zone displayed on the screen. This is perfect for getting a small file of the places around where you live. In the examples later in this chapter, I use a file I exported from this URL, `http://www.openstreetmap.org/export#map=16/48.8576/2.2949`. (Disclaimer: I do not live there. Unfortunately.)

The GeoFabrik website, `http://download.geofabrik.de/`, proposed by OSM, will allow you to download files for bigger zones (continents, countries, regions) free of charge. I encourage you to make business with them, should you need a special geo-dataset.

A small file may be imported via the Neo4j browser but I do not advise it for large files like a country, even a dense region. The import will fail with a lack of websockets but the animation will continue to turn and only tailing the log (`tail -f neo4j.log` on a Linux box) will tell you that there is a problem and you will have to kill the server process.

 In this case, running the `neo4j stop` command will not work, because no connection is possible when there are no websockets left. That is one reason why starting the server with `neo4j console` is good. Not only does it tail the log right after starting the server, but stopping the server is just a matter of pressing *Ctrl+C*.

Should you want to try, the query is of this form:

```
CALL spatial.importOSM("/home/jerome/map_ET_Paris.osm")
```

It will create a layer named after the file. You can also use the `spatial.importOSMToLayer` procedure to specify the layer name.

My file was 10+ MB. However, these new nodes are not labeled. So we have to run through properties to know what we have imported. In the Neo4j browser, look at the left column, click on the first tab--the one that looks like a pile of *crêpes*--and see the part titled 'Property Keys'. Among these is one named `amenity`. Let's have a look at the different amenities that we have:

```
MATCH (n) WHERE EXISTS(n.amenity)
RETURN DISTINCT n.amenity AS amenity, count(n) as nbr
ORDER BY nbr DESC, amenity ASC
```

The result list of this query contains a restaurant, cafe, ATM, toilets, and bench.

Should we want to propose to search by `amenity`, it would be useful to add an index to this `property`, but we cannot because these nodes have no label and an index creation is on a `property`, for a `Label`:

```
CREATE INDEX ON :Label(property)
```

So, we add a label like `Osm` to all the nodes with an `amenity`:

```
MATCH (n) WHERE EXISTS(n.amenity)
SET n:Osm
```

Then, the index creation is possible:

```
CREATE INDEX ON :Osm(amenity)
```

We could also add a label with the value of the `amenity` property, which is possible with APOC:

```
MATCH (n) WHERE EXISTS(n.amenity)
WITH n CALL apoc.create.addLabels(n, [n.amenity]) YIELD node
RETURN count(node)
```

Note that `RETURN` is mandatory after a `CALL`.

If we look at our data, we see that the coordinates are not on the node but on another, via a TAGS relation:

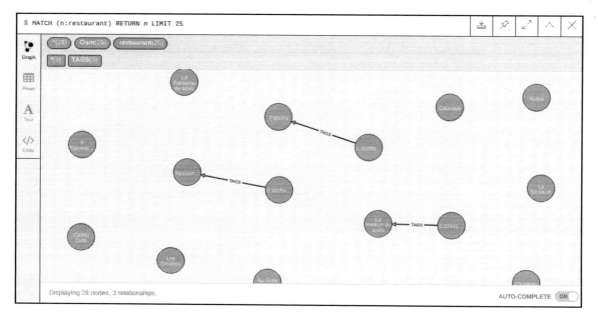

Coordinates tag restaurants

So, now, should we want to list the restaurants and their coordinates, the query is as follows:

```
MATCH (n)-[:TAGS]->(r:restaurant)
RETURN r.name, n.lat, n.lon
```

Do you notice what is wrong there? Yes, the label restaurant does not start with a capital R. We need a custom function (to capitalize the amenity value), whose result is to be passed to the addLabels procedure. Do it as an exercise.

Large OSM Imports

If you dig into the data, you will see how rich it is and also how much of the imported data you do not care about.

Easy way

When dealing with large datasets, do not start the import from the Neo4j browser, but instead use the Cypher-shell. On the command line, in `$NEO_HOME/bin`, run Cypher-shell and then type the Cypher query to call the import procedure:

```
jerome@nitendet ~/Tools/neo/neo4j-community-3.1.6/bin $ cypher-shell
username: neo4j
password: ********
Connected to Neo4j 3.1.6 at bolt://localhost:7687 as user neo4j.
Type :help for a list of available commands or :exit to exit the shell.
Note that Cypher queries must end with a semicolon.
neo4j> call spatial.importOSM('/home/jerome/OpenSource/spatial/map_ET_Paris.osm'
);
```

Importing with Cypher-shell

You must know that it may not be possible to import several OSM files in the same graph. There is a bug at the moment of writing this book; it depends on file content. I managed to import several OSM files but not two serious OSM files. An exception is raised about non-unicity for two `LegacyIndexProxy` instances. Fortunately, it should be solved as you read these lines.

 Also, be aware that the OSM files are extremely rich, like history of change for items. Much of this data will be of no use for you. Therefore, unless OSM data is at the core of your business, follow my advice NOT to use your main graph to import OSM data.

Use a secondary graph on another machine, import the zone that has your interest, then export what you need as CSV, and import that on your main server. The tougher way may also help.

The tougher way to import data

Another way to import an OSM file is to face the perils of Maven and Java on the command line. To get the sources of Neo4j spatial on your machine and build it, use the following query:

```
git clone git://github.com/neo4j-contrib/spatial.git
cd spatial
mvn clean install -DskipTests=true
```

Then, after getting the file you need (get the `.bz2` archive and unpack the `.osm` file within), type the following on the command line:

```
mvn dependency:copy-dependencies
java -cp target/classes:target/dependency/*
org.neo4j.gis.spatial.osm.OSMImporter new-osm-db bigBigFile.osm
```

This will create a new database: a full file hierarchy in a new folder named `new-osm-db`. This can prove useful to create a new graph without stopping one's server. Now, let's take a break from importing OSM and use some of the data imported.

Restroom please

In this closest-water story, let's imagine that we are at a known position and need to know the closest WC.

There is a procedure for that!

```
CALL spatial.closest('map_ET_Paris.osm', {lat:48.858093, lon:2.294694}, 1)
YIELD node
MATCH (node)-[:GEOM]-(geo)-[:TAGS]->(t:toilets)
RETURN coalesce(t.name,"unnamed") as name,coalesce(t.fee,'?') as fee,
geo.lat, geo.lon
```

Understanding WKT and BBOX

WKT is part of the list of new keywords that we saw earlier and stands for **well-known text**, as WKT is a text-based markup language and is human-readable. Its use is to represent objects on a map, like points, polygons, lines, and curves. WKT can express 2D, 3D, and even 4D coordinates.

However, you can now instantly recognize this point expressed in WKT:

```
POINT(48.858093 2.294694)
```

Indeed, it is the Parisian Eiffel Tower. Congratulations!

Now, not everybody sees what the next line represents:

```
POLYGON( 48.858093 2.294694, 49.858093 2.294696, 49.858093 2.294740)
```

If it represents anything at all! And where it is! (I chose numbers randomly).

You may see nodes with a WKT property in other kinds of layers. A **WKT layer** is the type to use if you want to give a shape to your layer. WKB is the binary version of WKT.

BBOX stands for **bounding box**, a rectangle defined by two points considered as opposite corners. Bounding boxes are used in queries to return all the nodes which have coordinates that place them in the box.

Removing all the geo data

You may want to remove all the indexed nodes from the spatial tree. You can do this by removing all the layers, which is a rather expeditive method indeed.

Try this code, which should return an empty list :

```
// Removing all spatial layers
CALL spatial.layers() YIELD name AS name
WITH collect(name) AS names
UNWIND names AS nameL
CALL spatial.removeLayer(nameL)  // enamel layer :)
call spatial.layers() YIELD name AS name2
WITH collect(name2) AS emptyNamesList
RETURN emptyNamesList
```

I hope you enjoyed this chapter, particularly rich in puns and wordplays.

Summary

In this chapter, we saw how to use geographical coordinates in Neo4j, be it without or with APOC, or with the Neo4j Spatial plugin. We saw what is geocoding and how to import geographic data provided by OpenStreetMap. Consequently, we can now imagine queries based on locations, like what restaurants are around me? or Where can I find a shared bicycle?

We just need to import the right datasets with the skills gained in Chapter 8, *Importing data into Neo4j*.

Now, let's see how to deal with the security of our data in the next chapter.

10
Security

In this chapter, you will learn what the security features of Neo4j are and how they apply, such as with their roles and access restrictions. If security is the number one priority to your admins it is because some data can be so sensitive that it has to be restricted to chosen groups of users. You would not want some unknown jerk to delete your data from somewhere on the internet, would you?

When users can be counted in hundreds, you need a directory (or to have more admins to create accounts; do not do that it is silly).

We will be covering the following topics in the chapter:

- Authentication and authorization
- Roles
- Users management
- Linking Neo4j to an LDAP directory
- Configuring Neo4j to use LDAP

Authentication and authorization

Authentication is the capacity for a system to ensure that who you claim to be is who you are and that you belong to the system users. This is usually realized using credentials like a login/password pair.

This pair can be managed by Neo4j or another system to which Neo4j will communicate the pair and receive a result leading to the user entering or not entering the system. These other specialized systems can be directories of the following technologies:

- LDAP
- Active directory
- Kerberos (along with LDAP)

Authorization is the capacity for a system to give different levels of access to different users, from being allowed to perform inconsequential commands like changing one's password to being allowed to add users or modify the graph. In most systems, this is achieved through the use of roles.

Roles

The following are the roles in Neo4j:

- No role
- Reader
- Editor
- Publisher
- Architect
- Admin

They are ordered by ascending possibilities, with admin being the most powerful. When created, users have no role, then an admin grants authorization level via roles.

The possibilities for each role are ascending and are based on those of the previous role. Let's browse the possibilities of each role:

- **No role**: This is the default role. It allows you to change one's password and see one's details. It doesn't allow much, and will make users sing, don't leave me this way.
- **Reader**: A reader can read the whole graph.
- **Editor**: An editor can read and modify the existing data for the whole graph. An editor can create new nodes with existing labels and existing properties, and new relations with existing names.
- **Publisher**: A publisher can create new nodes, new labels, and new relations.

- **Architect**: An architect has control over the indexes of the graph and over the constraints (CREATE and DROP).
- **Admin**: An admin can also create users, give them roles, and has a death right on running queries. Thus, the role that is the most fun and also the one with the most power. The Neo4j account has the admin role. (Did you change the password?)

Other roles

An admin may create and delete new roles with these commands:

```
CALL dbms.security.createRole('newRoleName')
CALL dbms.security.deleteRole('newRoleName')
```

These roles are to be used on custom procedures (see Chapter 06, *Extending Cypher*.) with the @Procedure annotation, as follows:

```
@Procedure(allowed='newRoleName')
```

You may have noticed a roles column in the result of the command:

```
CALL dbms.procedures()
```

This command is available for all users, starting with the reader role.

Users management

Admins can create new users in the Neo4j browser with this command, which brings up a user interface:

```
:server user add
```

Give a name, role, and password to the new user. Check whether the creation worked by viewing the list of users with the following command:

```
:server user list
```

From this list, it is possible to disable or delete a user.

Of course, you are not forced to use a web UI with inputs and buttons. There are more built-in procedures to manage users, accessible via the Neo4j browser or via the Cypher shell:

Create a user	`CALL dbms.security.createUser(`*username, password, requirePasswordChange*`)`
Delete a user	`CALL dbms.security.deleteUser(`*username*`)`
Assign a role to a user	`CALL dbms.security.addRoleToUser(`*roleName, username*`)`
Remove a role from a user	`CALL dbms.security.removeRoleFromUser(`*roleName, username*`)`
Create a role	`CALL dbms.security.createRole('`*newRoleName*`')`
Delete a role	`CALL dbms.security.deleteRole('`*newRoleName*`')`
Change a user's password	`CALL dbms.security.changeUserPassword(`*username, newPassword, requirePasswordChange*`)`
Change one's password	`CALL dbms.security.changePassword(`*password, requirePasswordChange*`)`
List all users	`CALL dbms.security.listUsers()`

Now, let's delegate some responsibilities to an LDAP server.

Linking Neo4j to an LDAP directory

I will start this paragraph with a piece of advice. If you are using a cluster, connecting each node to the same LDAP directory is the way to go as users are local to a node and are not propagated.

So, let's connect. We will use a Docker container based on an OpenLdap image.

Starting the directory

Let's prepare the folder where the configuration will be. In a shell, execute the following in your home folder:

```
mkdir data/ldap/environment -p
mkdir data/ldap/db -p
```

In this first new folder, create a file named users.ldif with the following content:

```
dn: dc=learningneo4j,dc=com
dc: learningneo4j
description: Directory of all the readers
objectClass: top
objectClass: dcObject
objectClass: organization
o: Readers Directory

dn: ou=users,dc=learningneo4j,dc=com
ou: users
objectClass: organizationalRole
cn: users

# =============================================================== ROLES
dn: ou=ldapreaders,dc=learningneo4j,dc=com
objectClass: top
objectClass: organizationalRole
roleOccupant: cn=ureader,ou=users,dc=learningneo4j,dc=com
cn: ldapreaders

dn: ou=ldapproducers,dc=learningneo4j,dc=com
objectClass: top
objectClass: organizationalRole
roleOccupant: cn=uproducer,ou=users,dc=learningneo4j,dc=com
cn: ldapproducers

dn: ou=ldaparchs,dc=learningneo4j,dc=com
objectClass: top
objectClass: organizationalRole
roleOccupant: cn=uarch,ou=users,dc=learningneo4j,dc=com
cn: ldaparchs

dn: ou=ldapadmins,dc=learningneo4j,dc=com
ou: ldapadmins
objectClass: top
objectClass: organizationalRole
roleOccupant: cn=uadmin,ou=users,dc=learningneo4j,dc=com
cn: ldapadmins
```

```
# ================================================================= USERS
dn: cn=ureader, ou=users,dc=learningneo4j,dc=com
objectclass: inetOrgPerson
sn: ureader
userpassword: ureader
memberOf: ou=ldapreaders,dc=learningneo4j,dc=com
cn: ureader

#ou=users,
dn: cn=uproducer,ou=users,dc=learningneo4j,dc=com
objectclass: inetOrgPerson
cn: Producer User
sn: uproducer
userpassword: uproducer
memberOf: ou=ldapproducers,dc=learningneo4j,dc=com

dn: cn=uarch,ou=users,dc=learningneo4j,dc=com
objectclass: inetOrgPerson
cn: Architect User
sn: uarch
userpassword: uarch
memberOf: ou=ldaparchs,dc=learningneo4j,dc=com

dn: cn=uadmin, ou=users,dc=learningneo4j,dc=com
objectclass: inetOrgPerson
cn: Admin User
sn: uadmin
userpassword: uadmin
memberOf: ou=ldapadmins,dc=learningneo4j,dc=com
```

LDIF stands for **LDAP data interchange format**. This is a human readable text format, although not very attractive. It is useful to load and update an LDAP directory.

Let's start a new container with the following:

```
docker run --name="ldapcon" --env
LDAP_ORGANISATION="LearningNeo4jWithJerome" --env
LDAP_DOMAIN="learningneo4j.com" --env
LDAP_BIND_DN="cn=admin,dc=learningneo4j, dc=com" --env
LDAP_BASE="dc=learningneo4j, dc=com" --env LDAP_ADMIN_PASSWORD="agentSmith"
-p389:389 --volume $HOME/data/ldap/environment:/container/environment/01-
custom --detach osixia/openldap:1.1.9
```

This gives away that we will run an LDAP server to learn Neo4j.com; we expose the default LDAP port 389 and allow the container to have access to the users.ldif file. Now, because I do not want you to do a lot of clicking, let's use this LDIF formatted file to create the tree of groups and users in our shiny organization, with the next command:

```
docker exec ldapcon ldapadd -x -D "cn=admin,dc=learningneo4j, dc=com" -w
agentSmith -f /container/environment/01-custom/users.ldif -H
ldap://127.0.0.1/ -v
```

It will execute the ldapadd command inside our container with the users.ldif file. The result is a tree, which I encourage you to see with a graphical interface such as JXplorer or Apache Directory Studio. The first being lighter and the second, better. Create connections to 127.0.0.1 on port 389, with the login as admin and password as agentSmith.

 If you wish to run a shell on your running container, the syntax is as follows:
```
docker exec -it ldapcon /bin/bash
```

Time to connect the dots and make Neo4j use our LDAP container.

Configuring Neo4j to use LDAP

You already know that the action takes place in $NEO_HOME/conf/neo4j.conf. What must be done is a mapping of the LDAP groups to the Neo4j default roles. Add these few lines at the end of the file:

```
dbms.security.auth_provider=ldap
dbms.security.ldap.host=ldap://127.0.0.1:389
dbms.security.ldap.use_starttls=false
dbms.security.ldap.authentication.mechanism=simple
dbms.security.ldap.authentication.user_dn_template=cn={0},ou=users,dc=learn
ingneo4j,dc=com
dbms.security.ldap.authentication.cache_enabled=false
dbms.security.ldap.authorization.use_system_account=true
dbms.security.ldap.authorization.system_username=cn=admin,dc=learningneo4j,
dc=com
dbms.security.ldap.authorization.system_password=agentSmith
dbms.security.ldap.authorization.user_search_base=dc=learningneo4j,dc=com
dbms.security.ldap.authorization.user_search_filter=(&(objectClass=*)(cn={0
}))
dbms.security.ldap.authorization.group_membership_attributes=memberOf
dbms.security.ldap.authorization.group_to_role_mapping=\
  "ou=ldapreaders,dc=learningneo4j,dc=com"= reader; \
```

```
"ou=ldapproducers,dc=learningneo4j,dc=com"= publisher; \
"ou=ldaparchs,dc=learningneo4j,dc=com"=architect; \
"ou=ldapadmins,dc=learningneo4j,dc=com"=admin
```

Now after restarting your Neo4j server, you will be able to log in with the credentials of the users defined in `users.ldif`, such as ureader/ureader or uadmin/uadmin as login/password pairs.

If you want to switch back to the previous authentication system, simply change the following line:

dbms.security.auth_provider=ldap

Replace the preceding line to this:

dbms.security.auth_provider=native

Test questions

A. What is a role for ?

    1. Grouping people for granting them authorization
    2. Grouping people for granting them authentication
    3. To be on stage

B. How many roles are there in Neo4j?

    1. Five
    2. Four
    3. More

C. What roles can manage users?

    1. Publisher
    2. Architect
    3. Admin

D. What advantage does using an LDAP directory bring?

1. Reusing existing hardware, software and procedures
2. Neo4j admin does not have to create all the users in Neo4j
3. All of the above
4. None

Summary

In this chapter specific for the Enterprise version of Neo4j, we have seen the use and importance of roles, how to give them to users, how to create roles, and how to restrict procedures calls to specific roles--which is perfect for restricting the view on the graph of users, provided they cannot access the web application we called Neo4j browser throughout this book (configure this in neo4j.conf).

We have seen how to run a containerized OpenLDAP server with a chosen dataset and connect this directory to a Neo4j server so that authentication becomes delegated to the OpenLDAP server. This way, the Neo4j admin does not have to recreate users in Neo4j and users do not have another password to remember.

In Chapter 11, *Visualization for Neo4j*, we will see a completely different domain and see how to do some visualization of our data.

11
Visualizations for Neo4j

In this chapter, we will look at the fascinating domain of graph visualizations within the context of the Neo4j Graph Database Management System. We will go into the reasons why these kinds of visualizations can be so wonderfully important, discuss different technical tools to help you with these visualizations, and finally, discuss some of the common dos and don'ts within this domain.

In this chapter, we will discuss the following topics:

- The power of visualizations, specifically graph visualizations
- The basic principles and components of a graph visualization solution
- Different visualization libraries and solutions on the market

With that, let's dive right in.

The power of graph visualizations

In this section, we will spend time discussing the reasons why graph visualizations are so important, and highlight some of the underpinning technologies that are used in the different solutions that we will zoom into later on.

Why graph visualizations matter!

A picture is worth a thousand words.

There are many reasons why the graph visualizations that we will discuss in this chapter, as well as the ones that we have seen previously and will show hereafter, are really nice. For a limited number of reasons, they are more than nice: they matter greatly and can have a massive impact on decisions being made--big or small. Let's discuss these.

Interacting with data visually

From a very early age, we are taught to interact with data in a cognitive way--focused on analysis, not understanding. We are not supposed to or encouraged to look at data in a creative, fun, or interesting way that induces insight. This, however, is now changing. There's an entirely new discipline emerging in the field of data science and analytics, which stresses the visual aspects of interacting with data. Visual interaction, as opposed to cognitive interaction, tends to have some quality for average human beings who do not have the technical or scientific background that some people may have. By extension, many different business managers may also find this new way of interacting quite interesting. Here are some reasons why:

- It allows people to extract key information at a glance. In an age of sub-second attention spans and massive information overload, this can be truly important to get a point across and help your audience sift through what is and what is not important.
- We all know the cliché: a picture says more than a thousand words. The reason it is a cliché, of course, is that it is true. Pictures are usually easier to understand and, perhaps more importantly, are also easier to remember.

We could expand on both points quite elaborately, but instead, we are going to recommend that you read up on books like Edward R. Tufte's for more details:

Edward Tufte's reference work on visualization

It is sufficient to say that graph visualizations can be truly powerful and that most Neo4j projects today will have some kind of visualization component to them for a combination of the previously stated reasons.

Looking for patterns

Expanding on and adding to the previous points on visualization, there is another great reason to interact with Neo4j in a visual way. The fact is that graph visualizations allow humans to really use an otherwise underused capacity of our brains: pattern recognition. When we interact with data in the traditional way (through lists of things, tabular structured reports, and summary statistics), it is very difficult for our brain to discern any kind of pattern. We would need to read, assimilate, and cognitively process all data before anything like that would become possible. However, with graph visualization, in many cases we can just leverage the primal capability that we have built into our machinery: the ability to recognize patterns. Pattern recognition is a key capability of the human brain and one we should leverage and exploit in our business life. Representing data in a visual way, like in a graph visualization, is a natural thing for us and can yield very powerful results. After all, that's why we whiteboard, mind-map, or doodle when we work and discuss with our colleagues, isn't it?

Spot what's important

Part of the power of these results will be in being able to separate the wheat from the chaff and find out what is truly important in a particular dataset. Sometimes, that important piece will be in the density of the connections between a particular data entity and other entities. Sometimes, it will be more in the intensity of the connections. At other times, it will be the outliers that will be the more important data elements--the ones with limited amounts of connectivity with the rest of the data structure. These data elements, which at a minimum will be interesting if not important, will jump out of a graph visualization immediately, whereas they may never surface in a long list of data elements that we could easily glance over.

For all of the mentioned reasons, graph visualization is truly important and should definitely be examined in detail by anyone interested in doing a Neo4j graph database project.

The basic principles of graph visualization

In order to visualize a graph structure, we need to take into account a number of aspects. As with any visualization, it is very easy to let the trees disappear into the forest--in graphs, we often talk about the **hairball** effect. Connected structures such as graphs can easily become very unclear and intransparent to the user; it takes a couple of very well-defined mechanisms to lay out the graph to the user in an intelligible way. More specifically, we tend to find three main mechanisms that are used by different technology solutions, which we will treat later on. Let's go through these mechanisms.

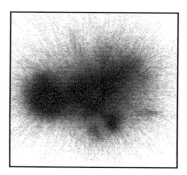

Graphs can quickly look like hairballs

 Before doing so, we want to specifically thank Alistair Jones for his insightful talks that gave me many of the ideas presented in this section. You can visit www.apcjones.com if you want to learn more.

Here are the three mechanisms to keep in mind:

- **Gravity:** In order for a graph visualization to make sense to a user, things that belong together need to be presented together. These items will need to gravitate to one another using some kind of force that will be calculated based on the characteristics of the nodes and relationships that will be stored in the Neo4j database management system.
- **Charge:** By the same logic, there needs to be a force that keeps items apart from one another. We call this **charge**, as we know from a long-forgotten course in school that substances with a similar positive or negative charge will repel each other. Similarly, we will associate a charge to different items in the graph to keep them from overlapping and make sure that they are visualized apart.

- **Springs**: As with many other data visualization solutions, it helps the effectiveness of the graph visualization greatly if the solution is presented in a dynamic and vivid fashion. In a graph database visualization like the ones that we want to hook up to Neo4j, this often means that we would appreciate some kind of springy behavior that displays the data in a way that is not static as usual but moves around on the screen as it is built or manipulated by the user. The spring analogy aims to explain that we will appreciate the type of visualization that will go back and forth a bit before it stabilizes on the screen.

With these three underlying techniques, a number of very interesting visualization libraries and fully-fledged solutions have been built. We will take the next couple of sections to highlight these briefly so that you know where you can find some potential components of your Neo4j solution.

Open source visualization libraries

Many developers that use Neo4j as their Graph Database Management System end up having some very specific needs to visualize the network and present it to their end users in an integrated way as part of their application. These Neo4j users, who are not afraid of getting their hands dirty with some code, will typically like to build the visualization using a library of tools that fit their purpose. There are several tools out there that could be used, so let's give you a little overview of the most popular ones.

D3.js

D3, pronounced **dee three**, is another way to refer to a library that is supposed to enable and provide data-driven documents. It is a JavaScript library to manipulate documents based on data. You can find the latest version on www.d3js.org. D3 helps you visualize data using HTML, SVG, and CSS. D3's emphasis on web standards gives you the full capabilities of modern browsers without tying yourself to a proprietary framework, combining powerful visualization components with a data-driven approach to the manipulation of the **Document Object Model** (**DOM**) that is the basis of HTML and XML documents.

As such, D3.js is not limited to the visualization of graphs--it aims to solve the heart of many data visualization problems: being able to manipulate a dataset interactively based on some kind of document. Once this is solved, the data can be manipulated independent of the format or representation, which offers great flexibility and has made the D3 libraries very popular with developers; this is why many other libraries are built on top of it.

D3 is the library used to make the Neo4j browser.

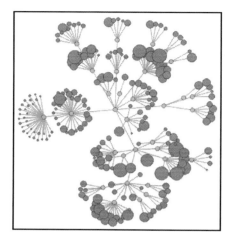

D3.js visualization of a graph

And now, let's see GraphViz.

GraphViz

GraphViz is an open source graph visualization software that you can download from
`www.graphviz.org`. It is often quoted as being the granddaddy of visualization software, but
is still very actively used and developed. It provides several main layout programs and
features web and interactive graphical interfaces as well as helper tools, libraries, and
language bindings. The core GraphViz team claims to not be able to put a lot of work into
GUI editors, but there are quite a few external projects and even commercial tools that
incorporate Graphviz.

The Graphviz layout programs take descriptions of graphs in a simple text language and
create diagrams in useful formats, for example, images and SVG for web pages and PDF or
Postscript for inclusion in other documents or for display in an interactive graph browser.

Graphviz has many useful features for concrete diagrams, such as options for colors, fonts,
tabular node layouts, line styles, hyperlinks, and custom shapes.

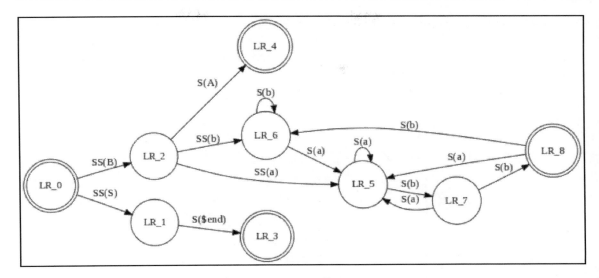

GraphViz visualization of a graph

And now, let's see `Sigma.js`.

Sigma.js

Sigma is a JavaScript library dedicated to graph drawing. You can find it on
`www.sigmajs.org`. It makes it easy to publish networks on web pages and allows developers
to integrate network exploration in rich web applications. Sigma provides a lot of built-in
features that are optimized for modern browsers, such as Canvas and WebGL renderers or
mouse and touch support. This is supposed to make network manipulation on web pages
smooth and fast for the user.

Sigma provides a lot of different settings to make it easy to customize drawing and
interaction with networks. You can also directly add your own functions to your scripts to
render nodes and edges the exact way you want. Sigma is a rendering engine, and it is up to
you to add all the interactivity you want.

The public API makes it possible to modify the data, move the camera, refresh the rendering, listen to events, and many other things. It's probably for some of these reasons that the visualization solution of `Linkurio.us`, which we will come back to later in this chapter, uses `Sigma.js` under the hood.

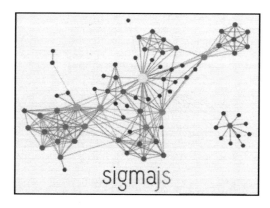

Sigma.js visualization of a graph

And now, let's see `Vivagraph.js`.

Vivagraph.js

Vivagraph is a free and fast graph drawing library for JavaScript. It is designed to be extensible and to support different rendering engines and layout algorithms. You can download the most recent version from `https://github.com/anvaka/VivaGraphJS` and see some very nice demos of it at `www.yasiv.com`. At the moment, it supports rendering graphs using WebGL, SVG, or CSS formats. Author Andrei Kashcha is also working on a library called `Ngraph` on which `Vivagraph` is built; you can find details of it on `https://github.com/anvaka/ngraph`.

Some of the `Vivagraph.js` examples on Yasiv are a lot of fun to use and powerfully illustrate that graphs can be used very well for things such as recommendations: it takes a split-second view of the Amazon recommendation graph, as shown in the following screenshot, to understand how one might use this:

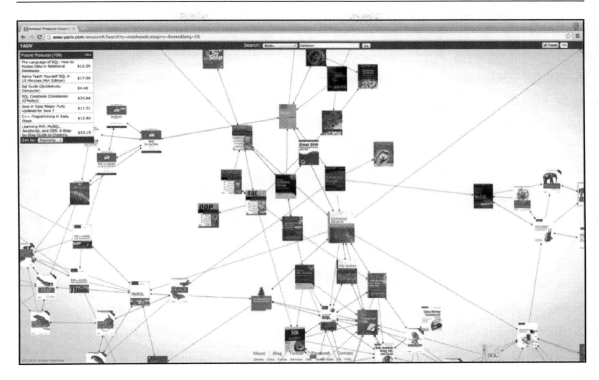

Vivagraph.js visualization of a graph

And now, let's see yWorks.

yWorks

yWorks yFiles for HTML is a powerful library. I have been particularly impressed by its automatic layout features and its capacity to untangle a graph automatically.

The main layouts available are:

- Hierachical layout
- Organic layout
- Orthogonal layout
- Tree layout
- Circular layout
- Balloon layout
- Radial layout
- Series parallel layout
- Routers

The usage is rather straightforward. Use the page template provided and then write the graph instructions within the script element.

These were probably some of the more popular open source visualization libraries out there.

Integrating visualization libraries in your application

Integrating libraries will always follow a similar pattern, as illustrated by the following figure:

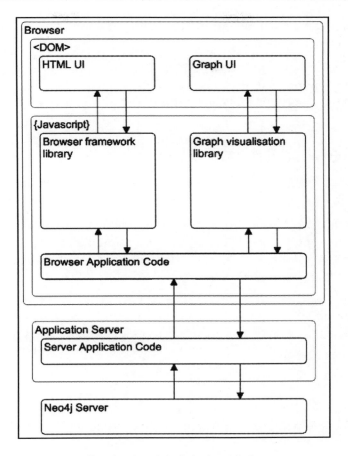

How to integrate graph visualizations in an application

The browser will contain two parts:

- The **DOM**, with the actual data. This contains the graph data as part of the total web page.
- The **JavaScript** part, with the browser framework as well as the graph visualization library (one of the ones mentioned before, possibly) and perhaps some other application code.

The application server will be on the other end of the Internet connection to provide the application interface to the user. This server will typically have some business logic hosted on it, but will most probably also have to integrate with a database management system like Neo4j.

The Neo4j server in the back will be serving up result sets based on queries generated by the aforementioned business logic.

This architecture allows us to understand how any of these libraries would need to be hooked into our application. With this, we will now turn our attention to some more packaged visualization solutions that can be used in combination with Neo4j.

Visualization solutions

We make a distinction between visualization libraries and visualization solutions for a very specific reason: they serve very different purposes.

Many members of the Neo4j user community have been developing their own application-specific visualization applications that are typically customized. They aim to solve a very specific visualization problem and use a library to do so, because it allows them to tweak the visualization to their liking at the expense of a bit more work.

There are, however, also those users of the Neo4j Graph Database Management System that require a more general, less optimized, but more readily available visualization solution. For these users, visualization *solutions* are a better option, as they are typically readily available, off-the-shelf solutions that require little or no customization to start adding value. These are the solutions that we will be discussing in this section of our book. So, let's take a look.

Note that we will be discussing these solutions in alphabetical order; there is no preference or order displayed in these pages, as we firmly believe that most of these tools are complementary to one another.

Gephi

Gephi is an interactive visualization and exploration platform for all kinds of networks and complex systems, dynamic graphs, and hierarchical graphs. It is developed by the Gephi Consortium, a not-for-profit legal entity in France created to ensure future developments of Gephi. They aim to develop a number of tools in an open source ecosystem, focused on the visualization and analysis of large networks in real time. Their tagline, *Like Photoshop but for data*, gives you a good feel of what they want to do: Gephi helps data analysts intuitively reveal patterns and trends, highlight outliers, and tell stories with their data.

The toolset runs on Windows, Linux, and Mac OS X and has a very extensible architecture (NetBeans platform plugins) that, for example, allows you to import and export Neo4j databases.

What makes Gephi interesting from my perspective is its capability to do both graph visualization and, at least for small-to-medium sized graphs, graph analytics. It can be of great help in discovering new patterns in your data--even those patterns that you are currently not aware of:

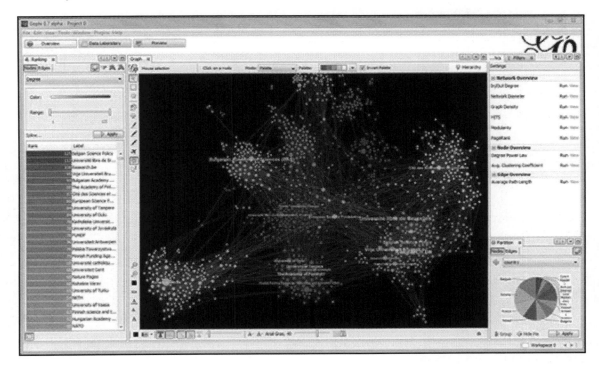

Gephi in action

Keylines

UK-based start-up Cambridge Intelligence (http://cambridge-intelligence.com/) has been building a very interesting toolkit for graph visualization called Keylines (http://keylines.com/) that has been gaining traction quite quickly in the law enforcement, fraud detection, counter terrorism, CRM, sales, and social network data sectors.

Keylines graph visualization

Keylines is interesting in many different ways from a technical perspective, mostly because it can be deployed on any browser or device without too much difference in architecture and support. It allows for both standard, out-of-the-box deployment, as well as deep customization using the System Development Kit that is provided with their commercial licenses.

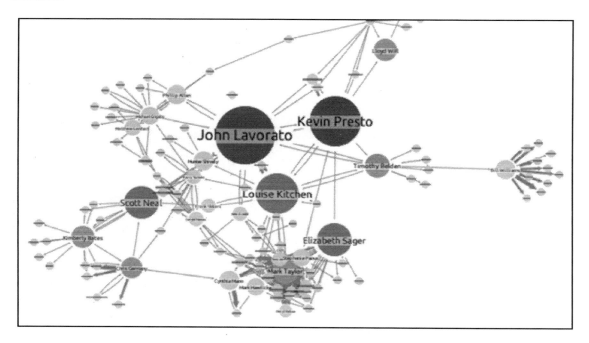

KeyLines in action

Linkurio.us

Linkurio.us (http://linkurio.us/) is probably one of the more interesting and newer additions to the graph visualization landscape. It was started in France by some of Gephi's original founders and contributors. They now offer a very well-rounded, moderately priced, easily accessible entry point for people that want an advanced graph visualization toolkit without having to jump through the hoops of building one.

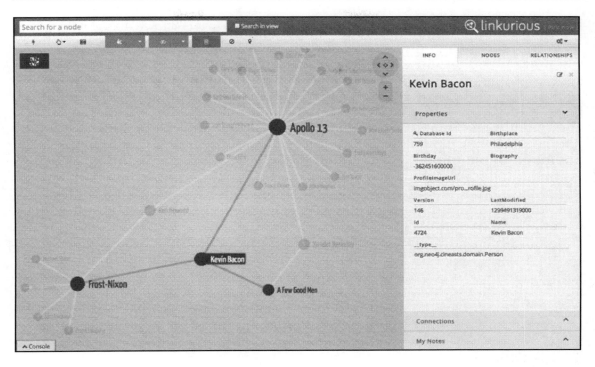

Linkurio.us graph visualization

Linkurio.us is a very nice alternative for graph visualizations, offering a packaged solution with lots of interesting features and a plug-and-play installation on top of an existing Neo4j database management system.

Neo4j Browser

With the arrival of Neo4j 2.0 in late 2013, the team at Neo Technology provided a new way of interacting with graph data, entirely based on an intuitive way to interact with the graph database using Cypher. This environment, called Neo4j Browser, is a bit of a hybrid between a data query tool and development environment.

It provides many of the tools that one would expect to use in an interactive exploration of graph data, allows you to save queries and do visual styling, and is gradually being expanded with more and more functionality.

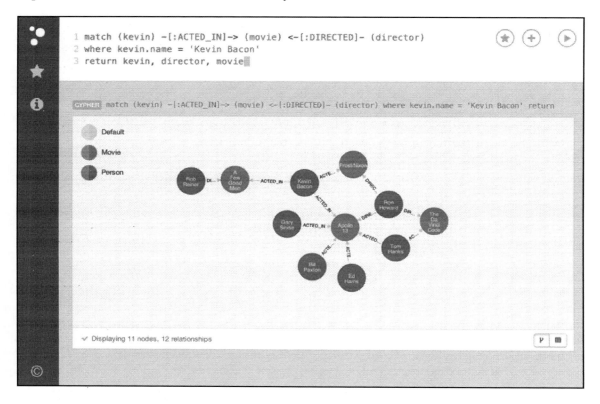

Neo4j Browser graph visualization and querying

Neo4j Browser is, at the time of this writing, still under development, with new features being constantly added.

One of the interesting new developments is that Neo Technology will actually allow the extraction and embedding of browser visualization functionality into your own applications.

Tom Sawyer Software for graph visualization

One of the lesser known alternatives for graph visualization, at least in Europe, is Tom Sawyer Software's Perspectives line of products.

Look at `https://www.tomsawyer.com` for the company's website and `https://www.tomsawyer.com/products/perspectives/index.php` for more information on Perspectives.

This is an advanced graphics-based software to build enterprise-class data relationship visualization and analysis applications. It features a complete **Software Development Kit (SDK)** with a graphics-based design and preview environment that lets you build, test, and deploy graph visualizations more easily, based on a reference architecture.

A visualization of **Tom Sawyer** graph is given as follows:

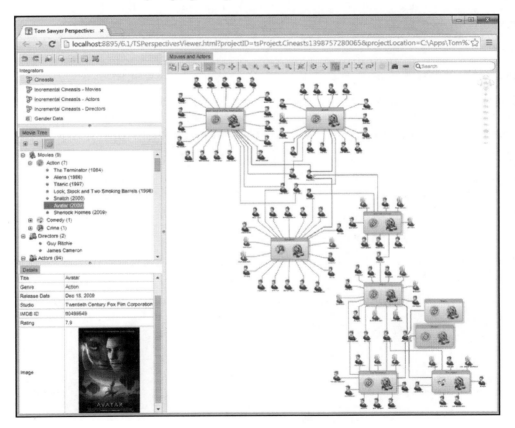

Tom Sawyer graph visualization

Tom Sawyer also offers standard data integration capabilities for Neo4j's Graph Database Management System.

With that, we are close to wrapping up the chapter of this book on graph visualizations. We do have a couple of closing remarks that we would like to add before we move on.

Closing remarks on visualizations - pitfalls and issues

It should be clear by now that once we have our data models in a Graph Database Management System like Neo4j, one of the great potential use cases for that system is tightly coupled with visualization capabilities. It is amazing what we can learn from visualizations, but we do want to point out two caveats that you should always keep in mind as you engage in a visualization project.

The fireworks effect

While graph visualizations usually have a very positive effect on their users, we--as IT people that are provided this as an interface to interact with data--must also be aware of the fact that these visualizations can be a bit too much sometimes.

We call this the *fireworks* effect, and while by no means specific to graph visualizations, it is an important thing to be aware of. The purpose of visualization can never be to attract oohs and aahs--that's what fireworks are supposed to do for the crowds of spectators that they attract.

Contrarily, the purpose of a visualization should always be to communicate with the beholders and transfer information from the software application that we are building on top of a Graph Database Management System such as Neo4j to its users.

This seems like a trivial point, but we know from experience that it is often forgotten. To demo this effect is easy, it just takes clicking on several nodes with many relations. Providing your graph is richer than the examples we loaded in Chapter 8, *Importing Data into Neo4j*; after a handful of double-clicks, the screen gets filled with nodes and the result is barely readable, making it useless.

The loading effect

With this purpose of visualizations in mind, we should also take into account another aspect that is crucially important in the world of data visualizations: the loading effect. This effect is, again, not specific to graph visualizations and is omnipresent in many charts and graphics presented by newspapers and television reports alike. We mean to highlight the effect that a particular type of presentation of the data has in the interpretation process of the user.

By making certain choices on how we present the data, the options that we present to the user, or even the colors that we choose for certain data elements, we may load the visualization with certain expectations and interpretations on behalf of the end user. Data visualizations should therefore always highlight and explain the choices made to the end user and offer different ways of representing the data if that would be of use.

Cytoscape example

In this paragraph, we will see an example of the usage of another graph library named Cytoscape.

 Cytoscape is open source, under MIT license, and can be found on GitHub at `https://github.com/cytoscape/cytoscape.js`, and its documentation can be found at `http://js.cytoscape.org/`.

The goal is to display data from our current database, showing usage of the JavaScript driver to get the list of operating systems of the Unix family.

Here is the result of the code to follow:

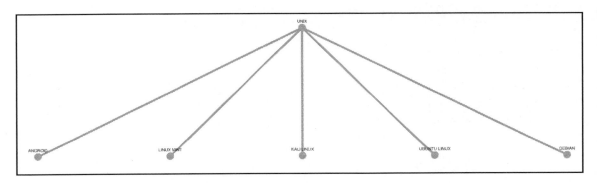

Our data with Cytoscape and its breadth-first layout

Even though my `javascript-fu` is weak (maybe even *undefined),* I managed to code this in a single page.

First, the style of cytograph sets the size of the display to show the graph. Then the libraries are loaded from their respective CDNs, then, a `div` element for the graph is created, the UNIX node is created at this stage, although it will be repeated in the result of the Cypher query. As it is not possible to create nodes with the same identifier, there is no merge in Cytoscape a check in the loop would be needed in order to not generate an error if the UNIX node (fam) creation was in the more natural place that is in the loop.

The neoElements array will then be used as the data source for the graph.

Thereafter, the Neo4j javascript driver is initialized, and it connects to localhost with `neo4j/password`. Yes, password is in clear text.
Of course, you should not do this in production; your page should call a REST endpoint instead of giving the credentials away.

The query is run when the document is ready, `then` the results are processed to create JS objects with the structure expected by Cytoscape in the `neoElements` array. Then is a JS keyword that enforces the sequence of the functions executions. Again, `then` is used to execute the `populate` function, which starts with the long definition of options that will be used for the layout (replace it with other definitions of the website to experiment).

Thereafter, Cytoscape is created (variable cy), nodes are added, and the layout gets created and run.

I encourage you to look at the documentation and experiment with this library.

Source code

Here is the course of our Cytoscape example:

```html
<!DOCTYPE html>
<html lang="en">
<head>
    <meta charset="utf-8">
    <meta http-equiv="X-UA-Compatible" content="IE=edge">
    <meta name="viewport" content="width=device-width, initial-scale=1">
    <title>Neo4j + Cytoscape</title>
    <style>
    #cytograph {
      width: 90%;
      height: 90%;
      position: absolute;
```

```
        top: 0px;
        left: 0px;
    }

    </style>
    <script type="text/javascript"
src="https://cdnjs.cloudflare.com/ajax/libs/jquery/2.2.4/jquery.min.js"></s
cript>
    <script
src="https://cdnjs.cloudflare.com/ajax/libs/cytoscape/3.1.4/cytoscape.js"><
/script>
    <script
src="https://cdn.rawgit.com/neo4j/neo4j-javascript-driver/1.1/lib/browser/n
eo4j-web.js"></script>
</head>

<body>
<h1>Basic cytoscape.js use with neo4j</h1>
<div id="cytograph"></div>

<script>
        var fam ; // first object is unix family.
        fam = new Object();
        fam.data = {}
        fam.data['group']= 'nodes';
        fam.data['id'] = 'UNIX';
        fam.data['name'] = 'UNIX';

        var neo = neo4j.v1;
        var driver = neo.driver("bolt://localhost", neo.auth.basic("neo4j",
"password")  );
        var session = driver.session();

        var neoElements = [];
        neoElements.push( fam );

$(document).ready( function () {
 session.run('MATCH (n:Os)--(f:OsFamily) RETURN n.name AS nname,f.name AS
fname').then
        (
        function (result) {
            var i = 1;
            result.records.forEach(
                function (r) {
                    var nouveau = new Object();
                        nouveau.data = {}
                        nouveau.data['group']  = 'nodes';
                        nouveau.data['id']      = ''+r._fields[0];
```

```
                              nouveau.data['name']   = ''+r._fields[0];

                    var rel = new Object();
                        rel.data = {}
                        rel.data['group']   = 'edges'
                        rel.data['id']      = r._fields[0]+r._fields[1];
                        rel.data['source']  = ''+r._fields[0];
                        rel.data['target']  = ''+r._fields[1];

                neoElements.push( nouveau );
                neoElements.push(rel);
              }
          );
      }
   )
   .then(
      function populate(result){
          var options = {
            name: 'breadthfirst',
            fit: true, // whether to fit the viewport to the graph
            directed: false, // whether the tree is directed downwards
(or edges can point in any direction if false)
            padding: 30, // padding on fit
            circle: false, // put depths in concentric circles if true,
put depths top down if false
            spacingFactor: 1.75, // positive spacing factor, larger =>
more space between nodes (N.B. n/a if causes overlap)
            boundingBox: undefined, // constrain layout bounds; { x1, y1,
x2, y2 } or { x1, y1, w, h }
            avoidOverlap: true, // prevents node overlap, may overflow
boundingBox if not enough space
            nodeDimensionsIncludeLabels: false, // Excludes the label
when calculating node bounding boxes for the layout algorithm
            roots: undefined, // the roots of the trees
            maximalAdjustments: 0, // how many times to try to position
the nodes in a maximal way (i.e. no backtracking)
            animate: false, // whether to transition the node positions
            animationDuration: 500, // duration of animation in ms if
enabled
            animationEasing: undefined, // easing of animation if enabled
            ready: undefined, // callback on layoutready
            stop: undefined // callback on layoutstop
          };

          var cy = cytoscape({ container:
document.getElementById('cytograph'),
                               elements: [],
                               style: cytoscape.stylesheet()
```

```
                              .selector('node')
                                .style({'content': 'data(id)'})
                              .selector('edge')
                                .style({
                                   'target-arrow-shape': 'triangle',
                                   'width': 8,
                                   'line-color': '#00ff00',
                                   'target-arrow-color': '#ff0000'
                                })
                              .selector('.highlighted')
                                .style({
                                   'background-color': '#61bffc',
                                   'line-color': '#61bffc',
                                   'target-arrow-color': '#61bffc',
                                   'transition-property': 'background-
color, line-color, target-arrow-color',
                                   'transition-duration': '0.5s'
                                })
                           });
      cy.add( neoElements );
      var leLayout = cy.layout(options);
      leLayout.run();
      cy.fit();
      });
});

</script>
</body>
</html>
```

Questions and answers

Question 1. If I wanted to build an application that included graph visualization, I would have to build that visualization from scratch.

1. True
2. False

Answer. False. While many applications benefit from a customized visualization solution, there are a number of solutions and libraries out there that can help you. At a minimum, these libraries and/or solutions will provide you with a baseline from which you can start.

Question 2. The three basic graph visualization forces used in many tools are:

1. Gravity, Obesity, Charge
2. Springs, Gravity, Charge
3. Charge, Gravity, Verbosity

Answer. Springs, Gravity, Charge.

Question 3. The well-known effect of data visualizations containing too much information, so much so that the user gets confused and cannot see the wood for the trees, is often referred to as:

1. The forest effect
2. The loading effect
3. The fireworks effect

Answer. The fireworks effect.

Summary

We conclude our chapter on graph visualization. In this chapter, we went through the reasons why graph visualizations matter greatly to modern-day data applications. We also illustrated different tools and techniques that can be used by application developers to create their graph database applications. We then wrapped up the chapter by pointing out some very important side effects of visualization solutions, and how we can take these effects into account when we engage in such a project.

The next chapter will cover data refactoring, because you know, the first time is not always perfect, and the model may evolve over time (spoiler: it always did, it always will).

12
Data Refactoring with Neo4j

This chapter is dedicated to the evolution of your graph.

Your data model will evolve over time. It could be because the first time is not perfect, most probably because of evolving requirements. We will start with the simple cases and go through increasingly complex cases.

We will be covering the following topics in the chapter:

- Capturing information of key pinpoints/locations
- Remodeling pinpoints/locations
- Extracting information from pinpoints/locations
- Adding and fetching locations

Preliminary step

You certainly know the proverb better to be safe than sorry and Murphy's law, don't you?

The advice is simple: back up your data! (See the Appendix, *Tips and Tricks*, for the ways to backup your server).

Before doing structural changes, you should play it safe. It is valid for all databases. Also, a backup procedure is in Schroedinger's state until validated.

Simple changes

I define simple changes as changes effecting individual nodes without impacting relations or other related nodes.

Renaming

There is no renaming feature in Cypher but there is a procedure for that in APOC.

The sentence *there is a procedure for that in APOC* is almost a mantra in the Neo4j community.

The longer version ends with--if there isn't , *ask Michael,* for Michael Hunger whom I already wrote about.

It is possible to rename labels, relations, node properties, and relation properties with APOC.

Currently, relations are named `types` so the procedures are as follows:

```
CALL apoc.refactor.rename.label(oldLabel, newLabel, [nodes])
CALL apoc.refactor.rename.type(oldType, newType, [rels])
CALL apoc.refactor.rename.nodeProperty(oldName, newName, [nodes])
or
CALL apoc.refactor.rename.typeProperty(oldName, newName, [rels])
```

You may optionally give a list of nodes or relations. Awesome.

Adding data

Adding data is enriching the current data model with new properties. This is rather safe. No risk of breaking changes here.

Adding data with a default value

Let's use the towers again, should we want to know if they host a restaurant or not. A yes/no field is a perfect fit for a `Boolean` property. We shall call this query, assuming it is a waste to build a tower and not fit a restaurant in it. We do this as follows:

```
MATCH (n:Tower)
SET n.hasRestaurant = toBoolean("true")
RETURN n
```

Notice the conversion to a `Boolean` value that then allows shortening of the queries:

```
MATCH (n:Tower)
WHERE n.hasRestaurant
RETURN n
```

Adding data with specific values

Should you want to specify a value for each node concerned, there are two main cases. Either the value is known or it has to be computed. If the value is known, you can certainly read it from a source, such as a JSON file, an XML file, or a CSV file.

In the first two cases, APOC will help you, or you may use LOAD CSV, as we saw in Chapter 08, *Importing Data into Neo4j*. The recipe will be as follows:

```
LOAD CSV  OR  CALL apoc.load.json(url) YIELD value
MATCH the node with its ID
SET the new property to the given value
```

If the value is not known and has to be computed from existing data, it gets a little trickier because there may be conversions to do from one field type to another to do. An example could be getting the street number from an address and storing it in a numerical field via the toInt method. The recipe is as follows:

```
MATCH the node to change and all  useful nodes and relations
SET newProperty = computed value
```

Checking our values

In either case, we cannot be sure that we can now make the assumption that the hasRestaurant property is present in all the Tower nodes. Fortunately, Cypher gets us covered as it is possible to find the unfinished nodes, thanks to NOT exists(node.property), like in this query:

```
MATCH (n:Tower)
WHERE NOT exists(n.hasRestaurant)
RETURN n
```

Then, it is up to you to flag the nodes as dirty (using a label of your choice), should you decide to exclude them from your queries via this label.

From the nodes, you can find a reason why the value is not set and improve your computation, which I advise you to code as a custom function (or procedure):

On a side note, I remind you that it is possible to define a constraint so that a label implies the existence of a property:

```
CREATE CONSTRAINT ON (t:Tower) ASSERT exists(t.hasRestaurant)
```

Removing data

Removing a property from nodes is as simple as follows:

```
MATCH   n
DELETE n.property
```

Be sure to filter your MATCH with labels, or face the dramatic consequence of data loss (but you have a backup, don't you?). Unlike when adding properties to your nodes, this can have consequences on the queries you use in your applications. We will get back to this in a later paragraph.

Great changes

When great changes are coming, you have to be prepared. Being philosophical, one could say know where you are and know where you go.

Know your model

To know where you are is to know your actual model. A previous feature of the APOC plugin, showing your meta-model as a graph is now a default feature of Neo4j and Cypher:

```
CALL db.schema()
```

As it is an instant view of your schema, I advise you to save this representation of your schema:

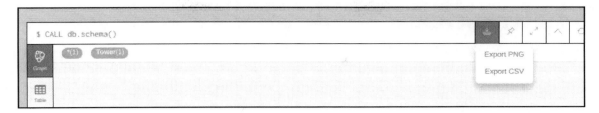

How to export a view of the schema

Export both formats. You can print the PNG image to use as a basis for your new modeling, while the CSV lists all the properties.

We will now see a panorama of the types of changes that you may have to perform.

Refactoring tools

To refactor our graph, we have two tools at our disposal. The first is standard Cypher and the second is APOC--in particular, the `apoc.refactor` package of procedures. Also mandatory is concentration and data backup, but you already know that.

Property to label

To add a label to a node based on a property, there are two steps:

- Add the label to the node
- Remove the property

For example, should we want to set a `hasRestaurant` label to towers with a restaurant, the queries would be as follows:

```
MATCH (t:Tower)
WHERE t.hasRestaurant
SET t:HasRestaurant
REMOVE t.hasRestaurant
RETURN t
```

This also illustrates the need of naming hygiene: `HasRestaurant` is a label because it starts with a capital letter while `hasRestaurant` is a property because it starts with a lowercase letter.

Property to node

Now, to dissociate a property from a node to a new node, for example, to share a value between nodes, we will see how to dissociate the countries of our towers from the `country` property to new nodes with the `:country` label, linked to the towers with a `:IN_COUNTRY` relation:

```
MATCH (t:Tower)
MERGE (c:Country {code: t.country})
CREATE UNIQUE (t)-[:IN_COUNTRY]->(c)
REMOVE t.country
RETURN t,c
```

You get extra points if you saw that, although a new kind of node is added, no constraint is created.

`CREATE UNIQUE` makes the relation unique. Run this code several times; there will be only one relation between the nodes.

Related node to label

Suppose we want to add a label to the towers based on the `country` nodes. If the label is known with a static value, an example query is as follows:

```
MATCH (t:Tower)--(c:Country)
SET t:HasCountry
```

This example makes little sense, but it shows you how to indicate any relation between two nodes. Therefore, it's worth it.

If the value of the label is dynamic, APOC is here to help--we already saw this procedure that can add an array of label.

This query will add the `Country` code as a label to the `Tower` nodes:

```
MATCH (t:Tower)--(c:Country)
CALL apoc.create.addLabels(id(t), [c.code]) YIELD node
RETURN node
```

Merging nodes

It is possible to merge several nodes together. Let's create some nodes:

```
CREATE (a:FIRST:MERGE {propF1: 'AF1',propF2: 'AF2'}), (b:SECOND:MERGE
{propS1: 'BS1',propS2: 'BS2'}), (c:THIRD:MERGE {propT1: 'CT1',propT2:
'CT2',propT3: 'CT3'})
```

Now let's see them:

```
MATCH (n:MERGE)
RETURN n
```

All right. Now, let's merge them onto the first node with this query:

```
MATCH (a:FIRST:MERGE), (b:SECOND:MERGE), (c:THIRD:MERGE)
CALL apoc.refactor.mergeNodes([a,b,c]) YIELD node
RETURN node
```

This results in a single node with four labels and the following properties (this is a copy/paste from the text view):

```
{"propF2":"AF2","propF1":"AF1","propS1":"BS1","propT2":"CT2","propT1":"CT1"
,"propS2":"BS2","propT3":"CT3"}
```

This was the expected result. Now what if these nodes had relations between them and properties with the same name? Let's see. We need to delete this node and recreate our limited dataset with the new specifications:

```
MATCH (n:MERGE)
DELETE n
CREATE (a:FIRST:MERGE {propF1: 'AF1',propF2: 'AF2'}), (b:SECOND:MERGE
{propS1: 'BS1',propS2: 'BS2',propF2:'VALUE FROM SECOND'}), (c:THIRD:MERGE
{propT1: 'CT1',propT2: 'CT2',propT3: 'CT3', propF1:'VALUE OF THIRD'})
```

If we merge the nodes like before, it results in the following:

```
{
  "propF2": "VALUE OF THIRD",
  "propF1": "VALUE OF THIRD",
  "propS1": "BS1",
  "propT2": "CT2",
  "propT1": "CT1",
  "propS2": "BS2",
  "propT3": "CT3"
}
```

This is the result we expected; for shared properties, values of node a are replaced by the values of node b, which get replaced by the values of node c.

Relations

To illustrate this paragraph, let's recreate the dataset with relations.

First, let's clear the graph:

```
MATCH (n:MERGE)
DETACH DELETE n
```

Now, let's create some data with the following query:

```
CREATE (a:FIRST:MERGE {name:'a',propF1: 'AF1',propF2: 'AF2'}),
(b:SECOND:MERGE {name:'b',propS1: 'BS1',propS2: 'BS2',propF2:'VALUE FROM
SECOND'}), (c:THIRD:MERGE {name:'c',propT1: 'CT1',propT2: 'CT2',propT3:
'CT3', propF1:'VALUE OF THIRD'})
CREATE (a)-[:A2B]->(b),(b)-[:B2B]->(b),(a)-[:A2C]->(c),(b)-[:B2C]->(c)
```

And check our small dataset with:

```
MATCH (n:MERGE)
RETURN n
```

Our start graph is as follows:

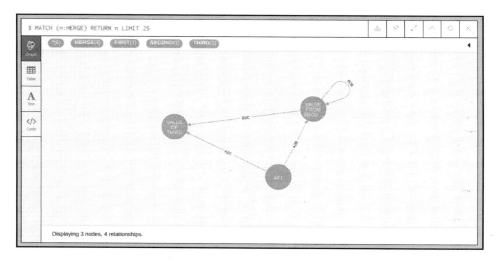

A graph well-named and well-oriented

We can now invert the relation A2B with the following:

```
MATCH (a:FIRST:MERGE)-[rel:A2B]-(b:SECOND:MERGE)
CALL apoc.refactor.invert(rel) YIELD output
RETURN output
```

Now, with this MATCH query:

```
MATCH (n:MERGE)
RETURN n
```

We can see that the relation A2B is now from B to A. It hurts the eyes and this creates an urgent need to rename the relation. The query to do so is as follows:

```
MATCH (a:FIRST:MERGE)-[rel:A2B]-(b:SECOND:MERGE)
CALL apoc.refactor.setType(rel, 'B2A') YIELD output
RETURN output
```

The A2B relation is renamed to B2A. Success.

We will continue to disrupt our logically named model to change the start and end nodes of relations. Let's make B2A start from the node c:

```
MATCH (a:FIRST:MERGE)-[rel:B2A]-(b:SECOND:MERGE), (c:THIRD)
CALL apoc.refactor.f
```

We get the graph as shown:

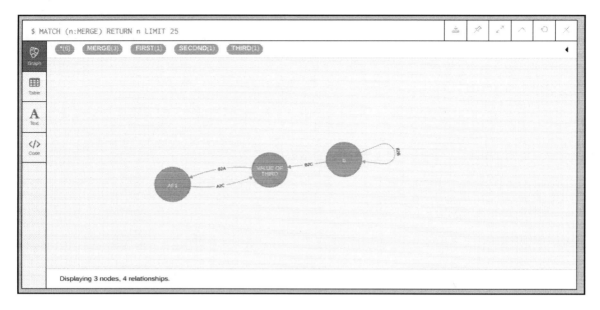

B2A starts from c now.

Now let's make the relation B2B end with the node a:

```
MATCH ()-[rel:B2B]-(), (a:FIRST)
CALL apoc.refactor.to(rel, a) YIELD output
RETURN output
```

This dramatically changes our graph to something very illogical, as shown:

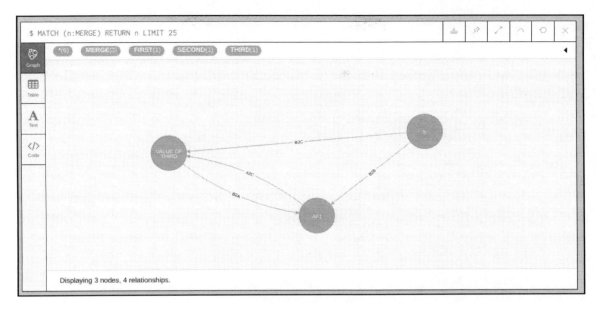

Spot the lying relation

Note that this works because there is only one node for each label--First, Second, and Third.

Extra points if you noticed the error of using capitals only for label names.

Consequences

There are two proverbs I like, which perfectly apply to our IT world:

> *With great power comes great responsibility ....*

> *To err is human, most catastrophes imply computers.*

Refactoring is a high risk of damaging your graph by accident. It is possible to lose information by removing properties on nodes that have not had that information transformed. It also impacts the queries that you have already written for your applications. Hopefully, breaking changes will appear by running your unit tests, which I am sure you have written.

Performance may be impacted too, as shorter queries tend to execute more quickly; there is a cost to adding more relations in a query.

Summary

We saw how to modify our graph of data for the most common updates. Undoubtedly, this will be useful to cope with the evolutions of your data projects during their lifespan (may they live long and prosper).

In the next chapter, we will talk about clustering several Neo4j Enterprise servers. A new frontier!

13
Clustering

This chapter is about clustering servers, and particularly about the causal clustering introduced in the Neo4j 3.2 Enterprise.

A cluster is a group of servers used to apply the proverbs, *United we stand, divided we fall* and *E pluribus unum* (Latin for several as one). To illustrate this, I will use several types of servers, two Linux laptops, and several Raspberry Pi.

As clustering is an enterprise version feature, it is not available in the community version. I will use the version 3.2.3 Enterprise in this chapter (available for free for 30 days on the Neo4j website).

This chapter covers the following topics:

- The need for clustering
- The concept of clustering
- Building a cluster
- Disaster recovery

Why set up a cluster?

The obvious reason to set up a cluster is that sometimes, a single server is not enough to serve the whole world. Scaling is needed. Setting several servers in several regions of the world could solve this, but separate servers imply other tasks such as reference data replication and sharing users. A cluster is the solution to these business needs. There are three main advantages to setting up a cluster:

- High throughput
- Data redundancy
- **High availability (HA)**

If you are working on a business project and you want 24/7 availability, you need a cluster.

Concepts

In a causal cluster, there can be two categories of servers. Core servers are the most important over read replica servers, as replicas are disposable and can be either added or removed during the scaling of the cluster. Let's go through their roles.

Core servers

Core servers are the most important servers of a cluster. The minimum number of core servers in a cluster is three for a transaction is reported as successful to the user who started it when the update generated is propagated to half the size of the cluster plus 1.

The roles of core servers are as follows:

- They are the targets of all the updating queries; they uphold data consistency via the consensus commit
- They are responsible for data safety
- They do the query routing, along with the bolt protocol drivers
- They copy data to read replicas (when polled)

Although this is transparent for the users, the admins know that, in a cluster, one server is the leader and is elected by the other core servers.

Read replica servers

Read replica servers are to be seen and used as **read-only servers**. Their data is updated by the core servers. A replica server may not be up to date at an instant T as transactions are considered good when core servers acknowledge the transaction. Use read replica servers for intensive reporting queries.

High throughput

When you put a server to work, the more users using it, the more server power will be needed.

Major websites do not buy bigger machines when their audience increases. The concept of load-balancing is having a single entry-point that delegates the requests to the next level. Most commonly, the next level is made of servers but it can be more load-balancers. Load-balancers may be hardware or software (like NGINX).

Neo4j's new protocol handles load balancing. Thus, creating a cluster with more replica servers in it allows more throughput while making the cluster a virtually bigger machine. Additionally, a query can be divided so that its parts are executed in parallel on several machines.

Data redundancy

Data redundancy is a solution to prevent data loss. The data is copied from node to node, asynchronously and automatically.

When a user updates data, the update is dispatched on enough core servers, then dispatched to remaining core servers and replica servers. You will not want to have all your servers in the same room, because disasters happen.

High availability

If you are a service provider, your contracts certainly have a clause about a 99 percent availability. High availability is achieved via the causal cluster architecture. If a server is failing, burning, or being moved to another site, the other servers online will automatically handle the requests.

Bolt

Bolt is a binary protocol used to communicate with a Neo4j server. Its three main qualities are to be lightweight, efficient, and type-safe (send a '1' character, get a character, not an integer). A variant of this protocol is **bolt+routing,** since version 3.1, load balancing is integrated in the drivers and protocol.

Building a cluster

The hardware elements that we will use are as follows:

- Two laptops as core servers, running Linux, connected to a home WiFi network
- Two raspberry Pi, 2 and 3, running as core servers

Read replica servers will be running as Docker containers. There will be five replicas running on my main laptop.

In a typical deployment, there are more read replicas than core servers. Of course, you can use any machine you want as long as it can connect to a network and run Neo4j. This can be more PCs, Macs, or any brand of credit card-sized computer running Linux.

Here, in a home environment, all servers are on the same network, plugged on the same router, and mostly in the same room (or not because of wifi and long cables). However, it is still relevant as an example and probably one of the cheapest options to do a cluster with hardware.

In a business environment, you may have to talk to your IT service, declare the machines, list which ports they use, and ask for safe passage of the network packets between them. This can take a long time.

The core servers

As the Raspberry Pis are running headless, I have not added a step of configuring their IP addresses and am relying on the DHCP of my router. If you are in the same situation, know that your machines may get a different IP address on reboot (or at the end of the DHCP bail timeout).

After the hardware part is completed, you should check how many hosts there are on your network; I have written a short shell script for that, which you can find in the `Appendix`, *Tips and Tricks*. Count the IPs returned. In my case, the router is listed and all other devices connected to the network are as well (such as smartphones, TV sets, and even some refrigerators).

Then comes the software part. It is recommended that you change the default password. Do it although I will advise you to use the same new password for all the Pis so to help remote connection. First, it must be possible to SSH from your main laptop to all the other machines. See `Appendix`, *Tips and Tricks*. Enable SSH on a Raspberry Pi if you cannot connect to your Pis.

Second comes the eventual installation of Java (`sudo aptitude install openjdk-8-jdk`).

Last but not least, install Neo4j (unzip as usual).

To copy the Neo4j archive from the main laptop to another host running SSH, use the scp command as follows:

```
scp neo4j.zip pi@192.168.0.20:/home/pi/
```

I would also recommend installing the APOC plugin on one of the hosts.

You may want to start Neo4j on each machine to check whether it starts and runs. Then stop them and delete the content of `$NEO_HOME/data/databases`. Now, list your servers, and choose which ones are to be core servers and which ones are to be read replicas. In my case, the core servers are those with the IP addresses finishing with 12, 15, and 16 (11 and 20 for the read replicas). There may be five or 20 servers, only two different configurations are to be written, one for the cores, a second for the replicas.

For the servers, add the following to the end of your `$NEO_HOME/conf/neo4j.conf` file:

```
dbms.mode=CORE
causal_clustering.expected_core_cluster_size=4
causal_clustering.initial_discovery_members=192.168.0.12:5000,192.168.0.15:5000,192.168.0.11:5000,192.168.0.20:5000
causal_clustering.discovery_listen_address=HostsIPAddress:5000
causal_clustering.transaction_listen_address=HostsIPAddress:6000
causal_clustering.raft_listen_address=HostsIPAddress:7000
dbms.connectors.default_advertised_address=HostsIPAddress
```

You must adapt the configuration file on each host and set the numeric value instead of HostsIPAddress. As some of my servers are headless, I want to be able to connect to their web interface from another host. Thus, I uncommented the following line in neo4j.conf:

dbms.connectors.default_listen_address=0.0.0.0

If you have enough hardware to set up some read replicas, the configuration is roughly the same, except for the first line, and shorter:

dbms.mode=READ_REPLICA
```
causal_clustering.expected_core_cluster_size=4
causal_clustering.initial_discovery_members=192.168.0.12:5000,192.168.0.15:
5000,192.168.0.11:5000,192.168.0.20:5000
```

> You should know that it is possible to host Neo4j in differents clouds and create a causal cluster. Should you want to build such a cluster, you need to contact a Neo4j sales representative.

Now, let's start the servers with the usual command:

neo4j start

It takes a little longer for single servers. You may follow the progress by tailing the log file:

tail -f neo4j.log

When you can read:

INFO Remote interface available at http://192.168.0.12:7474/

You may then open your web browser on the Neo4j home page. You will need to log in and set a new password for the Neo4j user. Only then will you read the role of that host in the left column in the first tab (the stack icon). The first to start will be the LEADER, while others will display FOLLOWER.

Now, let's check whether our data replicates. The simplest way is to open the browser of the LEADER core server host and create some data, then open the browser of another host and query for that data:

```
CREATE (:Person:RoleModel {name:'Didier'}), (:Person:Sun {name:'Anny'}),
(:Person:Mum {name:'Josiane'}), (:Person:Dad {name:'Jean-Pierre'})
```

In the time to run the query, the data is already available on the other hosts.

If you try to create nodes on a FOLLOWER, whether with the Neo4j browser or with the Cypher shell, you will get an error message. I'll get back to that later.

The read replicas

As mentioned earlier, we will use Docker containers as read replicas. To ensure that our data gets replicated, we will use local folders for the logs and data folders of each replica. It's not mandatory but will help us ensure that it works.

I will name the replicas a, b, c, d, e, and f. In my home folder, I will create a dedicated folder ReadReplicas and a subtree for each host.

On a Linux box, the shell commands are as follows:

```
cd ~
mkdir ReadReplicas
# Repeat lines below for each host
mkdir ReadReplicas/a/
mkdir ReadReplicas/a/logs
mkdir ReadReplicas/a/data
```

There are no plugins and no conf folders. So, to ensure that the configuration we want is used, some arguments will be needed. These arguments have to be translated into a new form:

```
causal_clustering.expected_core_cluster_size=4
 becomes
 NEO4J_causalClustering_expectedCoreClusterSize=4
```

Note the NEO4J_ prefix, dot turning to underlines, and underlines turning to camel-case.

Now, to launch a read replica, the Docker command is as follows:

```
docker run --name=replica-a --detach --env=NEO4J_dbms_mode=READ_REPLICA \
--env=NEO4J_causalClustering_expectedCoreClusterSize=4 \
--
env=NEO4J_causalClustering_initialDiscoveryMembers=192.168.0.12:5000,192.16
8.0.15:5000,\
192.168.0.11:5000,192.168.0.20:5000 \
--volume=$HOME/ReadReplicas/a/logs:/logs \
--volume=$HOME/ReadReplicas/a/data:/data neo4j:3.2.3-enterprise
```

Run it for each host with the adapted name. Between each, you can run, in the `ReadReplicas` folder, the following command to get the size of the folder, growing with time as replicas get the data from the core servers:

```
du -ch |grep total
```

As the usual ports are not published, you cannot access the Neo4j browser of the replicas.

The bolt+routing protocol

The bolt+routing protocol is a variant of the bolt protocol. Now, bolt is the default but you can (or must) also use bolt+routing as protocol in your client code. That will allow you to specify a FOLLOWER core server as the recipient of graph updates, as the couple server and driver will route the updates to the LEADER.

A FOLLOWER may become a LEADER if the LEADER fails. If this happens, the core servers will proceed to an election at the majority.

In order to be able to run an update query in the Neo4j browser of a FOLLOWER host, you may tick use bolt+routing in the left column in the tab with the gear icon. Then, an updating query like the following will work without error:

```
CREATE(ju:Person {name:"MonChéri"}), (am:Person {name:"MaPrincesse"})
```

As an exercise, you may try to stop your LEADER (neo4j stop) and see which other host becomes the LEADER.

Disaster recovery

Sometimes, servers fail to serve for so many possible reasons. If a read replica fails, so be it; replace it or add another one, it will get the data as it joins the cluster. If a core server fails, the cluster handles it too. The graph is recreated via the other cores. You can see it yourself:

1. Stop a core server.
2. Go through its folders, and remove data/databases and data/cluster-state.
3. Restart it (the more data, the more time it will take).
4. Watch the log file to see when it is ready.
5. Go to its Neo4j browser.
6. Be amazed.

This is so simple, it reminds me what a speaker said at a graph connect conference: "We do the hard things so you don't have to."

If all your core servers fail, first find the reason, for it is very unlikely on a real state-of-the-art deployment. If you want to roll your graph to the date of a previous backup, the steps are as follows:

1. Stop all instances (core and replicas).
2. Perform a backup restore on each instance (with the same backup file).
3. Restart all instances.

This will lead to unavailability during the procedure.

Summary

This chapter taught us why and how to create a Neo4j cluster with different kinds of servers. After the concepts, we saw how to build a cluster. We also saw the magic of the bolt+routing protocol.

You learned that we can grow from a cluster of several credit card-sized computers like Raspberry Pis (https://www.raspberrypi.org/) to a cluster made from several clouds (you'll need a strong credit card for that).

We also saw a disaster recovery procedure to which I'll add this tip:

> With any software, disaster recovery must always be team work. Otherwise, it is too easy to put the blame on one person because non-tech people need to act as inactivity makes them feel 'not in power' and blaming is so easy, as they believe failure should not have had happened first. No matter Murphy's law.
>
> If you are the one who understood what failed and how to solve the issue, and get the blame anyway instead the credit: change of shop. I saw firsthand that a client lost their best sysadmin as he got bored of that scheme.

Now let's see a use case example for Neo4j: impact analysis and simulation.

14
Use Case Example - Recommendations

In this chapter, we will look at how we can use the Neo4j graph database for a very specific use case, in which it shines. All the discussions so far have led us to this discussion, where we really want to zoom in on how one would practically use a database such as Neo4j for a very specific use case.

We will look at the following topics in this chapter:

- Modeling product relationships as a graph
- Using relationships to suggest recommendations
- Using relationships to detect fraud

Recommender systems dissected

We will take a look at so called recommender systems in this chapter. Such systems, broadly speaking, consist of two elementary parts:

- **A pattern discovery system**: This is the system that somehow figures out what would be a useful recommendation for a particular target group. This discovery can be done in many different ways, but in general, we see three ways to do so:

  - A **business expert** who thoroughly understands the domain of the graph database application will use this understanding to determine useful recommendations. For example, the supervisor of a do-it-yourself retail outlet would understand a particular pattern. Suppose that if someone came in to buy multiple pots of paint, they would probably also benefit from getting a gentle recommendation for a promotion of high-end brushes. The store has that promotion going on right then, so the recommendation would be very timely. This process would be a discovery process where the pattern that the business expert has discovered would be applied and used in graph databases in real time as part of a sophisticated recommendation.

  - A **visual discovery** of a specific pattern in the graph representation of the business domain. We have found that in many different projects, business users have stumbled on these kinds of patterns while using graph visualizations to look at their data. Specific patterns emerge, unexpected relations jump out, or, in more advanced visualization solutions, specific clusters of activity all of a sudden become visible and require further investigation. Graph databases such as Neo4j, and the visualization solutions that complement it, can play a wonderfully powerful role in this process.

  - An **algorithmic discovery** of a pattern in a dataset of the business domain using machine learning algorithms to uncover previously unknown patterns in the data. Typically, these processes require an iterative, raw number-crunching approach that has also been used on non-graph data formats in the past. It remains part-art part-science at this point, but can of course yield interesting insights if applied correctly.

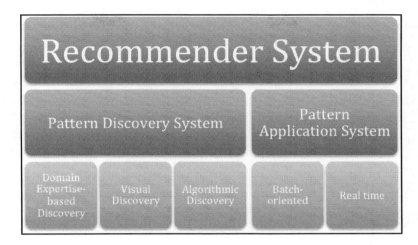

An overview of recommender systems

- **A pattern application system**: All recommender systems will be more or less successful based on not just the patterns that they are able to discover, but also based on the way that they are able to apply these patterns in business applications. We can look at different types of applications for these patterns:

- **Batch-oriented applications**: Some applications of these patterns are not as time-critical as one would expect. It does not really matter in any material kind of way if a bulk email with recommendations, or worse, a printed voucher with recommended discounted products, gets delivered to the customer or prospect at 10 am or 11 am. Batch solutions can usually cope with these kinds of requests, even if they do so in the most inefficient way.

- **Real-time oriented applications**: Some pattern applications simply have to be delivered in real time, in between a web request and a web response, and cannot be pre-calculated. For these types of systems, which typically use more complex database queries in order to match for the appropriate recommendation to make, graph databases such as Neo4j are a fantastic tool to have. We will illustrate this going forward.

With this classification behind us, we will look at an example dataset and some example queries to make this topic come alive.

Using a graph model for recommendations

We will be using a very specific data model for our recommender system. In total, we have the following:

- Ten products
- Three product brands
- Fifty relationships between existing person nodes and the mentioned products, highlighting that these persons bought these products

These are the products and brands that we added:

Node	Name	Label
100	iPad	Product
101	iPhone	Product
102	iPad Mini	Product
103	MacBook Pro	Product
104	MacBook Air	Product
105	ChromeBook	Product
106	Samsung Galaxy 4	Product
107	Samsung Galaxy Tab 3	Product
108	Google Nexus 5	Product
109	Google Nexus 7	Product

200	Apple	Brand
201	Google	Brand
202	Samsung	Brand

Adding products and brands to the dataset

The following diagram shows the resulting model:

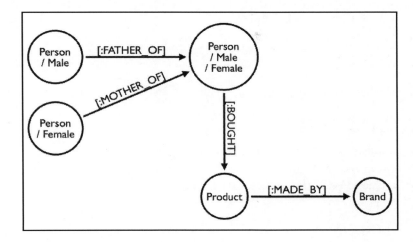

Our meta model

In Neo4j, this model will look something like the following:

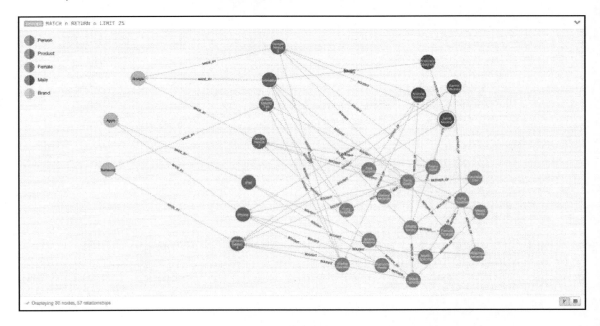

A view on our dataset

A dataset like this one, while of course a broad simplification, offers us some interesting possibilities for a recommender system. Let's take a look at some queries that could really match this use case and would allow us to either visually or in real time exploit the data in this dataset in a product recommendation application.

Specific query examples for recommendations

In this example dataset, we will explore a couple of interesting queries that would allow us--with the information that is available to us--to construct interesting recommendations for our hypothetical users. We will do so along different *axes*:

- Product purchases
- Brand loyalty
- Social and/or family ties

Let's start with the first and work our way through.

Recommendations based on product purchases

Let's build this thing from the ground up. The first query that we want to write is based on past purchasing behavior. We would like to find people that already share a couple of products that they have purchased in the past, but that also explicitly do not share a number of other products. In our data model, this Cypher query would go something as follows:

```
match (p1:Person)-[:BOUGHT]->(prod1:Product)<-[:BOUGHT]-(p2:Person)-
[:BOUGHT]->(prod2:Product)
where not(p1-[:BOUGHT]->prod2)
return p1.name as FirstPerson, p2.name as SecondPerson, prod1.name as
CommonProduct, prod2.name as RecommendedProduct;
```

In this query, the `match` clause gathers the pattern of users (`p1` and `p2`) that have bought a common product (`prod1`), but ensures that `p2` has actually bought one or more product's that `p1` has not bought.

The result is actually quite an extensive list of recommendations, as shown in the following screenshot:

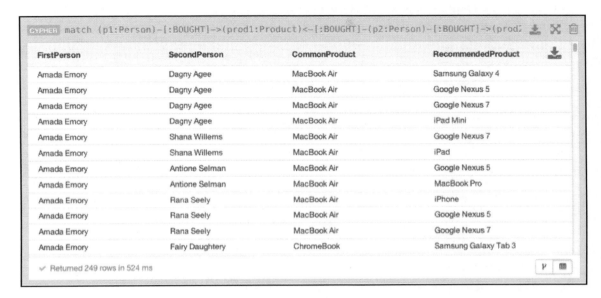

Extensive list of recommendations

So we can probably do with some refining here.

The next step in our recommendation process would therefore be to look at two people that have a stronger similarity. This means that the two people would need to have bought more than two products in common before the recommended product would actually be assumed to be attractive to the target audience.

Let's look at this query:

```
match (p1:Person)-[:BOUGHT]->(prod1:Product)<-[:BOUGHT]-(p2:Person)-
[:BOUGHT]->(prod2:Product)
with p1,p2,count(prod1) as NrOfSharedProducts, collect(prod1) as
SharedProducts,prod2
where not(p1-[:BOUGHT]->prod2) AND NrOfSharedProducts > 2
return p1.name as FirstPerson, p2.name as SecondPerson, extract(x in
SharedProducts | x.name) as SharedProducts, prod2.name as
RecommendedProduct;
```

As you can see, the basic query is the same as the previous one but we have added some filters for the number of shared products. We also worked with the collection of products (`collect(prod1)`) and extracted the names of these products in the final result. It looks like what is shown in the following screenshot:

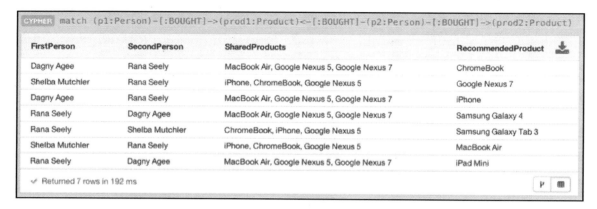

The refined recommendations based on product purchases

So let's now take a look at another type of recommendation, based on brand loyalty.

Recommendations based on brand loyalty

Obviously, we all understand that if we already own a product of a particular brand, it is likely that we will be more interested in other products that are manufactured by that same brand. So let's find the people that already have more than one product of a certain brand and see if we can recommend other products by that brand. Here's the query example:

```
MATCH (p:Person)-[b:BOUGHT]->(prod1:Product)-[:MADE_BY]->(br:Brand)<-
[MADE_BY]-(prod2:Product)
WITH p, br, prod2, count(prod1) as NrOfBrandProducts
WHERE not(p-[:BOUGHT]->prod2) and NrOfBrandProducts > 1
RETURN p.name as Person, br.name as Brand, collect(prod2.name) as
RecommendedProducts
ORDER BY Person ASC;
```

The pattern should be fairly similar, but the difference is that we are now counting the number of products of a certain brand and ensuring that the person in question has not yet bought the other products of that same brand. The result looks like this:

The recommendations based on brand

Again, this gives us some useful recommendations, based on a very different qualifier. Let's then bring in another parameter: our social relationships, in this case, based on the family ties that a particular user will have.

Recommendations based on social ties

In the next version of our recommendation queries, we will be using the relationships--in this particular dataset, based on family ties between parents and/or siblings--between our users to come up with some useful recommendations for their next purchase.

Let's look at the following query:

```
match (p:Person)-[b:BOUGHT]->(prod:Product),p<-[r1]-(parent:Person)-
[r2]->(sibling:Person)
where type(r1) in ["MOTHER_OF","FATHER_OF"] and type(r2) in
["MOTHER_OF","FATHER_OF"]
and not(sibling-[:BOUGHT]->prod)
return p.name as Person, prod.name as RecommendedProduct,
collect(sibling.name) as ForSiblings;
```

This would give us the products bought by a specific person, and looks for siblings (who have the same mother or father as the first person) who have not bought that specific product and may potentially benefit from it. Running the query gives us the following result set:

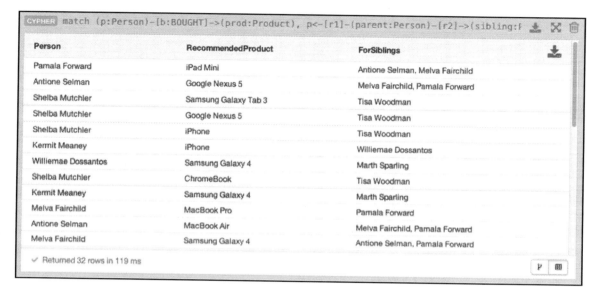

Person	RecommendedProduct	ForSiblings
Pamala Forward	iPad Mini	Antione Selman, Melva Fairchild
Antione Selman	Google Nexus 5	Melva Fairchild, Pamala Forward
Shelba Mutchler	Samsung Galaxy Tab 3	Tisa Woodman
Shelba Mutchler	Google Nexus 5	Tisa Woodman
Shelba Mutchler	iPhone	Tisa Woodman
Kermit Meaney	iPhone	Williemae Dossantos
Williemae Dossantos	Samsung Galaxy 4	Marth Sparling
Shelba Mutchler	ChromeBook	Tisa Woodman
Kermit Meaney	Samsung Galaxy 4	Marth Sparling
Melva Fairchild	MacBook Pro	Pamala Forward
Antione Selman	MacBook Air	Melva Fairchild, Pamala Forward
Melva Fairchild	Samsung Galaxy 4	Antione Selman, Pamala Forward

Returned 32 rows in 119 ms

The recommendations based on social ties

Again, a useful recommendation. Now, let's try to bring it all together and really try to make a complex, real-time recommendation based on all of this criteria: product purchase history, brand loyalty, and social/family networking.

Bringing it all together - compound recommendations

In the following query, we will try to mix all of the three aspects that we mentioned previously into one compound--and hopefully more relevant--recommendation. If we take into account all three angles for our recommendation system, then hopefully we will be able to make fewer, more powerful recommendations to the user.

Let's look at the following query:

```
match (p1:Person)-[:BOUGHT]->(prod1:Product)<-[:BOUGHT]-(p2:Person)-
[:BOUGHT]->(prod2:Product), p1<-[r1]-(parent:Person)-[r2]->p2, prod1-
```

```
[:MADE_BY]->(br:Brand)<-[:MADE_BY]-(prod2)
where type(r1) in ["MOTHER_OF","FATHER_OF"] and type(r2) in
["MOTHER_OF","FATHER_OF"] and not(p1-[:BOUGHT]->prod2)
return p1.name as FirstPerson, p2.name as SecondPerson, br.name as Brand,
prod2.name as RecommendedProduct;
```

What we are doing here is bringing the three aspects of our pattern together in the match clause. Here are the different parts explained:

1. The first part of the clause ensures that two people have bought common *and* different products
2. The second part ensures that the two people are siblings
3. The third part ensures that the products recommended would be based on the loyalty to a particular brand

Running this query is interesting. The result is shown in the following screenshot:

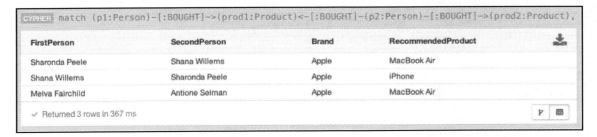

Compound recommendations

We immediately see that we get only three matches to this sophisticated pattern; however, as mentioned earlier, we have reason to believe that these recommendations will be more powerful.

This concludes our discussion of these core use cases around recommendations. Before closing this chapter, we would, however, like to spend a bit more time on some related topics around recommendations.

Business variations on recommendations

The entire principle of a recommender system, as we described before, can be generalized into a different kind of system that has many other business applications. Some people would call it a rules engine, which does some kind of sophisticated *if-this-then-that* matching and figures out what action to take at the other end of the decision tree. Other people may call it a pattern-matching system, which could be applied to any kind of pattern and tied to any kind of action. Most likely, graph databases such as Neo4j hold some characteristics of all of the above and provide you with an interesting infrastructural optimization that could serve well.

Before wrapping up this chapter, we would like to highlight some use cases that are extremely related to the recommender system use case. Let's go through some well-known sweet spot applications that essentially use the same principles underneath.

Fraud detection systems

We have seen a number of customers that are using graph database management systems such as Neo4j for fraud detection systems. The principle is quite simple: in many cases, the fraud of a particular nature is not defined by one transaction only, but by a chain of transactions that have their specific characteristics and that need to be compared to one another to see if they really do constitute a case of fraud.

In the following example, we are just looking at a suspect case of credit card fraud:

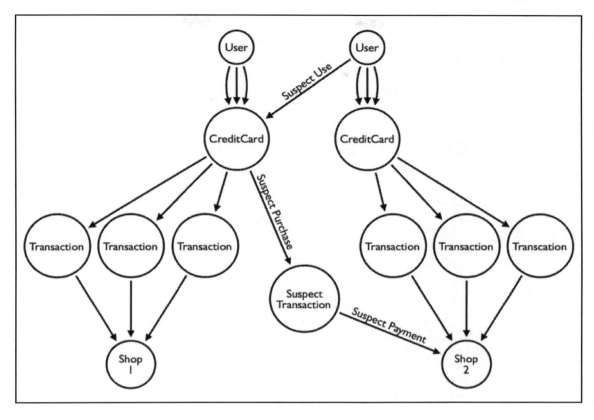

A suspect case of credit card fraud

A particular user always uses his credit card for transactions at a particular store. Another user uses his credit card for similar transactions at a different store. All of a sudden, there is this new transaction in the middle, which uses the credit card (let's say for a similar kind of transaction) in the other store. This kind of pattern may become flagged as a suspect pattern in some fraud detection systems.

The system would not necessarily immediately block the credit card, but the risk score of that particular transaction/card combination would definitely go up. If the score reaches a certain threshold, it would mean that there is an increased likelihood for that transaction to be fraudulent and the system would recommend that a particular action be taken.

The action would not be to recommend another product sale, but to put the credit card on hold and give the user a friendly customer service call to check whether this behavioral pattern is exceptional or not. The principle of this fraud detection system, however, would be very similar to that of a retail recommender system: define a pattern, detect a pattern, and act on the occurrence of that pattern with some kind of business-related measure.

Access control systems

Another example of a similar system that uses the principles of a recommender system--defining a pattern and then matching for its occurrences--for a different use case is an access control system:

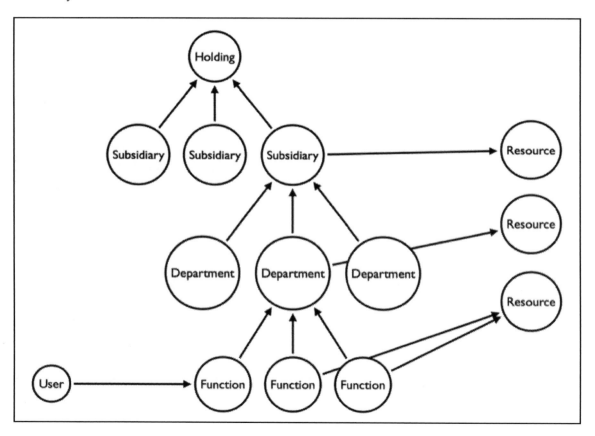

An access graph

Social networking systems

Obviously, there are a lot of recommender systems that will be very specific to a domain. In the past couple of years, with the massive rise of social networking tools and social apps all around us, the interest in social recommender systems has grown massively. Essentially, we are looking to make useful new connections between people that are effectively part of the same social circle, but may not have realized it yet.

Looking at the following sample network should clarify this immediately:

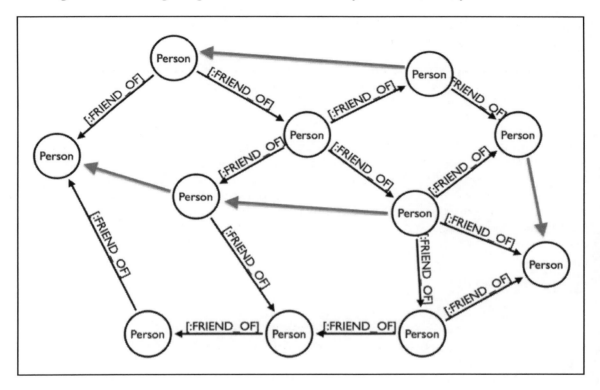

A social networking graph

In the preceding simple network, there is a very high likelihood that we can close some friendship loops very easily, by suggesting connections between new links between people. Very often, we will be using the graph theory principle of triadic closures, meaning that we will be closing the missing links of the triangles in the structure of our network.

So let's explore this social networking use case some more in the following chapter with a very specific set of examples.

Questions and answers

Q1: In order to build a recommendation system, I need an artificial intelligence engine that will take a look at my data and discover the recommendation patterns for me automatically.

1. True
2. False

Answer: **False**. Recommender systems can be based on business knowledge that your staff already has, a visual pattern you discover while browsing the data, or some kind of algorithmic machine learning process. All three can provide meaningful recommendation patterns for your business applications.

Q2: Recommender systems can only be applied in an Amazon-style retail environment, where you have a massive amount of data to base your recommendations on.

1. True
2. False

Answer: **False**. Recommendations are useful in many different business domains, not just retail product recommendations. Fraud detection systems (I recommend that you put this person in jail.) are just one example of a business application that has nothing to do with retail but that will use the same pattern matching capabilities to detect these more complicated fraud cases.

Summary

In this chapter, we gave you an overview of how graph databases such as Neo4j could be used in a recommender system. There are a lot of things that we did not discuss, which are out of the scope of this book, but that would probably be part of a true enterprise-class recommender system. Nevertheless, we hope to have illustrated that the querying power of Neo4j will open up a wealth of new opportunities for real-time recommender systems, where recommendations would no longer need to be pre-calculated but rather leveraged in near real time.

The next chapter will use an example of a use case to teach you about analyzing the impact change has on a process or system. It will also teach you how to analyze impact through graphs.

15
Use Case Example - Impact Analysis and Simulation

In this chapter, we will look at how we can use the Neo4j graph database for another very specific use case: **impact analysis**. All the discussions so far have led us to this discussion, where we really want to zoom in on how one would practically use a database such as Neo4j for a very specific use case.

In this chapter, we will see how to perform the following steps:

- Dissecting and understanding impact analysis systems. We will split the broader topic into two subtopics:
    - Impact analysis</li>
    - Impact simulation
- Applying impact analysis to a business process management use case using a detailed demonstration dataset.
- Applying impact simulation to a cost calculation use case, using another detailed demonstration dataset.

Let's get started straightaway.

Impact analysis systems dissected

In this chapter, we will spend time with specific types of systems that will allow corporations to perform some of the most complicated operations. In some cases, their information technology infrastructure will be set up to do this, and in others, this will not be the case. Analyzing and understanding their businesses in the context of its environment and the impact that the environment has on the business can be tremendously complex. In fact, doing this, means that companies need to do two very specific things:

- They need to understand how their business will react to specific impulses from the environment or other. Assuming that they have modeled their business as a set of interdependent processes, people, and resources, it is easy to see how graph databases could be very interesting tools to better understand what would happen to the rest of the network if a part of the network changes. We call this the core impact analysis use case.
- They need to be able to simulate different potential scenarios and choose the most optimal scenario to achieve their specific objectives. This, in one sense, becomes a variation of the previously mentioned scenario, but is different in the sense that it requires us to iterate on the previously mentioned scenario many times to determine what the optimal end state of the business would need to be to achieve the stated objectives. We will call this the impact simulation use case.

Let's now closely examine both of these use cases in some more detail and provide specific examples of both.

Impact analysis in business process management

In the business process management use case, we will be exploring how to use graph database technology to better understand the interdependencies of different business processes and some of their key resources. This is a use case that many large organizations call **business process management,** and is sometimes related to or part of a business continuity management discipline.

The idea is plain and simple: if you are a large corporation, it is essentially your responsibility to prepare for if something happens (a natural disaster, a large-scale power outage, a fire, a violent terrorist attack, or any other majorly disruptive event that could hit you as a corporation). The critical step in this preparation process is to understand what depends on what, which is where Neo4j as a graph database comes in: to enable that kind of understanding.

Modeling your business as a graph

The example we will use is that of a real-world use case, which combines a number of business concepts that are structured as a graph for better understanding. The concepts are as follows:

- **Business process**: These are the high-level business processes that one would typically consider at a top executive level.
- **Process**: These are the subprocesses that together make up a business process.
- **Return to operation objective**: Both Business processes and their subprocesses will have a maximum timeframe within which they absolutely must return to operation, in the case that an exceptional event causes them to suspend operations in the first place. This **return to operation objective (RTO)** can be anything from a few minutes to a few days.
- **Business line**: Processes will be used by one or more departments or business lines, which are organizational units that should enable the corporation to achieve their objectives.
- **Building**: Business lines are located at a specific site or building.
- **Application**: Processes can use specific information technology applications to facilitate their execution.

All of the mentioned concepts are connected to each other, as shown in the following figure:

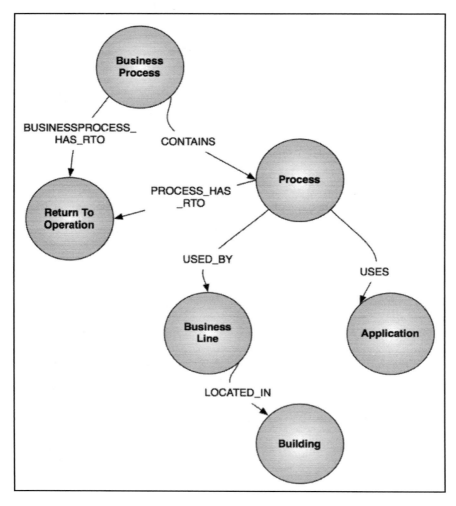

The Business Continuity Management model

We can then easily import a sample dataset into Neo4j. With a simple query, we can see how many relationships we have from a certain type to get some insight in the database:

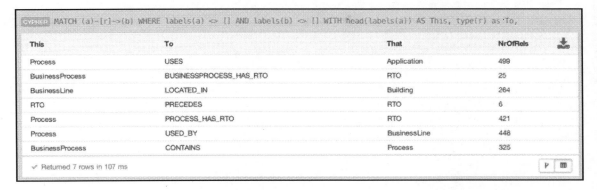

This	To	That	NrOfRels
Process	USES	Application	499
BusinessProcess	BUSINESSPROCESS_HAS_RTO	RTO	25
BusinessLine	LOCATED_IN	Building	264
RTO	PRECEDES	RTO	6
Process	PROCESS_HAS_RTO	RTO	421
Process	USED_BY	BusinessLine	448
BusinessProcess	CONTAINS	Process	325

✓ Returned 7 rows in 107 ms

The BCM database content

The sample dataset has, in total, 817 nodes and (as you can see from the preceding screenshot) 1,988 relationships. This is enough to ask some interesting questions that are appropriate for our use case.

Which applications are used in which buildings?

Let's say that we would like to use the graph model to determine which applications are used in specific locations/buildings of our corporation. Then, our Cypher query would look something as follows:

```
MATCH (app:Application)<-[:USES]-(proc:Process)-
[:USED_BY]->(bl:BusinessLine)-[:LOCATED_IN]->(b:Building) RETURN DISTINCT
app.name AS Application , b.name AS Building ORDER BY app.name ASC;
```

Note that this is quite an expensive query to run as it does not use any specific starting points in our graph traversals--it is a global query. However, the result comes back quickly for this dataset.

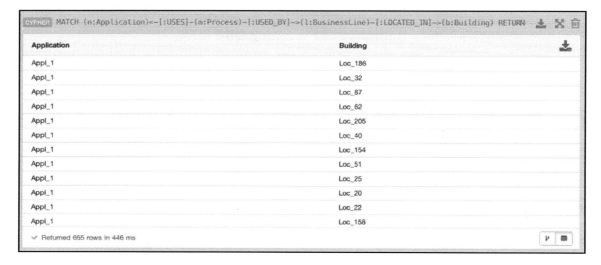

Results

This newfound understanding of the business then allows us to better take action if something happens to either the application or the building. Let's explore this a bit more.

Which buildings are affected if something happens to Appl_9?

This is a very local variety of the preceding query, and it answers the question very specifically for one. The application may be experiencing trouble at this particular moment. The query is similar to the following:

```
MATCH (app:Application {name:"Appl_9"})<-[:USES]-(proc:Process)-
[:USED_BY]->(bl:BusinessLine)-[:LOCATED_IN]->(b:Building) RETURN DISTINCT
app,proc,bl,b;
```

As we have returned the nodes rather than the properties on these nodes, our Neo4j browser returns a nice graphical representation that immediately provides the required insight:

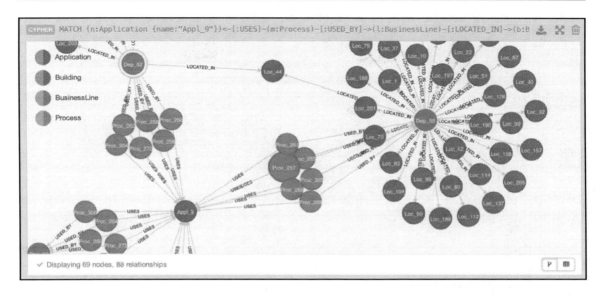

Buildings affected if something happens to Appl_9

Hopefully, this is a very good illustration of the use case already, but we can make it a bit more complex by including the RTO information. Let's examine one more query.

What business processes with an RTO of 0-2 hours would be affected by a fire at location Loc_100?

One thing that you may have already noticed is that there is something peculiar about the RTO characteristic. Most people would assume that such a characteristic would become a property of the (business) processes, but in our model, we have created separate nodes to represent these characteristics and linked them together in a chain of RTO values:

- An RTO of 0-2 hours precedes one of 2-4 hours
- An RTO of 2-4 hours precedes one of 4-24 hours
- An RTO of 4-24 hours precedes one of 1-7 days
- An RTO of 1-7 days precedes one of 7-14 days
- An RTO of 7-14 days precedes one of more than 14 days

You can see this in the following browser graph. The advantage of doing this is that we can now very easily slide along the RTO-line and figure out similar or close to RTO targets very easily.

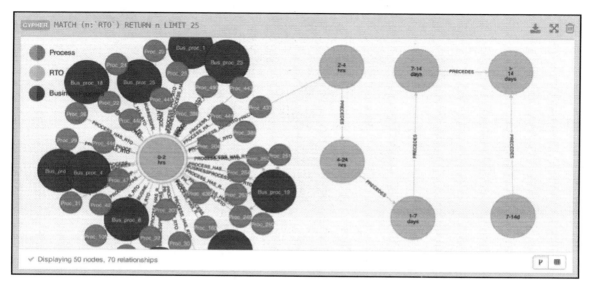

In-graph index of RTO times

So, then we can run the following query to answer the previous question:

```
MATCH (b:Building {name:"Loc_100"}), (rto:RTO {name:"0-2 hrs"})<-
[:BUSINESSPROCESS_HAS_RTO]-(bp:BusinessProcess) WITH b,bp MATCH p =
ShortestPath(b-[*..3]-bp) RETURN p;
```

The query uses `Building` and `RTO` as starting points for the traversal, and then uses the `ShortestPath` algorithm to find out which business processes would be affected. The result is immediately clear and visible for any business user who wants to analyze the impact of this event on the business environment that the company is operating.

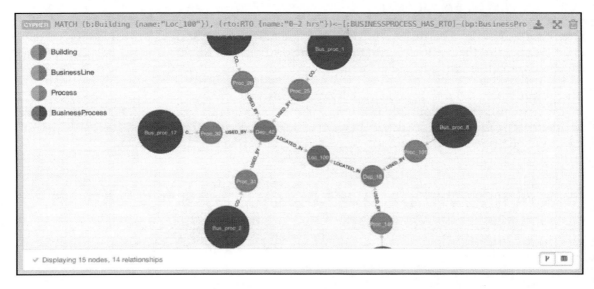

Business processes with RTO affected by incident at location

With these examples behind us, you have a good overview of how graph databases such as Neo4j can help with impact analysis systems. Now, we will explore another type of scenario that is related to this domain: **impact simulation**.

Impact simulation in a cost calculation environment

As discussed previously, the second impact-related use case that we would like to address in this chapter is the one that simulates the impact of a certain change to the network on the rest of the network. It basically addresses the question: how will we be impacted if a certain change occurs in the network? What would the optimal scenario if we were to change certain parameters in the graph structure?

The example that we will be using in this section uses a very common data structure that you may have seen in many other different use cases: a hierarchy or tree. During the course of this section, we will run through the different parts of tree structure and see what the impact of changes in the tree would be on the rest of the tree.

Modeling your product hierarchy as a graph

The use case that we are exploring uses a hypothetical dataset representing a product hierarchy. This is very common in many manufacturing and construction environments:

- A product is composed of a number of cost groups
- A cost group is composed of a number of cost types
- A cost type is composed of a number of cost subtypes
- A cost subtype is composed of costs
- Costs will be composed of components

The lowest part of the hierarchy structure, the components, will have a specific price. On my blog (`http://blog.bruggen.com/2014/03/using-neo4j-to-manage-and-calculate.html`), I have shown how you can create a sample dataset like this pretty easily. The model will be similar to the one shown in the following figure:

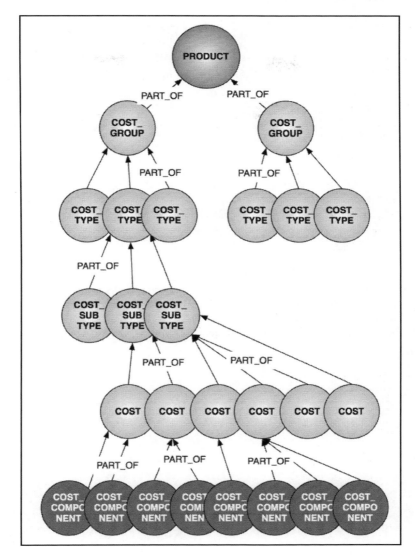

The product hierarchy data model for cost simulations

In the what if scenarios that compose our impact simulation, we will be exploring how we can efficiently and easily calculate and recalculate the price of the product if and when the price of one or more of the components changes. Let's get started with this.

Working with a product hierarchy graph

Let's take a look at how we could work with this product hierarchy graph in Neo4j. After adding the data to the graph, we have the following information in our neo4j database:

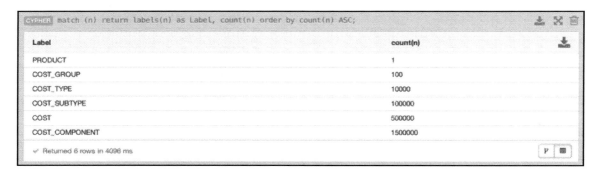

What do we have here, in this graph ?

In total, the product hierarchy graph is about 2.1 million nodes and the same number of relationships. This would be a sizeable product hierarchy by any measure. Doing a simple query on the hierarchy reveals the entire top-to-bottom structure:

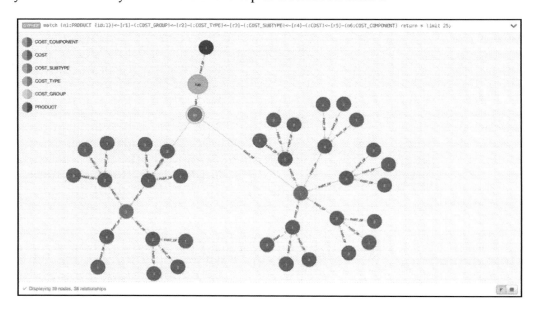

The product hierarchy in Neo4j's browser

Now that we have this hierarchy in place, we can start doing some queries on it. One of the key problems that we would like to solve is the price calculation problem: how do we run through the entire hierarchy structure and use the information stored in the hierarchy to (re)calculate the price of a product? This would typically be a terribly difficult and time-consuming query (as a matter of fact, it is a five-way join operation) on a relational system. So, what would it be on a graph-based database such as Neo4j? Let's find out.

In the following sections, we will actually present two different strategies to calculate the price of the product using the product hierarchy.

The first strategy will be by running through the entire tree, taking the lowest part of the tree for the pricing information and then multiplying that with the quantity information of all the relationships. When this full sweep of the tree reaches the top, we will have calculated the entire price of the product.

The second strategy will be using a number of intermediate calculations at every level of the tree. We will update all of the intermediate levels of the tree with the price calculations of everything lying underneath it at lower levels of the tree so that, effectively, we would need to run through a much smaller part of the tree to recalculate the price.

Let's take a look at this in more detail.

Calculating the price based on a full sweep of the tree

The first strategy that we will use to calculate the price of the product in our hierarchy will do a full sweep of the tree:

1. It will start from the product at the top.
2. Then, it will work its way down to every single cost component in the database.
3. Then, it will return the sum of the all total prices, calculated as a product of the price of each cost component with the quantities on the relationships that connect the cost component to the product at the top.

The query for this approach is similar to the following:

```
match
(n1:PRODUCT {id:1})<-[r1]-(:COST_GROUP)<-[r2]-(:COST_TYPE)<-[r3]-
(:COST_SUBTYPE)<-[r4]-(:COST)<-[r5]-(n6:COST_COMPONENT) return
sum(r1.quantity*r2.quantity*r3.quantity*r4.quantity*r5.quantity*n6.price)
as CalculatedPrice;
```

When we execute this query, it takes quite a bit of time as we need to run through all nodes and relationships of the tree to get what we want. With a tree of 2.1 million nodes and relationships, this took about 47 seconds on my laptop. Look at the result shown in the following screenshot:

Calculating the price based on a full sweep of the hierarchy

Now, anyone who has ever done a similar operation at similar scale in a relational system knows that this is actually a really impressive result. However, we think we can do better by optimizing our hierarchy management strategy and using intermediate pricing information in our queries. If we want to perform impact simulation--the subject of this section of the book--we really want this price calculation to be super fast. So, let's look at that now.

Calculating the price based on intermediate pricing

The strategy optimization that we will be using in this example will be to use intermediate pricing at every level of the tree. By doing so, we will enable our price calculation to span a much smaller part of the graph; only the part of the graph that changes-the node/relationship that changes and everything preceding it in the hierarchy-will need to be traversed when performing our impact simulations.

To do so, we need to add that intermediate pricing information to the hierarchy. Currently, only the lowest cost component level has pricing information. Also, we need to calculate that information for all levels of the hierarchy. We use a query similar to the following one to do so:

```
match (n5:COST)<-[r5]-(n6:COST_COMPONENT) with n5,
sum(r5.quantity*n6.price) as Sum set n5.price=Sum;
```

Essentially, what we do is we look at one level of the hierarchy, traverse upwards to the level above, and set the price of the upper level equal to the sum of all products of the price of the lower level and multiplied by the quantity of the relationship that connects it to the upper level.

As previously mentioned, we need to run that type of query for every level of our hierarchy:

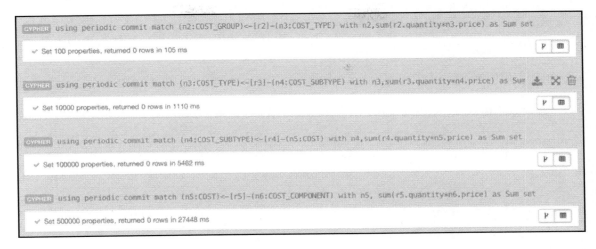

Adding intermediate pricing information

About 35 seconds later, this is all done, which is quite impressive.

Now that we have the intermediate pricing information, calculating the price of the product only needs to traverse one level deep. We use a query similar to the following one:

```
match (n1:PRODUCT {id:1})<-[r1]-(n2:COST_GROUP) return
sum(r1.quantity*n2.price);
```

Of course, this query is significantly faster, as it only touches a hundred or so nodes and relationships-instead of 2.1 million of each. So, note the super-fast query that yields an identical result to the full sweep of the tree mentioned previously:

Calculating price based on intermediate pricing

Now that we have done this optimization once, we can use this mechanism for our impact simulation queries.

Impact simulation on product hierarchy

Our original objective was all about impact simulation. We want to understand what happens to the price of the product at the top of our product hierarchy by simulating what happens if one or more cost component price changes. If this simulation would be sufficiently performant, then we could probably iterate on these changes quite frequently and use it as a way to optimize all the processes dependent on an appropriate price calculation of the product.

In the new, optimized strategy that we have previously outlined, we can very easily change the price of a cost component (at the bottom of the hierarchy), and as we update that price, recalculate all the intermediate prices that are set at the levels above the cost component (cost, cost subtype, cost type, cost group, and finally, the product). Let's look at the following query (which consists of multiple parts):

Part	Query
Part 1	`match (n6:COST_COMPONENT)    with n6, n6.price as OLDPRICE limit 1   set n6.price = n6.price*10   with n6.price-OLDPRICE as PRICEDIFF,n6`
Part 2	`match n6-[r5:PART_OF]->(n5:COST)-[r4:PART_OF]->(n4:COST_SUBTYPE)-[r3:PART_OF]->(n3:COST_TYPE)-[r2:PART_OF]->(n2:COST_GROUP)-[r1:PART_OF]-` `(n1:PRODUCT)`
Part 3	`set    n5.price=n5.price+(PRICEDIFF*r5.quantity),    n4.price=n4.price+(PRICEDIFF*r5.quantity*r4.quantity),` `n3.price=n3.price+(PRICEDIFF*r5.quantity*r4.quantity*r3.quantity),` `n2.price=n2.price+(PRICEDIFF*r5.quantity*r4.quantity*r3.quantity*r2.quantity),` `n1.price=n1.price+(PRICEDIFF*r5.quantity*r4.quantity*r3.quantity*r2.quantity*r1.quantity)` `return PRICEDIFF, n1.price;`

- **Part 1**: This looks up the price of one single cost component, changes it by multiplying it by 10, and then passes the difference between the new price and the old price (`PRICEDIFF`) to the next part of the query.
- **Part 2**: This climbs the tree to the very top of the hierarchy and identifies all of the parts of the hierarchy that will be affected by the change executed in part 1.
- **Part 3**: This uses the information of part 1 and part 2, and recalculates and sets the price at every intermediate level that it passes. At the top of the tree (n1), it will return the new price of the product.

Running this query on the dataset provide the following result:

PRICEDIFF	n1.price
7434	258471604678725120

✓ Set 6 properties, returned 1 row in 117 ms

Recalculating the price with one change in the hierarchy

This is really good; recalculating the price over a hierarchy of 2.1 million things all of a sudden only takes 117 milliseconds. Not too bad. Let's see if this also works if we change the price of more than one cost component. If we use the preceding query but change `limit 1` to `limit 100` and run this query, we get the following result:

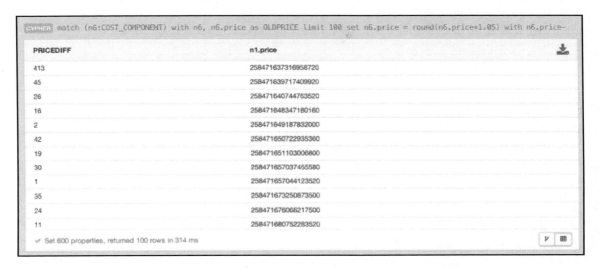

Recalculating the price based on 100 changes in the hierarchy

The effect of recalculating the price of the product based on a hundred changes in the hierarchy is done in 314 milliseconds--a truly great result. This sets us up for a fantastic way of simulating these impacts over our dataset.

This concludes our discussion of the impact simulation and allows us to wrap up this chapter.

Questions and answers

Q1. Analyzing impact often requires:

1. A lot of manual work in the database.
2. Complex join operations across multiple different types of information.
3. A simple path finding query over a graph database such as Neo4j.

A: 3. Path finding is a great use case for Neo4j.

Q2. Which of the following use cases is a great hierarchical use case for Neo4j?

1. Calculating the average selling price over a million different purchase transactions.
2. Calculating access control over a directory tree of users in groups and departments.
3. Calculating the shortest path on a road network between two cities.
4. Recommending a new product purchase to an existing client.

Answer: 2. Access control is typically a great hierarchical use case, as evidenced by the multiple hierarchically organized directory servers on the market today. Hierarchies, however, are just a specific type of graph and so they are typically also a great use case for Neo4j.

Summary

In this chapter, we illustrated that graph databases such as Neo4j are extremely well placed at playing a role in many enterprise architectures where impact analysis and simulation is important. There are many different fields where this may be useful, but we chose two specific domains to illustrate this use case. First, we took a look at a business process management use case, where analyzing and understanding the potential impact of a change in a network would be of primary interest to the user. Then, we took a look at an impact simulation use case, where we wanted to set up a use case in which we could iteratively simulate different impact scenarios and see what the result of those changes on the network would be, using a product hierarchy as an example to do so.

We hope we have given you a good overview of the use case and its potential.

Tips and Tricks

I am going to list a few tips and tricks to work efficiently on Neo4j.

Reset password

Even on a development machine that I use everyday, I may have forgotten the clever password I set up for the user Neo4j, as I have several versions installed on my machine.

The solution is to stop your server, then change the directory to the data/dbms subfolder, and remove the file named auth.

Check for other hosts

To know what hosts are running on your local network, with SSH access enabled, I offer you this little script:

```
#!/bin/bash

port=22
for ordi in `nmap -sn 192.168.0.1-100 /25 | egrep "scan report" | awk
'{print $5}'`
do
    echo Found IP $ordi on network.
    echo -------------------------------------
done
echo Now trying them for port $port , sorry for the timeout on successful
connections
echo
for ordi in `nmap -sn 192.168.0.1-100 /25 | egrep "scan report" | awk
'{print $5}'`
```

```
do
    echo Trying $ordi on port $port
    cat < /dev/tcp/$ordi/$port
    echo -----------------------------------
done
```

You may need to adapt this to change the IP range. Unix super users may wonder why there is a /25 instead of a /24. The answer is to avoid having the dot 254 IP in the loop, for it is the router and not a host.

Getting the first line of a CSV file

Getting the first line of a CSV file proves very useful to write the core of the Cypher queries. Why use a spreadsheet editor to copy/paste the first line when you can do it on a command prompt? This is even more useful if the file is huge and takes time to open.

On a Linux machine, try the following:

head -1 theBigHugeCSVFile.csv

If you want to create a Cypher file, try with the usual redirection:

head -1 theBigHugeCSVFile.csv > myFantasticImport.cyp

Now, you can open the .cyp file in your preferred text editor and replace the field separator with, at minimum, a line jump (\n), the equal sign, the name of the variable you want to use (such as line), and a dot.

This way, you have a block of all the fields in a usable form:

```
=line.field1
=line.field2
=line.field3
```

With your favorite text editor, you can easily turn the preceding lines into the following lines:

```
LOAD CSV WITH HEADERS FROM file:///theBigHugeCSVFile.csv' AS line
CREATE (a:SomeNodeLabel)
SET a.prop1=line.field1
SET a.prop2=line.field2
SET a.prop3=line.field3
```

Voilà, your import query is becoming real. (That reminds me to remind you to convert your fields to `toFloat`, `toInteger`, and `toBoolean`, wherever needed. Remember the input is strings).

Enabling SSH on a Raspberry Pi

When I installed the latest distribution on an SD card as the operating system for a brand new Raspberry Pi, unfortunately, I had no television to plug it to. Too bad, for it makes it impossible to run the usual setup. Worse, the Pi was running, doing nothing, and was inaccessible.

Fortunately, remote access is possible by enabling SSH, which is already installed.

When you have burnt the ISO to the SD card, two drives appear. One is the future root filesystem of your Pi, and the second named boot is where you must create an empty file named `ssh` (no extension).

There you go; plug a network cable and it is online. You can now log into it via SSH and run `raspi-config`.

 Earlier versions of Raspian had SSH enabled by default. Maybe the distribution you use has it. Anyway, you know what to do now.

Creating guides for the Neo4j browser

When you are in a situation where you need to display data to users but cannot create an application for that, an option to consider is to create guides, locally hosted so that your users just need to click on the queries to get the results. There is no risk if they have the reader role.

The first obvious option is to look at a guide and see how the source is structured. The second option is to look at the project neo4j guides available at `https://github.com/neo4j-contrib/neo4j-guides`.

This project proposes to convert a document in the asciidoc format to an HTML guide.

Here is a starter guide:

```
 == Learning Neo4j
:author: Jerome BATON
:twitter: wadael

=== Guides

Guides are very useful to quickly propose read-only queries to users.
See the arrows, I wrote no distinct source for that. Click it please
=== Add pictures

You can add pictures with this code
[source, text]
----
image::https://neo4j.com/wp-content/themes/neo4jweb/assets/images/neo4j-log
o-2015.png[height=150,float=right]
----


image::https://neo4j.com/wp-content/themes/neo4jweb/assets/images/neo4j-log
o-2015.png[height=400, float=right]
Neat.

== Queries

=== How many nodes ?
If you click on the query below, it will be copied in the input. You will
just have to run it.
[source, cypher]
----
MATCH (n)
RETURN count(n)
----
```

The steps are as follows:

1. Clone the project.
2. Paste the code into a file named `learning.adoc` at the root of the project.
3. Execute `./run.sh ./learning.adoc`.
4. (Optional: solve dependency issues with `apt-get install asciidoctor` and `gem install tilt`).
5. Add `browser.remote_content_hostname_whitelist=*` at the end of you `neo4j.conf` file. (Warning: it allows guides from the internet too.)

1. Execute Python `http-server.py`.
2. In the Neo4j browser, execute play `http://localhost:8001/html/learning.html`.
3. Enjoy testing your guide.
4. Deploy it on a production server.

Data backup and restore

Depending on the version you are using, the way to backup and restore your data will be different.

Community version

To back up your data of a community version server, only cold backup (offline) is possible.

A first way, very basic, but not to say DIY, is: first stop your server, then copy the whole `$NEO_HOME/data` folder to a secure storage. Then restart your server.

To restore backup data, stop your server, replace the `$NEO_HOME/data` folder with your backup, and restart your server.

Another way is to use the `neo4j-admin` utility program, installed with the server in `$NEO_HOME/bin`:

```
neo4j-admin dump --to=file --database=optionnalDBName
```

The *to* parameter should be a path to a file. The database parameter is optional and only needed if you have more than one database and want to dump a database other than `graph.db`.

To restore this dump of data, the command is as follows:

```
neo4j-admin load from=file
```

Enterprise version

The Enterprise version comes with an enriched version utility program: `neo4j-admin`, located in `$NEO_HOME/bin`. This version has two more functions: `backup` and `restore`.

To allow online backups, some configuration is needed; you need to uncomment the two lines in bold in $NEO_HOME/conf/neo4j.conf:

```
# Enable online backups to be taken from this database.
dbms.backup.enabled=true
# By default the backup service will only listen on localhost.
# To enable remote backups you will have to bind to an external
# network interface (e.g. 0.0.0.0 for all interfaces).
dbms.backup.address=0.0.0.0:6362
```

Tools

Let's have a look at a few of the tools.

Cypher-shell

Cypher-shell is a command-line tool that comes with the default installation of Neo4j.

You will find it in the $NEO_HOME/bin folder. As already stated, it allows you to run Cypher queries interactively on a Neo4j server, such as the Neo4j browser:

```
jerome@nitendet ~/Tools/neo/neo4j-enterprise-3.2.3/bin $ cypher-shell
username: uadmin
password: ******
Connected to Neo4j 3.2.3 at bolt://localhost:7687 as user uadmin.
Type :help for a list of available commands or :exit to exit the shell.
Note that Cypher queries must end with a semicolon.
neo4j> MATCH (n)
       RETURN count(n);
+-----------+
| count(n)  |
+-----------+
| 8         |
+-----------+

1 row available after 1 ms, consumed after another 0 ms
neo4j> :quit

Bye!
jerome@nitendet ~/Tools/neo/neo4j-enterprise-3.2.3/bin $
```

Cypher-shell, interactive mode

It is also possible to use it in a unix-ian way, as the destination of a file. Suppose that we have a file named `count.cy` containing this query:

```
MATCH (n)
RETURN count(n);
```

We can use Cypher-shell like this:

Cypher-shell, in 'like a sysadmin' mode

Data integration tools

Talend (`www.talend.com`) is an open source software vendor that provides data integration, data management, enterprise application integration, and Big Data software and services. They have a very extensible, visual, and powerful development environment for all kinds of integration services that can be connected together in a workflow designer style environment.

MuleSoft (`www.mulesoft.com`), headquartered in San Francisco, California, provides an integration platform to connect any application, datasource, or API, whether in the cloud or on-premises. Just like Talend, it offers a visual environment to integrate other datasources in the polyglot persistence architecture with the Neo4j graph database management system. To do so, Mulesoft provides a well-documented connector for Neo4j that allows you to integrate data very easily.

Modeling tools

Modeling for graph databases is just as important as ever. Even though there is no external schema overlooking our data model by default, there is still a clear and important need to model. The way to define the structure of the data that we are planning to store in Neo4j needs to be documented in a clear and understandable fashion. In this section of our book, we will outline two frequently used tools that we can suggest for the development of our graph models.

Arrows

Originally started by Neo Technology's Alistair Jones (`www.apcjones.com`) as a side project for graph documentation and visualization, the Arrows toolset today enables very easy and usable documentation of graph database models. The tool is available online at `www.apcjones.com/arrows` and provides very basic but advanced graph drawing capabilities.

The nicest thing about the Arrows model is that it enables the mapping of the property graph model of Neo4j to the drawing canvas. Its automatic scaling and alignment features are also extremely useful.

The Arrows toolset, which is an open source project publicly available on `https://github.com/apcj/arrows`.

OmniGraffle

OmniGraffle (`http://www.omnigroup.com/omnigraffle/`) is a diagramming application made by The Omni Group (`http://www.omnigroup.com/`). OmniGraffle is built only for Mac OS X and iPad. It may be used to create diagrams, flow charts, org charts, illustrations, and graph database models. It features a drag-and-drop WYSIWYG interface. **Stencils**--groups of shapes to drag and drop--are available as extensions for OmniGraffle, and users can create their own stencils, for example, to get easy access to property graph editing requirements. In many of these respects, OmniGraffle is similar to Microsoft Visio.

Community projects

These are projects definitely worth having a look at:

- `https://github.com/cleishm/libcypher-parser`: libcypher-parser is a parser library and validation (lint) tool for Cypher, the graph query language.
- Structr (`https://structr.org`): Struct is an application generator, do their `sample application tutorial`, watch the video, and you will be amazed !
- `https://neo4j-client.net/`: Another command-line client.
- `https://github.com/anvaka/ngraph.path`: A JS library for fast path finding in arbitrary graphs.

- There is another visualization library worth your time, which is `Popoto.js` (`http://www.popotojs.com/`). It is built preceding `D3.js`.
- `https://github.com/neo4j-contrib/neo4j-graph-algorithms`: More efficient graph algorithms for Neo4j.

Online documentation

Neo4j Inc. provides a very good amount of documentation on its product; see `https://neo4j.com/docs/`.

The YouTube channel, `https://www.youtube.com/c/neo4j`, provides the videos of the graph connect events (and more).

Find the APOC userguide at `https://neo4j-contrib.github.io/neo4j-apoc-procedures/`.

Community

As open source users, we sometimes seek for help and sometimes offer our help. There is a Neo4j tag on StackOverflow, `https://stackoverflow.com/questions/tagged/neo4j`, for all the Neo4j questions.

There are several **Slack** channels; see `https://neo4j.com/developer/slack/`.

If you use Twitter, follow them all: `@neo4j`, `@mesirii`, `@emileifrem`, `@rvanbruggen`, `@craigtaverner`, `@Aethelraed`, `@darthvader42`, `@tb_tomaz`, `@lyonwj`, `@maxdemarzi`, `@markhneedham`, `@BarrasaDV`, `@ryguyrg`, `@andres_taylor`, `@iansrobinson`, `@apcj`, `@jimwebber`, (and maybe `@wadael`, too).

Graph Connect conferences and local meetups are a very good way to meet fellow graphistas, exchange tips, and push job offers.

More proverbs

To close this book on a lighter note but with wisdom anyway, here are some proverbs.

(As Lili said:) *Trash in ! trash out !* Meaning if you do not put in the maximum care when you import data, you will get the data you deserve as query results!

Take care of the nulls, do not import numbers as strings, and use booleans when needed.

Everything is misplaced when you mistake latitude and longitude!

Having one's child's name on a book cover makes family happy!

The joy of learning calls for the joy to teach!

Authors love feedback!

Index

Made in the USA
San Bernardino, CA
11 August 2018